LAW OF PRESS IN MEDIA

LAW OF PRESS IN MEDIA

By

Dheeraj Razdan

2008

CYBER TECH PUBLICATIONS
4264/3, Ansari Road, Daryaganj, New Delhi-110002 (India)
Ph.: 011-23244078. Fax: 011-23280028
E-Mail: cyberpublicationsdelhi@yahoo.com

LAW OF PRESS IN MEDIA

Dheeraj Razdan

First Edition 2008

Reprint 2024

Published by :

G.S. Rawat for **Cyber Tech Publications**
4264/3, Ansari Road, Daryaganj, New Delhi-110002 (India)
Ph.: 011-23244078. Fax: 011-23280028
E-Mail: cyberpublicationsdelhi@yahoo.com

Printed at : **Amit Enterprises**, Maujpur, Delhi, (9810878184)

Preface

Press in all countries work under a pre defined boundary laid by the government concerned. However it is said to be the fourth estate and a very respectable status it holds in the society. But alongwith the framework for its proper functioning a number of laws, codes and ethics are also being made for the press. The laws include all aspects of the press viz. duty of journalists, salaries and facilities and works required. For the same purpose in India. The press council of India was established, it delivers, amends, and make new laws whenever required for the Indian press. The book beings with principles and Ethics of journalism, fundamentals and journalism, History of press council is India, press council and Indian Government, freedom of press worldwide and the present day mass media and press and includes all important factors of these fields.

All important laws of the press are discussed in this book. Author sincerely hopes that this book will provide idea about the working of press to the students of journalism and other general students.

Your feedbacks are heartily welcome.

—Author

Contents

1

Principles and Ethics of Journalism

In 1997, an organization then administered by PEJ, the Committee of Concerned Journalists, began a national conversation among citizens and news people to identify and clarify the principles that underlie journalism. After four years of research, including 20 public forums around the country, a reading of journalism history, a national survey of journalists, and more, the group released a Statement of Shared Purpose that identified nine principles. These became the basis for The Elements of Journalism, the book by PEJ Director Tom Rosenstiel and CCJ Chairman and PEJ Senior Counselor Bill Kovach. Here are those principles, as outlined in the original Statement of Shared Purpose.

A STATEMENT OF PURPOSE

After extended examination by journalists themselves of the character of journalism at the end of the twentieth century, we offer this common understanding of what defines our work. The central purpose of journalism is to provide citizens with accurate and reliable information they need to function in a free society.

This encompasses myriad roles—helping define community, creating common language and common knowledge, identifying a community's goals, heros and villains, and pushing people beyond complacency. This purpose also involves other requirements, such as being entertaining, serving as watchdog and offering voice to the voiceless.

Over time journalists have developed nine core principles to meet the task. They comprise what might be described as the theory of journalism:

Journalism's First Obligation is to the Truth

Democracy depends on citizens having reliable, accurate facts put in a meaningful context. Journalism does not pursue truth in an absolute or philosophical sense, but it can—and must—pursue it in a practical sense. This "journalistic truth" is a process that begins with the professional discipline of assembling and verifying facts. Then journalists try to convey a fair and reliable account of their meaning, valid for now, subject to further investigation. Journalists should be as transparent as possible about sources and methods so audiences can make their own assessment of the information. Even in a world of expanding voices, accuracy is the foundation upon which everything else is built—context, interpretation, comment, criticism, analysis and debate. The truth, over time, emerges from this forum. As citizens encounter an ever greater flow of data, they have more need—not less—for identifiable sources dedicated to verifying that information and putting it in context.

Its First Loyalty is to Citizens

While news organizations answer to many constituencies, including advertisers and shareholders, the journalists in those organizations must maintain allegiance to citizens and the larger public interest above any other if they are to provide the news without fear or favor. This commitment to citizens first is the basis of a news organization's credibility, the implied covenant that tells the audience the coverage is not slanted for friends or advertisers. Commitment to citizens also means journalism should present a representative picture of all constituent groups in society. Ignoring certain citizens has the effect of disenfranchising them. The theory underlying the modern news industry has been the belief that credibility builds a broad and loyal audience, and that economic success follows in turn. In that regard, the business people in a news organization also must nurture—not exploit—their allegiance to the audience ahead of other considerations.

Its Essence is a Discipline of Verification

Journalists rely on a professional discipline for verifying information. When the concept of objectivity originally evolved, it did not imply that journalists are free of bias. It called, rather, for a consistent method of testing information—a transparent approach to evidence—precisely so that personal and cultural biases would not undermine the accuracy of their work. The method is objective, not the journalist.

Seeking out multiple witnesses, disclosing as much as possible about sources, or asking various sides for comment, all signal such standards. This discipline of verification is what separates journalism from other modes of communication, such as propaganda, fiction or entertainment. But the need for professional method is not always fully recognized or refined. While journalism has developed various techniques for determining facts, for instance, it has done less to develop a system for testing the reliability of journalistic interpretation.

Its Practitioners must Maintain an Independence from those they Cover

Independence is an underlying requirement of journalism, a cornerstone of its reliability. Independence of spirit and mind, rather than neutrality, is the principle journalists must keep in focus. While editorialists and commentators are not neutral, the source of their credibility is still their accuracy, intellectual fairness and ability to inform—not their devotion to a certain group or outcome. In our independence, however, we must avoid any tendency to stray into arrogance, elitism, isolation or nihilism.

It must Serve as an Independent Monitor of Power

Journalism has an unusual capacity to serve as watchdog over those whose power and position most affect citizens. The Founders recognized this to be a rampart against despotism when they ensured an independent press; courts have affirmed it; citizens rely on it. As journalists, we have an obligation to protect this watchdog freedom by not demeaning it in frivolous use or exploiting it for commercial gain.

It must Provide a Forum for Public Criticism and Compromise

The news media are the common carriers of public discussion, and this responsibility forms a basis for our special privileges. This discussion serves society best when it is informed by facts rather than prejudice and supposition. It also should strive to fairly represent the varied viewpoints and interests in society, and to place them in context rather than highlight only the conflicting fringes of debate. Accuracy and truthfulness require that as framers of the public discussion we not neglect the points of common ground where problem solving occurs.

It must Strive to Make the Significant Interesting and Relevant

Journalism is story-telling with a purpose. It should do more than gather an audience or catalogue the important. For its own survival, it must balance what readers know they want with what they cannot anticipate but need. In short, it must strive to make the significant interesting and relevant. The effectiveness of a piece of journalism is measured both by how much a work engages its audience and enlightens it. This means journalists must continually ask what information has most value to citizens and in what form. While journalism should reach beyond such topics as government and public safety, a journalism overwhelmed by trivia and false significance ultimately engenders a trivial society.

It must keep the News Comprehensive and Proportional

Keeping news in proportion and not leaving important things out are also cornerstones of truthfulness. Journalism is a form of cartography: it creates a map for citizens to navigate society. Inflating events for sensation, neglecting others, stereotyping or being disproportionately negative all make a less reliable map. The map also should include news of all our communities, not just those with attractive demographics. This is best achieved by newsrooms with a diversity of backgrounds and perspectives. The map is only an analogy; proportion and comprehensiveness are subjective, yet their elusiveness does not lessen their significance.

Its Practitioners must be Allowed to Exercise their Personal Conscience

Every journalist must have a personal sense of ethics and responsibility—a moral compass. Each of us must be willing, if fairness and accuracy require, to voice differences with our colleagues, whether in the newsroom or the executive suite. News organizations do well to nurture this independence by encouraging individuals to speak their minds. This stimulates the intellectual diversity necessary to understand and accurately cover an increasingly diverse society. It is this diversity of minds and voices, not just numbers, that matters.

ETHICS OF JOURNALISM

The Assembly affirms the following ethical principles for journalism and believes that they should be applied by the profession throughout Europe.

News and Opinions

1. In addition to the legal rights and obligations set forth in the relevant legal norms, the media have an ethical responsibility towards citizens and society which must be underlined at the present time, when information and communication play a very important role in the formation of citizens' personal attitudes and the development of society and democratic life.
2. The journalist's profession comprises rights and obligations, freedoms and responsibilities.
3. The basic principle of any ethical consideration of journalism is that a clear distinction must be drawn between news and opinions, making it impossible to confuse them. News is information about facts and data, while opinions convey thoughts, ideas, beliefs or value judgments on the part of media companies, publishers or journalists.
4. News broadcasting should be based on truthfulness, ensured by the appropriate means of verification and proof, and impartiality in presentation, description and narration. Rumour must not be confused with news.

News headlines and summaries must reflect as closely as possible the substance of the facts and data presented.

5. Expression of opinions may entail thoughts or comments on general ideas or remarks on news relating to actual events. Although opinions are necessarily subjective and therefore cannot and should not be made subject to the criterion of truthfulness, we must ensure that opinions are expressed honestly and ethically.

6. Opinions taking the form of comments on events or actions relating to individuals or institutions should not attempt to deny or conceal the reality of the facts or data.

The right to information as a fundamental human right-Publishers, proprietors and journalists

7. The media's work is one of "mediation", providing an information service, and the rights which they own in connection with freedom of information depends on its addressees, that is the citizens.

8. Information is a fundamental right which has been highlighted by the case-law of the European Commission and Court of Human Rights relating to Article 10 of the European Convention on Human Rights and recognised under Article 9 of the European Convention on Transfrontier Television, as well as in all democratic constitutions. The owner of the right is the citizen, who also has the related right to demand that the information supplied by journalists be conveyed truthfully, in the case of news, and honestly, in the case of opinions, without outside interference by either the public authorities or the private sector.

9. The public authorities must not consider that they own information. The representativeness of such authorities provides the legal basis for efforts to guarantee and extend pluralism in the media and to ensure that the necessary conditions are created for exercising freedom of expression and the right to information and precluding censorship. Moreover, the Committee of Ministers is aware of this fact, as demonstrated by its Declaration

on the Freedom of Expression and Information adopted on 29 April 1982.

10. When dealing with journalism it must be borne in mind that it relies on the media, which are part of a corporate structure within which a distinction must be made between publishers, proprietors and journalists. To that end, in addition to safeguarding the freedom of the media, freedom within the media must also be protected and internal pressures guarded against.

11. News organisations must consider themselves as special socio-economic agencies whose entrepreneurial objectives have to be limited by the conditions for providing access to a fundamental right.

12. News organisations must show transparency in matters of media ownership and management, enabling citizens to ascertain clearly the identity of proprietors and the extent of their economic interest in the media.

13. Inside the news organisation, publishers and journalists must co-exist, bearing in mind that the legitimate respect for publishers' and owners' ideological orientations is limited by the absolute requirements on truthful news reporting and ethical opinions. This is essential if we are to respect the citizens' fundamental right to information.

14. These requirements are such that we must reinforce the safeguards of the journalist's freedom of expression, for they must in the last instance operate as the ultimate sources of information. In this connection we must legally expand and clarify the nature of the conscience clause and professional secrecy vis-à-vis confidential sources, harmonising national provisions on this matter so that they can be implemented in the wider context of democratic Europe.

15. Neither publishers and proprietors nor journalists should consider that they own the news. News organisations must treat information not as a commodity but as a fundamental right of the citizen. To that end, the media should exploit neither the quality nor the substance of

the news or opinions for purposes of boosting readership or audience figures in order to increase advertising revenue.

16. If we are to ensure that information is treated ethically, its target audience must be considered as individuals and not as a mass.

17. Information and communication as conveyed by journalism through the media, with powerful support from the new technologies, has decisive importance for the development of the individual and society. It is indispensable for democratic life, since if democracy is to develop fully it must guarantee citizens participation in public affairs. Suffice it to say that such participation would be impossible if the citizens were not in receipt of the information on public affairs which they need and which must be provided by the media.

18. The importance of information, especially radio and television news, for culture and education was highlighted in Assembly Recommendation 1067. Its effects on public opinion are obvious.

19. It would be wrong to infer from the importance of this role that the media actually represent public opinion or that they should replace the specific functions of the public authorities or institutions of an educational or cultural character such as schools.

20. This would amount to transforming the media and journalism into authorities or counter-authorities ("mediocracy"), even though they would not be representative of the citizens or subject to the same democratic controls as the public authorities, and would not possess the specialist knowledge of the corresponding cultural or educational institutions.

21. Therefore journalism should not alter truthful, impartial information or honest opinions, or exploit them for media purposes, in an attempt to create or shape public opinion, since its legitimacy rests on effective respect for the citizen's fundamental right to information as part of respect for democratic values. To that end, legitimate investigative journalism is limited by the veracity and

honesty of information and opinions and is incompatible with journalistic campaigns conducted on the basis of previously adopted positions and special interests.

22. In journalism, information and opinions must respect the presumption of innocence, in particular in cases which are still sub judice, and must refrain from making judgments.

23. The right of individuals to privacy must be respected. Persons holding office in public life are entitled to protection for their privacy except in those cases where their private life may have an effect on their public life. The fact that a person holds a public post does not deprive him of the right to respect for his privacy.

24. The attempt to strike a balance between the right to respect for private life, enshrined in Article 8 of the European Convention on Human Rights, and the freedom of expression set forth in Article 10, is well documented in the recent case-law of the European Commission and Court of Human Rights.

25. In the journalist's profession the end does not justify the means; therefore information must be obtained by legal and ethical means.

26. At the request of the persons concerned, the news media must correct, automatically and speedily, and with all relevant information provided, any news item or opinion conveyed by them which is false or erroneous. National legislation should provide for appropriate sanctions and, where applicable, compensation.

27. In order to harmonise the application and exercise of this right in the member states of the Council of Europe, we must implement Resolution (74) 26 on the right of reply _ Position of the individual in relation to the press, adopted by the Committee of Ministers on 2 July 1974, and also the relevant provisions of the European Convention on Transfrontier Television.

28. In order to ensure high-quality work and independence on the part of journalists, they must be guaranteed decent pay and proper working conditions and facilities.

29. In the relations which the journalist must maintain in the course of his duties with the public authorities or the various economic sectors, care should be taken to avoid any kind of connivance liable to affect the independence and impartiality of journalism.

30. In journalism, controversial or sensational items must not be confused with subjects on which it is important to provide information. The journalist must not exploit his duties for the principal purpose of acquiring prestige or personal influence.

31. In view of the complexity of the process of providing information, which is increasingly based on the use of new technologies, speed and conciseness, journalists must be required to have appropriate professional training.

32. Within the newspaper business, publishers, proprietors and journalists must live side by side. To that end, rules must be drawn up for editorial staff in order to regulate professional relations between the journalists and the publishers and proprietors within the media, separately from the normal requirements of labour relations. Such rules might provide for the setting up of editorial boards.

33. In society, situations of tension and conflict sometimes arise under the pressure of factors such as terrorism, discrimination against minorities, xenophobia or war. In such circumstances the media have a moral obligation to defend democratic values: respect for human dignity, solving problems by peaceful, tolerant means, and consequently to oppose violence and the language of hatred and confrontation and to reject all discrimination based on culture, sex or religion.

34. No-one should remain neutral vis-à-vis the defence of democratic values. To that end the media must play a major role in preventing tension and must encourage mutual understanding, tolerance and trust between the various communities in regions where conflict prevails, as the Secretary General of the Council of Europe has set out to do with her confidence-building measures in the former Yugoslavia.

35. Having regard to the very specific influence of the media, notably television, on the attitudes of children and young people, care must be taken not to broadcast programmes, messages or images glorifying violence, exploiting sex and consumerism or using deliberately unsuitable language.

36. Having regard to the requisite conditions and basic principles enumerated above, the media must undertake to submit to firm ethical principles guaranteeing freedom of expression and the fundamental right of citizens to receive truthful information and honest opinions.

37. In order to supervise the implementation of these principles, self-regulatory bodies or mechanisms must be set up comprising publishers, journalists, media users' associations, experts from the academic world and judges; they will be responsible for issuing resolutions on respect for ethical precepts in journalism, with prior commitment on the part of the media to publish the relevant resolutions. This will help the citizen, who has the right to information, to pass either positive or negative judgment on the journalist's work and credibility.

38. The self-regulatory bodies or mechanisms, the media users' associations and the relevant university departments could publish each year the research done a posteriori on the truthfulness of the information broadcast by the media, comparing the news with the actual facts. This would serve as a barometer of credibility which citizens could use as a guide to the ethical standard achieved by each medium or each section of the media, or even each individual journalist. The relevant corrective mechanisms might simultaneously help improve the manner in which the profession of media journalism is pursued.

PUBLIC SERVICE BROADCASTING

While all countries of the region have legislative frameworks governing the freedom of speech, expression, information and publication, the effect of such laws is to indicate the limits of expression negatively so as to protect the rights of individuals, the interests of the state, law and order and public security. The specific statutes pertaining to radio and television also relate to the content of programmes and the obligation not to condone or incite crime, not to blaspheme or offend religious beliefs and susceptibilities and not to offend good taste or decency. Regulations may also be framed to ensure that these standards are observed.

But state ownership of most radio and television stations puts the onus of monitoring programmes and ensuring the observance of standards on the government itself. There is now in India an attempt to create an independent monitoring body and forum for redressing complaints under the provisions of the Prasar Bharati Act. In Sri Lanka a Media Council Act has been advocated to carry out similar functions.

The structural constraint of state ownership of the electronic media also engenders functional constraints. There is an absence of editorial autonomy for the broadcaster, who is ultimately responsible to the political authorities. Although the five countries under study claim to be democracies, a culture of dialogue that also respects the opinions of dissenters is lacking. For the most part the state in the respective countries uses the public-funded electronic media in a politically partisan manner. The state's justification for such use is that the government of the day needs to project its development activities to the public as an expression of accountability.

In doing so the state overlooks the requirement of the media to inform the public on matters of public interest and to act as a watchdog of governance. This is difficult to realise in a culture of compliance, the absence of authentic professionalism and observance of a concomitant ethic.

The state's attitude to the information process has traditionally been to disclose as little as possible to the media, secrecy being the norm. Where it chooses the path of disclosure it is usually to further the interest of the regime or to embarrass its political opponents. The manipulation of the electronic media that function under government auspices leads to officialisation of the information process. Thereby broadcasters are denied their editorial independence and the professional obligation to observe ethical norms of communication such as accuracy, fairness, objectivity, right of reply and of dissent, and responsiveness to social need.

The absence of a clearly articulated media policy in respect of public-funded media organisations in pluralist societies such as the South Asian often results in propagandist and partisan use of such media, resort to self-censorship and cronyism among communicators.

HUMAN RIGHTS AND JOURNALISTIC ETHICS

The foregoing critique of state-run and public-funded electronic media institutions is also valid for newspapers that function under state auspices. Some such criticism is also valid for newspapers that are privately owned and deny editorial autonomy to journalists. Nor do such newspapers foster the observance of journalistic ethics in day-to-day functioning by providing for professional training and observance of ethical norms.

Although the newspaper enterprise in most South Asian countries is over 150 years old (except explicitly in Bangladesh and Pakistan for reasons of their recent creation as separate nations) there has been no formal code until recently. However, there are laws pertaining to newspapers and printing presses and the general law, several provisions of which are incorporated in the Penal Code.

It was noted earlier in this essay that private newspapers that were supportive of the ruling power in the respective countries experienced a sense of political, social and economic power. Consequently, they could hire and fire journalists at will and felt that their newspapers had no moral obligation to serve the public interest or to accommodate news and views favourable to those with whom they disagreed or whom they disliked.

It was the intensely partial, divisive and restrictive stance of some newspapers, albeit influential with the ruling elites, which led to public clamour for press commissions in some countries of South Asia. Partly, they were inspired by the initiatives taken in Britain (Royal Commission on the Press,

1947-1949) and in the United States with the publication in 1947 of "A Free and Responsible Press." An independent Commission on the Freedom of the Press issued it. Its report deals with the responsibilities of the owners and managers of the press to their consciences and the common good for the formation of public opinion. The Commission comprised persons of standing drawn from civil society.

The special significance of the US commission is that it predates the Universal Declaration of Human Rights of 1948 and the International Covenant on Civil and Political Rights in 1976, in particular Articles 14, 17 and 19. The Commission focused on the moral aspect of freedom of expression, the right being based on the duty of a person to the common good and to his own thought. "In the absence of moral duties, there are no moral rights," the report states.

The jurisprudence derived from the recognition of human rights and duties, the inspirational religious and cultural values of the South Asian civilisations and a shared public repugnance at the abuse of power by some newspapers and journalists supportive of regimes that were authoritarian led to the appointment of press commissions.

In India the first press commission was set up in 1952 and reported on the status of the press. Its unique feature is that it is multi-lingual, publishing in as many as 90 languages. The ownership pattern of some 25,000 newspapers and journals is varied, the largest number (nearly two thirds) being published by individuals. Their combined share of circulation is about equal to that of newspapers published by joint stock companies. The number of company newspapers is only about one eighteenth of the number published by private individuals. Societies and associations, firms and partnerships, trusts, cooperative societies and educational institutions are among the other publishers of newspapers. This varied pattern of ownership, the multi-lingual character of the press, the diversity of the readership and the absence of an ethic shared by journalists and the public compound the issue of a common code of communication ethics.

The Press Council of India, set up by an Act of Parliament in 1965, was empowered to draft a code of conduct for newspapers, news agencies and journalists in accordance with high professional standards. But it refrained from doing so, hoping that a code would evolve from its own deliberations.

In 1984 the Press Council published an 11-point set of guidelines, which could serve as norms in the event of editors and journalists themselves deciding to draft a code. They were as follows.

- Accuracy and fairness
- Verification before publication
- Respect for privacy
- Recognition of the right of reply
- Restraint in the coverage of communal disputes/clashes
- Avoidance of plagiarism
- Principles regarding recording interviews and phone conversations
- Avoidance of vulgarity and obscenity
- Caution in criticising judicial actions
- Restraint in the use of photographs of bodies of victims of crime/accidents
- Avoidance of crass commercialism

It has been observed that there is a low degree of voluntary compliance with the code. Nevertheless, public faith in the Press Council as a forum for redressing complaints against newspapers is borne out by the number of complaints it receives and investigates. The Council has on occasion deplored conflict between owners and editors that tends to affect editorial freedom as well as the proper functional relationship between the proprietors and the staff engaged in the production of the paper.

A cause of conflict between owners and editors is the interlocking of the press with industry. Consequently, owners warn editors not to be too critical of the government, fearing reprisals that may affect their business interests.

Another ethical issue arises from the attitude to the newspaper as a saleable commodity, expressed by the Managing

Director of Benett Coleman and Company, publishers of "The Times of India."

Such an attitude negates the human rights basis of media ethics. It is refreshing therefore to find a Code of Ethics of the All-India Newspapers Editors Conference. In several respects it is similar to the Guidelines of the Indian Press Council.

Significant departures from the Council principles are that journalists are enjoined to promote the unity of the country and to be circumspect in dealing with movements and ideas which promote regionalism at the cost of national unity; the integrity of the country is to be regarded as sacrosanct; confidentiality and professional secrecy; obligations of propriety to fellow journalists, and personal integrity of conduct.

The Code of Conduct 1993 for Newspapers, News Agencies and Journalists of Bangladesh framed under the Press Council Act of 1974 introduces the expression "moral duty" in several of its provisions. Among such moral duties is that the editor must accept full and sole responsibility for all that is published in his newspaper; that journalists should highlight degeneration of moral values in Bangladesh society; and exercise caution in publishing news of man-woman relationships or any report relating to women.

In Nepal the preamble to the Code of Conduct for Journalists (1992) states that the country's new Constitution (1990) has established democratic principles and values, and by enhancing the dignity of the press has placed a greater responsibility on its practitioners to fulfil the professional duty entrusted to them by making it responsible to society.

The Code, issued by the Press Council (initially set up in 1970 and reconstituted in 1992) requires journalists to "always remain dedicated to human values, democratic behaviour, national interest and public welfare."

Another article of the Code states that "news and views leading to communal fighting, terrorism and differences between different races, religious groups and communities should not be entertained."

Another provision states that resort to blackmail through journalism for economic or other benefit "is a serious moral crime." In other respects the Code is comparable with codes elsewhere.

In 1993 the Nepal Journalists Association adopted a Code of Conduct for Journalists, also called the Birgunj Declaration 1993 after the venue of the meeting. While it is similar to other codes for journalists, it is significant in that it requires journalists to be dedicated to ensuring that the people's right to be informed is secured. They are also required to "remain dedicated to human values, democratic culture, the country's well-being and for the public well-being."

The relaxation of restrictions on the Nepalese press owes a great deal to a 1981 Royal Commission on the Press that led to the enactment of the Press and Publications Act of 1982, a measure of reform.

The Constitution of 1990 reinforced the liberalisation. Of special interest is Article 16, which states, "Every person shall have the right to demand and receive information on any matter of public importance." The Press and Publications Act of February 1992 further consolidated the earlier gains.

Pakistan's articulation of media ethics is unique in that it illustrates how Islam tends to reshape the values and ethics of Pakistan's society.

The authoritarian regime of Field Marshal Ayub Khan had in 1963 promulgated the restrictive Press and Publications Ordinance. It was replaced by a mild regulatory law, the Registration of Press and Publications Ordinance of 1988, as a result of the Federal Shariat Court judgement on a petition which entailed examination of the 1963 Ordinance.

In its judgment the Shariat Court relied heavily on the Islamic Declaration for the mass media prepared and published by the Islamic Press Union. According to the Islamic Declaration, Islam lays great emphasis on freedom of expression and human dignity. It not only gives people the right of dissent but also makes it obligatory on them to protest against tyranny, injustice and oppression.

The Declaration adds, "Islam aims at creating a disciplined society where the rights and obligations of the individuals are in harmony with the broader interests of the community.

"These rights and obligations must not be curtailed, abrogated, suspended or transgressed by individuals, governments, parliaments or other institutions."

The Declaration articulates in some detail the rights of freedom of expression, or protest against injustice and evil and the individual's right to privacy. It goes on to spell out the concept of authenticity, which the media are required to uphold in practice.

Article 19 of the Constitution of the Islamic Republic of Pakistan, besides guaranteeing to citizens freedom of speech and expression, also guarantees freedom of the press, subject, however, to reasonable restrictions imposed by law "in the interest of the glory of Islam, of the integrity, security or defence of Pakistan or any part thereof, friendly relations with foreign states, public order, decency or morality, or in relation to contempt of court, defamation or incitement to any offence."

The Sri Lanka Press Council Code of Ethics for journalists was drawn up in consultation with a group of editors and approved by parliament in October 1981. The Press Council was established in 1973 by an act of parliament. Its institution was recommended by the Press Commission of 1963, which recommended the broadbasing of the ownership of the press besides other matters.

The Code of Ethics is comparable with codes in most Western countries, but many journalists are not aware of its existence nor does it form part of whatever training is provided in newspaper establishments. Even some legislators are unaware that the Code has been there since 1981. The principles enshrined in the Code derive from the human rights jurisprudence, which draws attention to both rights and duties.

OBSERVANCE OF MEDIA ETHICS

The South Asian experience points to a gulf between the values and norms enshrined in the respective codes and the actual practice of journalism. It derives partly from a mistaken notion that the press is in a privileged position and that journalists are entitled to greater freedom of expression than ordinary citizens. Further, breach of the code of ethics is not punishable by courts except where the infringement is also an offence against some statutory provision.

While freedom of expression is exercised, at times to the point of license, there is insufficient evidence of the duty of care and respect for the rights of others. That the right of expression and publication has to be exercised with responsibility for accuracy, objectivity, fairness and balance appears not to be part of a professional code.

It requires an activist Press Council and a self-regulatory professional body of journalists to ensure high standards of journalism and promotion of the ethical values that the codes seek to uphold. Nevertheless, the interventionist role of the Press Council is minimal. It often acts only on complaints by aggrieved readers. It does not in addition perform a monitoring role. In any case, after inquiry all that the Press Council can do is to order the newspaper to publish a correction; an apology where it is required; and it could reprimand the offending newspaper. It has no penal power. So it tends to be regarded as toothless.

The situation is further compounded by the absence of a public ethic based on a concept of morality and respect for human rights. At times readers tend to consider public curiosity about the private lives of politicians and celebrities a matter of public interest although the private conduct of such persons does not always impinge on the performance of their public duty.

The fact that newspapers are in a competitive industry is another functional constraint on the observance of media ethics. Papers not only strive to be first with the news, but also tend to sensationalise it to get the edge on competitors.

The link between newspaper circulation and advertising also tends to blur the ethical dimension. Dramatisation of news promotes sales and circulation and helps increase advertising revenue. Note the cynical attitude of the proprietors of The

Times of India who regard the newspaper primarily as a saleable commodity.

Journalism schools endeavour to instil an awareness of the ethics of principle. But only a very small proportion of South Asian journalists have had pre-entry training in such schools of journalism. In-plant training is mainly craft-oriented. Even if media ethics is part of the curriculum of such training, the practice of journalism leaves much to be desired.

The absence of professional bodies of journalists comparable with bodies for such professions as law, medicine, engineering and accountancy is a drawback to the self-regulation of the profession.

While there are many associations of journalists in the respective countries they function more like trade unions and are concerned mainly with working conditions, salaries, pensions, ancillary facilities and security of service.

The need for codes of media ethics is unquestionable. But codes alone have not been effective in raising ethical standards in the media. This was the consensus of a three-day seminar on "Communication Ethics from a

South Asian Perspective," held in Colombo, Sri Lanka, in November 1993.

The participants included 20 senior journalists and communication scholars from the South Asian region. The seminar was organised by the Asian Media Information and Communication Centre (AMIC) Singapore, the World Association of Christian Communication, UK, and the International Centre for Ethnic Studies, Colombo, with support from the Friedrich Ebert Foundation, Colombo.

The seminar recommended replacement of press councils by media councils, which, unlike the former, should not be perceived as an extension of the state but as genuinely independent bodies. They should comprise respected media practitioners and eminent persons from public life chosen through a mechanism ensured by appropriate legislation.

The seminar also commented on the paucity of professional bodies of media practitioners in the region and called for the status of such bodies to be recognised by both the state and the social community. It would be the responsibility of such bodies to promote observance of ethical standards among media practitioners and a greater sense of social responsibility among media institutions.

While there is a growing degree of awareness among senior media practitioners of the need for adherence to media ethics there is little evidence of discussion of media ethics at the level of media owners. However, there is discussion by media owners on what they perceive as the intrusive role of the state in introducing new regulatory measures especially in relation to electronic media.

Perhaps the weakest aspect of media ethics in South Asia is the absence of an articulate public ethic that could act as a countervailing force to both the state and media institutions. The restraint on such a cohesive public ethic emerging is media audiences being heterogeneous in composition and values, levels of appreciation of media content, diverse in taste and apparently shunning an activist role in safeguarding cultural values and promoting high standards of media performance.

JOURNALISM CODES OF ETHICS NOW FOCUSED MORE ON FINANCIAL SUCCESS

What a beautiful idea! Bonnie Brennen and Lee Wilkins, researchers at the Missouri School of Journalism recently analyzed and compared two early codes, the 1923 American Society of Newspaper Editors (ASNE) code and the 1934 American Newspaper Guild (ANG) code, with the 2003 New York Times code of ethics. They found that changes to the journalism code of ethics have played a significant part in the negative perception of today's media.

The whole Article: For the past 15 years, the public's perception of the news media has been becoming more negative, causing historic professional stress for journalists. The industry has moved from privately owned to publicly traded and toward conglomeration of ownership in order to maximize profits. Readership of newspapers and viewership of broadcast news have fallen. A new study by researchers at the University of Missouri-Columbia found that changes to the journalism code of ethics have played a significant part in the negative perception of today's media.

Two journalism professors at MU's School of Journalism, Bonnie Brennen and Lee Wilkins, recently analyzed and compared two early codes, the 1923 American Society of Newspaper Editors (ASNE) code and the 1934 American Newspaper Guild (ANG) code, with the 2003 New York Times code of ethics and found several significant changes and shifts in professional thinking.

> *"The ASNE code set out to maintain the rights and dignity of the profession and tried to establish ethical standards for journalistic conduct," said Brennen. "For example, the ASNE code says that invasions of privacy should be avoided unless the public warrants such intrusion, and editors are asked to not publish unofficial charges without giving the people the opportunity to defend themselves."*

The ANG code, Brennen and Wilkins found, insists that reporters respect the rights of individuals by crafting factual and fair news reports that accurately represent an unbiased account of the news. It gives reporters little room for exceptions or extenuating conditions.

When the researchers looked at the Times code, they found striking differences from the ASNE and ANG code. The Times code focuses mainly on conflicts of interest, economic health and financial success. For example, staff members are prohibited from free-lance work that competes with the Times while noting that the Times sphere of influence is larger than ever. Also, according to the code:

> *"Staff members may not appear on broadcasts that directly compete with the Times' own offerings on television or the Internet...As the paper moves further into these new fields, its direct competitors, clients or potential clients will undoubtedly grow in number."*

In terms of conflicts of interest, the code, Brennen and Wilkins said, interprets the subject broadly, linking conflict of interest to perception of the newspaper's impartiality, neutrality and the integrity of news reports. Other elements that influence the integrity of the news reports, such as accuracy and tough-minded evaluation of both sources and the information they provide, are not mentioned in the Times code.

Brennen and Wilkins found that the sections in the code based on economic and financial success of the Times are one of the main fault lines in the profession: the tension between economic goals and the traditional view of journalism as a public service, something emphasized in the earlier codes. The Times, they believe, has placed its economic health on an equal footing with the public trust.

"If the recent Jayson Blair incident is any indication, management's financial concerns as articulated in the ethics code ? Have their parallels in real life," Brennen and Wilkins said. "The emphasis reveals something central about the profession: concerns about financial profitability do remain on an equal footing with journalistic duty and service."

2

Fundamentals of Journalism

Journalism is a discipline of writing. News-oriented journalism is sometimes described as the "first rough draft of history" (attributed to Phil Graham), because journalists often did record important events, however producing news articles on short deadlines. While under pressure to be first with their stories, news media organizations usually edit and proofread their reports prior to publication, adhering to each organization's standards of accuracy, quality, and style. Many news organizations claim proud traditions of holding government officials and institutions accountable to the public, while media critics have raised questions about holding the press itself accountable.

Digitalization of news-production and the diffusion capabilities of the internet are challenging the traditional journalistic professional culture. The concept of participatory or citizen journalism proposes that amateur reporters can actually produce stories inside or outside professional media outlets, ending the information production monopoly of the press.

REPORTING

Journalism's main activities include stating who, what, when, where, why and how, and stating the significance and effects of certain events or trends. Journalism exists in a number of media: newspapers, television, radio, magazines and, most recently, the World Wide Web through the Internet.

The subject matter of journalism can be anything and everything that they choose, and journalists report and write on a wide variety of subjects: politics on the international, national, provincial and local levels, economics and business on the same four levels, health and medicine, education, sports, hobbies and recreation, life-styles, clothing, food, pets, and relationships; journalists report on anything that news organizations think consumers will read. Journalists can report for general interest news outlets like newspapers, news magazines and broadcast sources; general circulation specialty publications like trade and hobby magazines or for news publications and outlets with a select group of subscribers. Journalists are usually expected and required to go out to the scene of a story to gather information for their reports, and often may compose their reports in the field. They also use the telephone, the computer and the internet to gather information. However, more often those reports are written, and they are almost always edited in newsrooms, the offices where journalists and editors work together to prepare news content.

Journalists, especially if they cover a specific subject or area (a "beat") are expected to cultivate sources, people in the subject or area, that they can communicate with, either to explain the details of a story, or to provide leads to other subjects of stories yet to be reported. They are also expected to develop their investigative skills to better research and report stories.

PRINT JOURNALISM

Print journalism can be split into several categories: newspapers, news magazines, general interest magazines, trade magazines, hobby magazines, newsletters, private publications, online news pages and others. Each genre can have its own requirements for researching and writing reports.

For example, newspaper journalists in the United States have traditionally written reports using the inverted pyramid style, although this style is used more for straight or hard news reports rather than features. Written hard news reports are expected to be spare in the use of words, and to list the most important information first, so that, if the story must be cut because there is not enough space for it, the least important facts will be automatically cut from the bottom. Editors usually ensure that reports are written with as few words as possible. Feature stories are usually written in a looser style that usually depends on the subject matter of the report, and in general granted more space.

News magazine and general interest magazine articles are usually written in a different style, with less emphasis on the inverted pyramid. Trade publications can be more news-oriented, while hobby publications can be more feature-oriented.

BROADCAST JOURNALISM

Radio journalists must gather facts to present them fairly and accurately, but also must find and record relevant and interesting sounds to add to their reports, both interviews with people involved in the story and background sounds that help characterize the story. Radio reporters may also write the introduction to the story read by a radio news anchor, and may also answer questions live from the anchor.

Television journalists rely on visual information to illustrate and characterize their reporting, including on-camera interviews with people involved in the story, shots of the scene where the story took place, and graphics usually produced at the station to help frame the story. Like radio reporters, television reporters also may write the introductory script that a television news anchor would read to set up their story. Both radio and television journalists usually do not have as much "space" to present information in their reports as print journalists.'

ON-LINE (CYBER) JOURNALISM

The growth of the Internet and World Wide Web has spawned the newest medium for journalism, on-line (Cyber) journalism. The speed at which news can be disseminated on the web, and the profound penetration to anyone with a computer and web browser, have greatly increased the quantity and variety of news reports available to the average web user.

The bulk of on-line journalism has been the extension of existing print and broadcast media into the web via web versions of their primary products. New reports that were set to be released at expected times now can be published as soon as they are written and edited, increasing the deadline pressure and fear of being scooped many journalists must deal with.

Most news websites are free to their users-one notable exception being the Wall Street Journal website, for which a subscription is required to view its contents-but some outlets, such as the New York Times website, offer current news for free but archived reports and access to opinion columnists and other non-news sections for a periodic fee. Attempts to start unique web publications, such as Slate and Salon, have met with limited success, in part because they do or did charge subscription fees.

Many newspapers are branching into new mediums because of the Internet. Their websites may now include video, podcasts, blogs and slide-shows. Story chat, where readers may post comments on an article, has changed the dialogue newspapers foster. Traditionally kept to the confines of the opinion section as letters to the editor, story chat has allowed readers to express opinions without the time delay of a letter or the approval of an editor.

The growth of blogs as a source of news and especially opinion on the news has forever changed journalism. Blogs now can create news as well as report it, and blur the dividing line between news and opinion. The debate about whether blogging is really journalism rages on.

VARIATIONS OF JOURNALISM

Feature Journalism

Newspapers and periodicals often contain features written by journalists, many of whom specialize in this form of in-depth journalism.

Feature articles usually are longer than straight news articles, and are combined with photographs, drawings or other "art." They may also be highlighted by typographic effects or colors.

Writing features can be more demanding than writing straight news stories, because while a journalist must apply the same amount of effort to accurately gather and report the facts of the story, the reporter must also find a creative and interesting way to write the article, especially the lead, or the first one or two paragraphs of the story. The lead must grab the reader's attention yet accurately embody the ideas of the article. Often the lead of a feature article is dictated by its subject matter. Journalists must work even harder to avoid cliched images and words when writing the lead and the rest of the article.

In the last half of the 20th Century the line between straight news reporting and feature writing blurred as more and more journalists and publications experimented with different approaches to writing an article. Tom Wolfe, Gay Talese, Hunter S. Thompson and other journalists used many different approaches to writing news articles. Urban and alternative weekly newspapers went even further blurring the distinction, and many magazines fan more features than straight news.

Some television news shows experimented with alternative formats, and many TV shows that claimed to be news shows were not considered as such by many critics, because their content and methods did not adhere to accepted journalistic standards. National Public Radio, on the other hand, is considered a good example of a good mixture of straight news reporting, features, and combinations of the two, usually meeting standards of high quality. Other U.S. public radio news organizations have achieved similar results. A majority of newspapers still maintain a clear distinction between news and features, as do most television and radio news organizations.

SPORTS JOURNALISM

Sports journalism covers many aspects of human athletic competition, and is an integral part of most journalism products, including newspapers, magazines, and radio and television news broadcasts. While some critics don't consider sports journalism to be true journalism, the prominence of sports in Western culture has justified the attention of journalists to not just the competitive events of sports, but also to athletes and the business of sports.

Sports journalism in the United States has traditionally been written in a looser, more creative and more opinionated tone than traditional journalistic writing; the emphases on accuracy and underlying fairness is still a part of sports journalism. An emphasis on the accurate description of statistical performances of athletes is also an important part of sports journalism.

SCIENCE JOURNALISM

Science journalism is a relatively new branch of journalism, in which journalists' reporting conveys information on science topics to the public. Science journalists must understand and interpret very detailed, technical and sometimes jargon-laden information and render it into interesting reports that are comprehensible to consumers of news media.

Scientific journalists also must choose which developments in science merit news coverage, as well as cover disputes within the scientific community with a balance of fairness to both sides but also with a devotion to the facts.

Many, but not all, journalists covering science have training in the sciences they cover, including several medical journalists who cover medicine.

INVESTIGATIVE JOURNALISM

Investigative journalism, in which journalists investigate and expose unethical, immoral and illegal behavior by individuals, businesses and government agencies, can be complicated, time-consuming and expensive-requiring teams of journalists, months of research, interviews (sometimes repeated interviews) with numerous people, long-distance travel, computers to analyze public-record databases, or use of the company's legal staff to secure documents under freedom of information laws.

Because of its inherently confrontational nature, this kind of reporting is often the first to suffer from budget cutbacks or interference from outside the news department. Investigative reporting done poorly can also expose journalists and media organizations to negative reaction from subjects of investigations and the public, and accusations of gotcha journalism. When conducted correctly it can bring the attention of the public and government problems and conditions that the public deem need to be addressed, and can win awards and recognition to the journalists involved and the media outlet that did the reporting.

GONZO JOURNALISM

Gonzo journalism is a type of journalism popularized by the American writer Hunter S. Thompson, author of Fear and Loathing in Las Vegas, Fear and Loathing: On the Campaign Trail of '72, among other stories and books. Gonzo journalism is characterized by its punchy style, rough language, and ostensible disregard for conventional journalistic writing forms and customs. Gonzo journalism attempts to present a multi-disciplinary perspective on a particular story, drawing from popular culture, sports, political, philosophical and literary sources. Gonzo journalism has been styled eclectic or untraditional. It remains a feature of popular magazines such as Rolling Stone magazine. It has a good deal in common with on-line journalism.

'CELEBRITY' OR 'PEOPLE' JOURNALISM

Another area of journalism that grew in stature in the 20th Century is 'celebrity' or 'people' journalism, which focuses on the personal lives of people, primarily celebrities, including movie and stage actors, musical artists, models and photographers, other notable people in the entertainment industry, as well as people who seek attention, such as politicians, and people thrust into the attention of the public, such as people who do something newsworthy.

Once the province of newspaper gossip columnists and gossip magazines, celebrity journalism has become the focus of national tabloid newspapers like the National Enquirer, magazines like People and Us Weekly, syndicated television shows like Entertainment Tonight, Inside Edition, The Insider, Access Hollywood, and Extra, cable networks like E!, A&E Network and The Biography Channel, and numerous other television productions and thouasands of websites. Most other news media provide some coverage of celebrities and people.

Celebrity journalism differs from feature writing in that it focuses on people who are either already famous or are especially attractive, and in that it often covers celebrities obsessively, to the point of these journalists behaving unethically in order to provide coverage. Paparazzi, photographers who would follow celebrities incessantly to obtain potentially embarrassing photographs, have come to characterize celebrity journalism.

CONVERGENCE JOURNALISM

An emerging form of journalism, which combines different forms of journalism, such as print, photographic and video, into one piece or group of pieces. Convergence Journalism can be found in the likes of CNN and many other news sites. The Washington Post has a notable amount of such.

ROLE OF JOURNALISM IN SOCIETY

In the 1920s, as modern journalism was just taking form, writer Walter Lippmann and American philosopher John Dewey debated over the role of journalism in a democracy. Their differing philosophies still characterize a debate about the role of journalism in society and the nation-state.

Lippmann understood that journalism's role at the time was to act as a mediator or translator between the public and policymaking elites. The journalist became the middleman. When elites spoke, journalists listened and recorded the information, distilled it, and passed it on to the public for their consumption. His reasoning behind this was that the public was not in a position to deconstruct a growing and complex flurry of information present in modern society, and so an intermediary was needed to filter news for the masses. Lippman put it this way: The public is not smart enough to understand complicated, political issues. Furthermore, the public was too consumed with their daily lives to care about complex public policy.

Therefore the public needed someone to interpret the decisions or concerns of the elite to make the information plain and simple. That was the role of journalists. Lippmann believed that the public would affect the decision making of the elite with their vote. In the meantime, the elite (i.e. politicians, policy makers, bureaucrats, scientists, etc.) would keep the business of power running. In Lippman's world, the journalist's role was to inform the public of what the elites were doing. It was also to act as a watchdog over the elites as the public had the final say with their votes. Effectively that kept the public at the bottom of the power chain, catching the flow of information that is handed down from experts/elites.

Dewey, on the other hand, believed the public was not only capable of understanding the issues created or responded to by the elite, it was in the public forum that decisions should be made after discussion and debate. When issues were thoroughly vetted, then the best ideas would bubble to the surface. Dewey believed journalists not only had to inform the public, but should report on issues differently than simply passing on information. In Dewey's world, a journalist's role changed. Dewey believed that journalists should take in the information, then weigh the consequences of the policies being enacted by the elites on the public. Over time, his idea has been implemented in various degrees, and is more commonly known as "community journalism."

This concept of Community Journalism is at the center of new developments in journalism. In this new paradigm, journalists are able to engage citizens and the experts/elites in the proposition and generation of content. It's important to note that while there is an assumption of equality, Dewey still celebrates expertise. Dewey believes the shared knowledge of many is far superior to a single individual's knowledge. Experts and scholars are welcome in Dewey's framework, but there is not the hierarchical structure present in Lippman's understanding of journalism and society. According to Dewey, conversation, debate, and dialogue lie at the heart of a democracy.

While Lippman's journalistic philosophy might be more acceptable to government leaders, Dewey's approach is a better descriptor of how many journalists see their role in society, and, in turn, how much of society expects journalists to function. Americans, for example, may criticize some of the excesses committed by journalists, but they tend to expect journalists to serve as watchdogs on government, businesses and other actors, enabling people to make informed decisions on the issues of the time.

THE ELEMENTS OF JOURNALISM

According to The Elements of Journalism by Bill Kovach and Tom Rosensteil, there are nine elements of journalism. In order for a journalist to fulfill their duty of providing the people with the information they need to be free and self-governing, they must follow these guidelines:

1. Journalism's first obligation is to the truth.
2. Its first loyalty is to the citizens.
3. Its essence is discipline of verification.
4. Its practitioners must maintain an independence from those they cover.
5. It must serve as an independent monitor of power.
6. It must provide a forum for public criticism and compromise.
7. It must strive to make the significant, interesting, and relevant.
8. It must keep the news comprehensive and proportional.
9. Its practitioners must be allowed to exercise their personal conscience.

PROFESSIONAL AND ETHICAL STANDARDS

Since the development of professional journalism at the beginning of the 20th Century, journalists have been expected to follow a stringent code of journalistic conduct that requires them to, among other things:

- Use original sources of information, including interviews with people directly involved in a story, original documents and other direct sources of information, whenever possible, and cite the sources of this information in reports;
- Fully attribute information gathered from other published sources, should original sources not be available (to not do so is considered plagiarism; some newspapers also note when an article uses information from previous reports);

- Use multiple original sources of information, especially if the subject of the report is controversial;
- Check every fact reported;
- Find and report every side of a story possible;
- Report without bias, illustrating many aspects of a conflict rather than siding with one;
- Approach researching and reporting a story with a balance between objectivity and skepticism.
- Use careful judgment when organizing and reporting information.
- Be careful about granting confidentiality to sources (news organizations usually have specific rules that journalists must follow concerning grants of confidentiality);
- Decline gifts or favors from any subject of a report, and avoid even the appearance of being influenced;
- Abstain from reporting or otherwise participating in the research and writing about a subject in which the journalist has a personal stake or bias that cannot be set aside.

This was in stark contrast to the media climate prior to the 20th Century, where the media market was dominated by smaller newspapers and pamphleteers who usually had an overt and often radical agenda, with no presumption of balance or objectivity.

RECOGNITION OF EXCELLENCE IN JOURNALISM

There are several professional organizations, universities and foundations that recognize excellence in journalism. The Pulitzer Prize, administered by Columbia University in New York City, is awarded to newspapers, magazines and broadcast media for excellence in various kinds of journalism. The Columbia University Graduate School of Journalism gives the Alfred I. duPont-Columbia University Awards for excellence in radio and television journalism, and the Scripps Howard Foundation gives the National Journalism Awards in 17 categories. The Society of Professional Journalists gives the Sigma Delta Chi Award for journalism excellence. In the television industry, the National Academy of Television Arts & Sciences gives awards for excellence in television journalism

FAILING TO UPHOLD STANDARDS

Such a code of conduct can, in the real world, be difficult to uphold consistently. Journalists who believe they are being fair or objective may give biased accounts—by reporting selectively, trusting too much to anecdote, or giving a partial explanation of actions. Even in routine reporting, bias can creep into a story through a reporter's choice of facts to summarize, or through failure to check enough sources, hear and report dissenting voices, or seek fresh perspectives.

As much as reporters try to set aside their prejudices, they may simply be unaware of them. Young reporters may be blind to issues affecting the elderly. A 20-year veteran of the "police beat" may be deaf to rumors of departmental corruption. Publications marketed to affluent suburbanites may ignore urban problems. And, of course, naive or unwary reporters and editors alike may fall prey to public relations, propaganda or disinformation.

News organizations provide editors, producers or news directors whose job is to check reporters' work at various stages. But editors can get tired, lazy, complacent or biased. An editor may be blind to a favorite reporter's omissions, prejudices or fabrications. Provincial editors also may be ill-equipped to weigh the perspective (or check the facts of) a correspondent reporting from a distant city or foreign country.

A news organization's budget inevitably reflects decision-making about what news to cover, for what audience, and in what depth. Those decisions may reflect conscious or unconscious bias. When budgets are cut, editors may sacrifice reporters in distant news bureaus, reduce the number of staff assigned to low-income areas, or wipe entire communities from the publication's zone of interest.

Publishers, owners and other corporate executives, especially advertising sales executives, can try to use their powers over journalists to influence how news is reported and published. Journalists usually rely on top management to create and maintain a "firewall" between the news and other departments in a news organization to prevent undue influence on the news department. One journalism magazine, Columbia Journalism Review, has made it a practice to reveal examples of executives who try to influence news coverage, of executives who do not abuse their powers over journalists, and of journalists who resist such pressures.

REPORTING VERSUS EDITORIALIZING

Generally, publishers and consumers of journalism draw a distinction between reporting-"just the facts"-and opinion writing, often by restricting opinion columns to the editorial page and its facing or "op-ed" (opposite the editorials) page. Unsigned editorials are traditionally the official opinions of the paper's editorial board, while op-ed pages may be a mixture of syndicated columns and other contributions, frequently with some attempt to balance the voices across some political or social spectrum.

The distinction between reporting and opinion can break down. Complex stories often require summarizing and interpretation of facts, especially if there is limited time or space for a story. Stories involving great amounts of interpretation are often labelled "news analysis," but still run in a paper's news columns. The limited time for each story in a broadcast report rarely allows for such distinctions.

AMBUSH JOURNALISM

Ambush journalism refers to aggressive tactics practiced by journalists to suddenly confront with questions people who otherwise do not wish to speak to a journalist. The practice has particularly been applied by television journalists, such as those on the CBS-TV news show 60 Minutes and by Geraldo Rivera, currently on the Fox News cable channel, and by hundreds of American local television reporters conducting investigations.

The practice has been sharply criticized by journalists and others as being highly unethical and sensational, while others defend it as the only way to attempt to provide those subject to it an opportunity to comment for a report. Ambush journalism has not been ruled illegal in the United States, although doing it on private property could open a journalist to being charged with trespassing.

GOTCHA JOURNALISM

Gotcha journalism refers to the deliberate manipulation of the presentation of facts in a report in order to portray a person or organization in a particular way that varies from an accurate portrayal based on balanced review of the facts available. In particular it is applied to broadcast journalism, where the story, images and interviews are tailored to create a particular impression of the subject matter.

It is considered highly unethical to engage in gotcha journalism. Many subjects of reporting have claimed to have been subjected to it, and some media outlets are guilty of deliberately biased reporting.

LEGAL STATUS

Journalists around the world often write about the governments in their nations, and those governments have widely varying policies and practices towards journalists, which control what they can research and write, and what press organizations can publish. Many Western governments guarantee the freedom of the press, and do relatively little to restrict press rights and freedoms, while other nations severely restrict what journalists can research and/or publish.

Journalists in many nations have enjoyed some privileges not enjoyed by members of the general public, including better access to public events, crime scenes and press conferences, and to extended interviews with public officials, celebrities and others in the public eye. These privileges are available because of the perceived power of the press to turn public opinion for or against governments, their officials and policies, as well as the perception that the press often represents their consumers. These privileges extend from the legal rights of journalists but are not guaranteed by those rights. Sometimes government officials may attempt to punish individual journalists who irk them by denying them some of these privileges extended to other journalists.

Nations or jurisdictions that formally license journalists may confer special privileges and responsibilities along with those licenses, but in the United States the tradition of an independent press has avoided any imposition of government-controlled examinations or licensing. Some of the states have explicit shield laws that protect journalists from some forms of government inquiry, but those statutes' definitions of "journalist" were often based on access to printing presses and broadcast towers. A national shield law has been proposed.

In some nations, journalists are directly employed, controlled or censored by their governments. In other nations, governments who may claim to guarantee press rights actually intimidate journalists with threats of arrest, destruction or seizure of property (especially the means of production and dissemination of news content), torture or murder.

Journalists who elect to cover conflicts, whether wars between nations or insurgencies within nations, often give up expectation to protection by government, if not giving up their rights to protection by government. Journalists who are captured or detained during a conflict are expected to be treated as civilians and to be released to their national government.

RIGHTS OF JOURNALISTS VERSUS THOSE OF PRIVATE CITIZENS AND ORGANIZATIONS

Journalists enjoy similar powers and privileges as private citizens and organizations. The power of journalists over private citizens is limited by the citizen's rights to privacy. Many who seek favorable representation in the press (celebrities, for example) do grant journalists greater access than others enjoy. The right to privacy of a private citizen may be reduced or lost if the citizen is thrust into the public eye, either by their own actions or because they are involved in a public event or incident.

Citizens and private organizations can refuse to deal with some or all journalists; the powers the press enjoy in many nations often make this tactic ineffective or counter-productive.

Citizens in most nations also enjoy the right against being libeled or defamed by journalists, and citizens can bring suit against journalists who they claim have published damaging untruths about them with malicious disregard for the truth. Libel or defamation lawsuits can also become conflicts between the journalists' rights to publish versus the private citizen's right to privacy. Some journalists have claimed lawsuits brought against them and news organizations-or even the threat of such a lawsuit-were intended to stifle their voices with the threat of expensive legal proceedings, even if plaintiffs cannot prove their cases. This is referred to as the Chilling effect.

In the United Kingdom, it is up to the journalist and/or their employers to defend against claims of defamation, opposed to other nations where the burden of proof is on the claimant.

In many nations, journalists and news organizations must function under similar threat of retaliation from private individuals or organizations as from governments. Criminals and criminal organizations, political parties, some zealous religious organizations, and even mobs of people have been known to punish journalists who speak or write about them in ways they do not like. Punishments can include threats, physical damage to property, assault, torture and murder.

RIGHT TO PROTECT CONFIDENTIALITY OF SOURCES

Journalists' interaction with sources sometimes involves confidentiality, an extension of freedom of the press giving journalists a legal protection to keep the identity of a source private even when demanded by police or prosecutors; withholding sources can land journalists in contempt of court, or jail-time.

The scope of rights granted journalists varies from nation to nation; in the United Kingdom, for example, the government has had more legal rights to protect what it considers sensitive information, and to force journalists to reveal the sources of leaked information, than the United States. Other nations, particularly Zimbabwe and the People's Republic of China, have a reputation of persecuting journalists, both domestic and foreign.

In the United States, there has never been a right to protect sources in federal court. Some states provide varying degrees of such protection. However, federal courts will refuse to force journalists to reveal sources, unless the information the court seeks is highly relevant to the case, and there's no other way to get it. Journalists, like all citizens, who refuse to testify even when ordered to can be found in contempt of court and fined or jailed.

RIGHT OF ACCESS TO GOVERNMENT INFORMATION

Like sources, journalists depend on the rights granted by government to the public and, by extension, to the press, for access to information held by the government. These rights also vary from nation to nation and, in the United States, from state to state. Some states have more open policies for making information available, and some states have acted in the last decade to broaden those rights. New Jersey, for example, has updated and broadened its Sunshine Law to better define what kinds of government documents can be withheld from public inquiry.

In the United States, the Freedom of Information Act (FOIA) guarantees journalists the right to obtain copies of government documents, although the government has the right to redact, or black out, information from documents in those copies that FOIA allows them to withhold. Other federal legislation also controls access to information.

HISTORY OF JOURNALISM

The history of journalism, or the gathering and transmitting of news, spans the growth of technology and trade, marked by the advent of specialized techniques for gathering and disseminating information on a regular basis that has caused, as one history of journalism surmises, the steady increase of "the scope of news available to us and the speed with which it is transmitted."

Prehistoric, Ancient and Medieval Periods

Early methods of transmitting news began with word of mouth, which limited its content to what people saw and relayed to others; accuracy in new depended on the scope of the event being described and its relevance to the listener. Ancient monarchial governments developed ways of relaying written reports, including the Roman Empire from Julius Caesar onward, which recorded and distributed a daily record of political news and acts to Roman colonies. After the empire collapsed, news dissemination depended on travelers' tails, songs, ballads, letters, and governmental dispatches.

Renaissance and the Printing Press

The invention of the movable type printing press, attributed to Johannes Gutenberg in 1456, led to the wide dissemination of the Bible and other printed books. The first newspapers appeared in Europe in the 17th century. The first printed periodical was Mercurius Gallobelgicus, first appearing in Cologne, now Germany, in 1594; written in Latin, it was largely concerned with what was by then a dying Roman Empire. Nevertheless, it was distributed widely and found its way to readers in England.

The first regularly published newspaper in English (as opposed to the earlier "news books", published in 8-to 24-page quarto formats) was the Oxford Gazette (later the London Gazette, and published continually ever since), which first appeared in 1665. It began publication while the British royal court was in Oxford to avoid the plague in London, and was published twice a week. When the court moved back to London, the publication moved with it. An earlier newsbook, the Continuation of Our Weekly News, had been published regularly in London since 1623.

The first daily newspaper, the Daily Courant, appeared in 1702 and continued publication for more than 30 years. Its first editor was also the first woman in journalism, although she was replaced after only a couple of weeks. By this time, the British had adopted the Press Restriction Act, which required that the printer's name and place of publication be included on each printed document.

JOURNALISM IN AMERICA

The first printer in Britain's American colonies was Stephen Day in Cambridge, Massachusetts, who began in 1638. The British regulation of printing extended to the Colonies. The first newspaper in the colonies, Benjamin Harris's Public

Occurrences both Foreign and Domestic, was suppressed in 1690 after only one issue under a 1662 Massachusetts law that forbade printing without a license. The publication of a story suggesting that the King of France shared a bed with his son's wife probably also contributed to the suppression.

A second newspaper, the Boston News-Letter, appeared in 1704. It was not suppressed, but it was late reporting local and European news and survived until 1722. The first newspaper published outside New England was Andrew Bradford's American Weekly Mercury, which published between 1719 and 1746.

The first real colonial newspaper was the New England Courant, published as a sideline by printer James Franklin, brother of Benjamin Franklin. Like many other Colonial newspapers, it was aligned with party interests and did not publish balanced content. Ben Franklin was first published in his brother's newspaper, under the pseudonym Silence Dogood, in 1722, and even his brother did not know. Ben Franklin's pseudonymous publishing represented a common practice of newspapers of that time of protecting writers from retribution from those they criticized, often to the point of what would be considered libel today.

After James Franklin suspended publication of the Courant, Ben Franklin moved to Philadelphia in 1728 and took over the Pennsylvania Gazette the following year. Ben Franklin expanded his business by essentially franchising other printers in other cities, who published their own newspapers. By 1750, 14 weekly newspapers were published in the six largest colonies. The largest and most successful of these could be published up to three times per week.

AMERICAN INDEPENDENCE

By the 1770s, 89 newspapers were published in 35 cities. "Most papers at the time of the American Revolution were anti-royalist, chiefly because of opposition to the Stamp Act taxing newsprint." Though the tax was imposed on newsprint, not publication itself, Colonial governments could suppress newspapers "by denying the stamp or refusing to sell approved paper to the offending publisher."

Newspapers flourished in the new republic-by 1800, there were about 234 being published-and tended to be very partisan about the form of the new federal government, which was shaped by successive Federalist or Republican presidencies. Newspapers directed much abuse toward various politicians, and the eventual dual between Alexander Hamilton and Aaron Burr was fueled by controversy in newspaper pages.

As the 19th century progressed in America, newspapers began functioning more as private businesses with real editors rather than partisan organs, though standards for truth and responsibility were still low. "Other than local news, much of the reporting was simply copied from other newspapers, sometimes verbatim. In addition to news stories, there might be poetry or fiction, or (especially late in the century) humorous columns."

Newspapers in general remained political with strong bias toward the government; Andrew Jackson started his own newspaper, funneled government printing work to it, and forced his Washington competition out of business.

RISE OF PROMINENT AMERICAN NEWSPAPERS

As American cities like New York, Philadelphia, Boston and Washington grew with the growth of the Industrial Revolution, so did newspapers. Larger printing presses, the telegraph and other technological innovations allowed newspapers to print thousands of copies, boost circulation and increase revenue.

The first newspaper to fit the modern definition as a newspaper was the New York Herald, founded in 1835 and published by James Gordon Bennett. It was the first newspaper to have city staff covering regular beats and spot news, along with regular business and Wall Street coverage. In 1838 Bennett also organized the first foreign correspondent staff of six men in Europe and assigned domestic correspondents to key cities, including the first reporter to regularly cover Congress.

Not to be outdone was the New York Tribune, which began publishing in 1841 and was edited by Horace Greeley. It was the first newspaper to gain national prominence; by 1861, it shipped thousands of copies daily to other large cities, including 6,000 to Chicago, while other Eastern newspapers published weekly editions for shipment to other cities. Greeley also organized a professional news staff and embarked on frequent publishing crusades for causes he believed in. The Tribune was the first newspaper, in 1886, to use the linotype machine, invented by Ottman Mergenthaler, which "rapidly increased the speed and accuracy with which type could be set."

The New York Times, now considered one of the best newspapers in the world, was founded in 1851 by George Jones and Henry Raymond. It established the principle of balanced reporting in high-quality writing. At the time, it did not achieve the circulation and success it now enjoys.

Growth of Newspapers Outside Eastern Cities

The influence of these large newspapers in New York and other Eastern cities slowly spread to smaller cities and towns, Weekly newspapers gave way to dailies, and competition between newspapers even in small towns became fierce.

In the Midwest and beyond, there was a boom for local newspapers, which remained more focused on local news and services than the larger urban newspapers. Many newspapers flourished during the conquest of the West, as homesteaders were required to publish notices of their land claims in local newspapers. Many of these papers died out after the land rushes ended.

THE RISE OF THE WIRE SERVICES

The American Civil War had a profound effect on American journalism. Large newspapers hired war correspondents to cover the battlefields, with more freedom than correspondents today enjoy. These reporters used the new telegraph and expanding railways to move news reports faster to their newspapers. The cost of sending telegraphs helped create a new concise or "tight" style of writing which has became a standard for journalism through the next century.

The ever-growing demand for urban newspapers to provide more news led to the organization of the first of the wire services, a cooperative between six large New York City-based newspapers led by David Hale, the publisher of the Journal of Commerce, and James Gordon Bennett, to provide coverage of Europe for all of the papers together. What became the Associated Press received the first cable transmission ever of European news through the trans-Atlantic cable in 1858.

NEW FORMS OF JOURNALISM

The New York dailies continued to redefine journalism. James Bennet's Herald, for example, didn't just write about the disappearance of David Livingstone in Africa; they sent Henry Stanley to find him, which he did, in Uganda. The success of Stanley's stories prompted Bennett to hire more of what would turn out to be investigative journalists. He also was the first American publisher to bring an American newspaper to Eurpoe by founding the Paris Herald, which was the precursor of the International Herald Tribune.

Charles Anderson Dana of the New York Sun developed the idea of the human interest story and a better definition of news value, including uniqueness of a story.

Era of Hearst and Pulitzer

William Randolph Hearst and Joseph Pulitzer both owned newspaper chains in the American West, and both established papers in New York City: Hearst's New York World in 1883 and Pulitzer's New York Journal in 1896. Their stated missions to defend the public interest, their circulation wars and their embrace of sensational reporting, which spread to many other newspapers, led to the coinage of the phrase "yellow journalism." While the public may have benefitted from the beginnings of "muckraking" journalism, their often excessive coverage of juicy stories with sensational reporting turned many readers against them.

Muckraking journalism continued into the 20th Century, led by well-known investigative journalists Lincoln Steffens, Ida Tarbell and Upton Sinclair. Their work exposed the dismal conditions of the Chicago slums and meat-packing industry, the monopolistic practices of the Standard Oil Co. and more.

Muckraking Publications

Smaller newspapers and magazines engaged in more investigative reporting than the larger dailies, and took greater risks. This gave rise, over time, to an alternative press movement, which today is typified by alternative weekly newspapers like The Village Voice in New York City and The Phoenix in Boston, as well as political magazines like Mother Jones and The Nation.

Rise of the African-American Press

The rampant and flagrant segregation of and discrimination against African-Americans did not prevent them from founding their own daily and weekly newspapers, especially in urban areas. These newspapers and other publications flourished because of the loyalty their readers had to them.

Foreign-Language Newspapers

As immigration rose dramatically during the last half of the 19th century, many immigrants published newspapers in their native languages to cater to their fellow expatriots. One good example were many newspapers published in Yiddish for the thousands of Jews who left Eastern Europe.

Birth of Broadcasting in the 20th Century

Guglielmo Marconi and colleagues in 1901 used a wireless radio transmitter to send a signal from the United States to Europe. By 1907, his invention was in wide use for transatlantic communications.

HISTORY OF AMERICAN NEWSPAPERS

The history of American newspapers spans the history of the United States from 1700 till today.

Colonial Period

Public Occurrences

The first multi-page newspaper printed in America was Public Occurrences Both Foreign and Domestic. It was printed for one issue before being shut down by the government, its publisher arrested and all known copies destroyed. This was a four page periodical published by Benjamin Harris. Was first published in North America in 1690.

The New England Courant

It was James Franklin, Benjamin Franklin's older brother, who first made a news sheet something more than a garbled mass of stale items, "taken from the Gazettes and other Public Prints of London" some six months late. James Franklin, "encouraged by a number of respectable characters, who were desirous of having a paper of a different cast from those then published,...began the publication, at his own risk, of a third newspapers, entitled The New England Courant." These respectable characters were known as the Hell-Fire Club; they succeeded in publishing a paper "of a different cast," which, although it shocked New England orthodoxy pretty thoroughly, nevertheless proved vastly entertaining and established a kind of literary precedent. Instead of filling the first page of the Courant with the tedious conventionalities of governors' addresses to provincial legislatures, James Franklin's club wrote essays and satirical letters after the manner of The Spectator just ten years after the first appearance of The Spectator in London.

As a result, the very look of an ordinary first page of the Courant is like that of a Spectator page. After the more formal introductory paper on some general topic, such as zeal or hypocrisy or honour or contentment, the facetious letters of imaginary correspondents commonly fill the remainder of the Courant's first page. Timothy Turnstone addresses flippant jibes to Justice Nicholas Clodpate in the first extant number of the Courant Tom Pen-Shallow quickly follows, with his mischievous little postscript: "Pray inform me whether in your Province Criminals have the Privilege of a Jury."

Tom Tram writes from the moon about a certain "villainous Post master" he has heard rumours of. (The Courant was always perilously close to legal difficulties and had, besides, a lasting feud with the town postmaster.) Ichabod Henroost complains of a gadding wife. Abigail After with would like to know when the editor of the rival paper, the Gazette, "intends to have done printing the Carolina Addresses to their Governor, and give his Readers Something in the Room of them, that will be more entertaining." Homespun Jack deplores the fashions in general, and small waists in particular. Some of these papers represent native wit, with only a general approach to the model; others are little more than paraphrases of The Spectator. And sometimes a Spectator paper is inserted bodily, with no attempt at paraphrase whatever

Ben Franklin, Journalist

When Benjamin Franklin established himself in Philadelphia, shortly before 1730, the town boasted two "wretched little" news sheets, Andrew Bradford's American Mercury, and Keimer's Universal Instructor in all Arts and Sciences, and Pennsylvania Gazette. This instruction in all arts and sciences consisted of weekly extracts from Chambers's Universal Dictionary, actually commencing with A, and going steadily on towards Z, followed by installments of Defoe's Religious Courtship, called by the editor "a scarce and delightful piece of History." Franklin quickly did away with all this when he took over the Instructor, and made it The Pennsylvania Gazette.

The Gazette soon became Franklin's characteristic organ, which he freely used for satire, for the play of his wit, even for sheer excess of mischief or of fun. From the first he had a way of adapting his models to his own uses. The series of essays called The Busy-Body, which he wrote for Bradford's American Mercury in 1729, followed the general Addisonian form, modified already to suit homelier conditions. The thrifty Patience, in her busy little shop, complaining of the useless visitors who waste her valuable time, is related to the ladies who address Mr. Spectator. The Busy-Body himself is a true Censor Morum, as Isaac Bickerstaff had been in the Tatler. And a number of the fictitious characters, Ridentius, Eugenius, Cato, and Cretico, represent traditional eighteenth-century classicism. Even this Franklin could use for contemporary satire, since Cretico, the "sowre Philosopher," is evidently a portrait of Franklin's rival, Samuel Keimer. As time went on, Franklin depended less on his literary conventions, and more on his own native humour.

In this there is a new spirit-not suggested to him by the fine breeding of Addison, or the bitter irony of Swift, or the stinging completeness of Pope. The brilliant little pieces Franklin wrote for his Pennsylvania Gazette have an imperishable place in American literature. It is none the less true that they belong to colonial journalism.

The Pennsylvania Gazette, like most other newspapers of the period was often poorly printed. Franklin was busy with a hundred matters outside of his printing office, and never seriously attempted to raise the standards of his trade. Nor did he ever properly edit or collate the chance medley of stale items which passed. for news in the Gazette. His influence on the practical side of journalism was very small. On the other hand, his advertisements of books show his very great interest in popularizing secular literature.

Undoubtedly his paper contributed to the broader culture which distinguished Pennsylvania from her neighbours before the Revolution. Starting with the custom of importing a stray volume or two along with stationer's supplies, Franklin gradually developed a book shop in his printing office. There was nothing unusual in this fact, by itself.

The South Carolina Gazette

Franklin's influence in journalism was not confined to Pennsylvania. He often assisted young journeymen in the establishment of newspapers in distant towns. Thomas Whitemarsh, for instance, went to Charleston, South Carolina, in 1731, as Franklin's partner in a new enterprise, which soon included a new paper, The South Carolina Gazette. Naturally, Whitemarsh filled his front page with essays, sometimes reprinted from The Spectator, but often original, with a facetious quality suggesting Franklin. Essays of one sort or another were always popular in The South Carolina Gazette. Here may be found interesting notices of the various performances (probably professional) of Otway's Orphan, Farquhar's Recruiting Officer, and other popular plays of the period which were given at the Charleston theatres for twenty or thirty years before the first wandering professional companies began to play in the Northern colonies.

The Virginia Gazette

Early theatrical notices may also be followed in The Virginia Gazette, a paper of unusual excellence, edited by William Parks in Williamsburg, the old capital of Virginia. Here The Busy-Body, The Recruiting Officer, and The Beaux-Stratagem were all performed, often by amateurs, though professionals were known as early as 1716 in Williamsburg. Life in Williamsburg in 1736 had a more cosmopolitan quality than in other towns. A sprightly essay-serial called The Monitor, which fills the first page of The Virginia Gazette for twenty-two numbers, probably reflects not only the social life of the capital, but also the newer fashion in such periodical work. It is dramatic in method, with vividly realized characters who gossip and chat over games of piquet or at the theatre. The Beaux-Stratagem, which had been played in Williamsburg three weeks before, is mentioned as delightful enough to make one of the ladies commit the indiscretion of giggling. The Monitor represents a kind of light social satire unusual in the colonies.

Politics in the Later Newspapers

After 1750, general news became accessible, and the newspapers show more and more interest in public affairs. The literary first page was no longer necessary, though occasionally used to cover a dull period. A new type of vigorous polemic gradually superseded the older essay. A few of the well-known conventions were retained, however. We still find the fictitious letter, with the fanciful signature, or a series of papers under a common title, such as The Virginia-Centinel, or Livingston's Watch-Tower. The former is a flaming appeal to arms, running through The Virginia Gazette in 1756, and copied into Northern papers to rouse patriotism against the French enemy. The expression of the sentiment, even thus early, seems national. Livingston's well-known Watch-Tower, a continuation of his pamphlet-magazine The Independent Reflector, has already the keen edge of the Revolutionary writings of fifteen and twenty years later. The fifty-second number even has one of the popular phrases of the Revolution: "Had I not sounded the Alarm, Bigotry would e'er now have triumphed over the natural Rights of British Subjects."

Revolutionary Epoch and Early National Era: 1770-1820

The Massachusetts Spy

Isaiah Thomas's Massachusetts Spy was constantly on the verge of being suppressed, from its establishment in 1770 to the American Revolution, it carried radicalism to its logical conclusion. When the Spy began to be reprinted in other papers, as "the most daring production ever published in America," the country as a whole was ready for Tom Paine's Common Sense (1775). The turbulent years between 1775 and 1783 were a time of great trial and disturbance among newspapers. Interruption, suppression, and lack of support checked their growth substantially.

Although there were forty-three newspapers in the United States when the treaty of peace was signed (1783), as compared with thirty-seven on the date of the battle of Lexington (1775), only a dozen remained in continuous operation between the two events, and most of those had experienced delays and difficulties through lack of paper, type, and patronage. Not one newspaper in the principal cities, Boston, New York, and Philadelphia, continued publication throughout the war.

When the colonial forces were in possession, royalist papers were suppressed, and at times of British occupation Revolutionary papers moved away, or were discontinued, or they became royalist, only to suffer at the next turn of military fortunes. Thus there was an exodus of papers from the cities along the coast to smaller inland places, where alone it was possible for them to continue without interruption. Scarcity of paper was acute; type worn out could not be replaced. The appearance of the newspapers deteriorated, and issues sometimes failed to appear at all. Mail service, never good, was poorer than ever; foreign newspapers, an important source of information, could be obtained but rarely; many of the ablest writers who had filled the columns with dissertations upon colonial rights and government were now otherwise occupied.

News from a distance was less full and regular than before; yet when great events happened reports spread over the country with great rapidity, through messengers in the service of patriotic organizations. The newspapers made use of such assistance, and did service in further spreading the tidings, though they seldom overtook the flying word of mouth. Naturally, reporting was still imperfect. The Salem Gazette printed a full but coloured account of the battle of Lexington, giving details of the burning, pillage, and barbarities charged to the British, and praising the militia who were filled with "higher sentiments of humanity." The Declaration of Independence was published by Congress, 6 July, 1776, in the Philadelphia Evening Post, from which it was copied by most of the papers; but some of them did not mention it until two weeks later, and even then found room for only a synopsis. When they were permitted to do so they printed fairly full accounts of the proceedings of provincial assemblies and of Congress, which were copied widely, as were all official reports and proclamations. On the whole, however, a relatively small proportion of such material and an inadequate account of the progress of the war is found in the contemporaneous newspapers.

The general spirit of the time found fuller utterance in mottoes, editorials, letters, and poems. In the beginning both editorials and communications urged united resistance to oppression, praised patriotism, and denounced tyranny; as events and public sentiment developed these grew more vigorous, often a little more radical than the populace. Later, the idea of independence took form, and theories of government were discussed. More interesting and valuable as specimens of literature than these discussions were the poems inspired by the stirring events of the time.

Long narratives of battles and of heroic deaths were mingled with eulogies of departed heroes. Songs meant to inspire and thrill were not lacking. Humour, pathos, and satire sought to stir the feelings of the public. Much of the poetry of the Revolution is to be found in the columns of dingy newspapers, from the vivid and popular satires and narratives of Philip Freneau to the saddest effusions of the most commonplace schoolmaster.

The newspapers of the Revolution were an effective force working towards the unification of sentiment, the awakening of a consciousness of a common purpose, interest, and destiny among the separate colonies, and of a determination to see the war through to a successful issue. They were more single-minded than the people themselves, and they bore no small share of the burden of arousing and supporting the often discouraged and indifferent public spirit. Many of the papers, however, which were kept alive or brought to life during the war could not adapt themselves to the new conditions of peace.

Perhaps a dozen of the survivors held their own in the new time, notably the Boston Gazette, which declined rapidly in the following decade, The Connecticut Courant of Hartford, The Providence Gazette, and The Pennsylvania Packet of Philadelphia, to which may be added such representative papers as The Massachusetts Spy, the Boston Independent Chronicle, the New York Journal and Packet, the Newport Mercury, The Maryland Gazette of Annapolis, The Pennsylvania Gazette and The Pennsylvania Journal, both of Philadelphia.

Practically all were of four small pages, each of three or four columns, issued weekly. The Pennsylvania Packet, which appeared three times a week, became in 1784 the first daily paper. In the same year the New York Journal was published twice a week, as were several of the papers begun in that year. There was a notable extension to new fields. In Vermont, where the first paper, established in 1781, had soon died, another arose in 1783; in Maine two were started in 1785. In 1786 the first one west of the Alleghanies appeared at Pittsburg, and following the westward tide of immigration The Kentucky Gazette was begun at Lexington in 1787.

Conditions were hardly more favourable to newspapers than during the recent conflict. The sources of news were much the same; the means of communication and the postal system were little improved. Newspapers were not carried in the mails but by favour of the postmen, and the money of one state was of dubious value in another. Consequently circulations were small, rarely reaching a thousand; subscribers were slow in paying; and advertisements were not plentiful.

Newspapers remained subject to provincial laws of libel, in accordance with the old common law, and were, as in Massachusetts for a short time in 1785, subject to special state taxes on paper or on advertisements. But public sentiment was growing strongly against all legal restrictions, and in general the papers practised freedom, not to say license, of utterance.

With independence had come the consciousness of a great destiny. The collective spirit aroused by the war, though clouded by conflicting local difficulties, was intense, and the principal interest of the newspapers was to create a nation out of the loose confederation. Business and commerce were their next care; but in an effort to be all things to all men, the small page included a little of whatever might "interest, instruct, or amuse." Political intelligence occupied first place; news, in the modern sense, was subordinated. A new idea, quite as much as a fire, a murder, or a prodigy, was a matter of news moment. There were always a few items of local interest, usually placed with paragraphs of editorial miscellany. Correspondents, in return for the paper, sent items; private letters, often no doubt written with a view to such use, were a fruitful source of news; but the chief resource was the newspapers which every office received as exchanges, carried in the post free of charge, and the newspapers from abroad.

3

Press Council of India: History

Press Council is a mechanism for the Press to regulate itself. The raison d'etre of this unique institution is rooted in the concept that in a democratic society the press needs at once to be free and responsible.

If the Press is to function effectively as the watchdog of public interest, it must have a secure freedom of expression, unfettered and unhindered by any authority, organised bodies or individuals. But, this claim to press freedom has legitimacy only if it is exercised with a due sense of responsibility. The Press must, therefore, scrupulously adhere to accepted norms of journalistic ethics and maintain high standards of professional conduct.

Where the norms are breached and the freedom is defiled by unprofessional conduct, a way must exist to check and control it. But, control by Government or official authorities may prove destructive of this freedom. Therefore, the best way is to let the peers of the profession, assisted by a few discerning laymen to regulate it through a properly structured representative impartial machinery. Hence, the Press Council.

A need for such a mechanism has been felt for a long time both by the authorities as well as the Press itself all over the world, and a search for it resulted in the setting up of the first Press Council known as the Court of Honour for the Press in Sweden in 1916. The idea gained quick acceptance in other Scandinavian countries, and later in other parts of Europe, Canada, Asia, Australia and New Zealand. Today, the Press Councils or similar other media bodies are in place in more than four dozen nations.

BASIC CONCEPT

The basic concept of self-regulation in which the Press Councils and similar media bodies world over are founded, was articulated by Mahatma Gandhi, who was an eminent journalist in his own right, thus: " The sole aim of journalist should be service. The newspaper press is a great power, but just as unchained torrent of water submerges the whole country side and devastates crops, even so an uncontrolled pen serves but to destroy. If the control is from without, it proves more poisonous than want of control. It can be profitable only when exercised from within."

Pandit Jawaharlal Nehru while defending Press freedom, warning of the danger its irresponsible exercise entails stressed: " If there is no responsibility and no obligation attached to it, freedom gradually whithers away. This is true of a nation's freedom and it applies as much to the Press as to any other group, organisation or individual."

The First Press Commission (1954) came across in some section of the Press, instances of yellow journalism of one type or another, scurrilous writing-often directed against communities or groups, sensationalism, bias in presentation of news and lack of responsibility in comment, indecency and vulgarity and personal attacks on individuals. The Commission, however, pointed out that the well-established newspapers had, on the whole. Maintained a high standard of journalism. They had avoided "cheap senstationalism and unwarranted intrusion into private lives." But it remarked that " whatever the law relating to the Press may be, there would still be a large quantum of objectionable journalism which, though not falling within the purview of the law, would still require to be checked." It was of the view that the best way of maintaining professional standards of journalism would be to bring into existence a body of people principally connected with the industry whose responsibility it would be to arbitrate on doubtful points and to censure any one guilty of infraction of the code of journalistic ethics.

The Commission recommended the setting up of a Press Council. Among the objectives visualised for the Council were: " to safeguard the freedom of the press", " to ensure on the part of the Press the maintenance of High standards of public taste and to foster due sense of both the rights and responsibilities of citizenship" and " to encourage the growth of sense of responsibility and public service among all those engaged in the profession of journalism." The Commission, recommended the establishment of the Council on a statutory basis on the ground that the Council should have legal authority to make inquiries as otherwise each member, as well as the Council as a whole, would be subject to the threat of legal action from those whom it sought to punish by exposure.

The Commission said that the Council should consist of men who would command general confidence and respect of the profession and should have 25 members excluding the Chairman. The Chairman was to be a person who was or had been a Judge of the High Court and was to be nominated by the Chief Justice of India.

The Press Council of India was first constituted on 4th July, 1966 as an autonomous, statutory, quasi-judicial body, with Shri Justice J R Mudholkar, then a Judge of the Supreme Court, as Chairman. The Press Council Act, 1965, listed the following functions of the Council in furtherance of its objects:

- to help newspapers to maintain their independence;
- to build up a code of conduct for newspapers and journalists in accordance with high professional standards;
- to ensure on the part of newspapers and journalists the maintenance of high standards of public taste and foster a due sense of both the rights and responsibilities of citizenship;
- to encourage the growth of a sense of responsibility and public service among all those engaged in the profession of journalism;
- to keep under review any development likely to restrict the supply and dissemination of news of public interest and importance;
- to keep under review such cases of assistance received by any newspaper or news agency in India from foreign sources, as are referred to it by the Central Government.

Provided that nothing in this clause shall preclude the Central Government from dealing with any case of assistance received by a newspaper or news agency in India from foreign sources in any other manner it thinks fit;

- to promote the establishment of such common service for the supply and dissemination of news to newspapers as may, from time to time, appear to it to be desirable;
- to provide facilities for the proper education and training of persons in the profession of journalism;
- to promote a proper functional relationship among all classes of persons engaged in the production or publication of newspapers;
- to study developments which may tend towards monopoly or concentration of ownership of newspapers, including a study of the ownership or financial structure of newspapers, and if necessary, to suggest remedies therefor;
- to promote technical or other research;
- to do such other acts as may be incidental or conducive to the discharge of the above functions.

The Act of 1965 provided that the Council shall consist of a Chairman and 25 other members. Of the 25 members, 3 were to represent the two houses of Parliament, 13 were to be from amongst the working journalists, of which not less than 6 were to be editors who did not own or carry on the business of management of newspapers and the rest were to be the persons having special knowledge or practical experience in respect of education and science, law, literature and culture. By an amendment of the Act in 1970, the membership of the Council was raised by one to provide a seat for persons managing the news agencies.

The Chairman under the Act on 1965, was to be nominated by the Chief Justice of India. Of the three Members of Parliament, two representing Lok Sabha were to be nominated by the Speaker of the Lok Sabha and one representing Rajya Sabha, was to be nominated by the Chairman of the Rajya Sabha. The remaining 22 members were to be selected by a three-man Selection Committee comprising the Chief Justice of India, Chairman of the Press Council and a nominee of the President of India. The Chairman and the members were to hold office for a period of three years provided that no member could hold office for a period exceeding six years in the aggregate.

When in the early years of the Council's existence a grievance was aired about the selection of a category of members, Parliament embarked on a search for a meticulous formula which would ensure uncompromising impartiality and fairness in the selection of Chairman and other members. This led to the amendment of the 1965 Act entrusting this work to a Committee comprising the incumbent of the three highest offices which are considered as an embodiment of these attributes, namely, Chairman of Rajya Sabha, Speaker of Lok Sabha and Chief Justice of India. But, the pursuit for still less subjective scheme continued. Even a statistical formula was evolved for equitable presentation of the various representative organisations of the profession.

As has been referred to earlier, composition of the nominating committee was changed by an amendment of the said Act in 1970, according to which the Chairman and the members from the press were to be nominated by a Nominating Committee consisting of the Chairman of the Rajya Sabha, the Chief Justice of India and the Speaker of the Lok Sabha.

The amending Act of 1970 introduced several other provisions in the Act. The manner of selection of persons of special knowledge or practical experience was specified. It provided that of the three persons to be nominated from among such people, one each shall be nominated by the University Grants Commission, the Bar Council of India and the Sahitya Academy. It also provided for raising the membership of the Council to give one seat to the persons managing the news agencies. Out of the six seats for proprietors and managers of newspapers, two each were earmarked for big, medium and small newspapers. No working journalist who owned or carried on the business of management of newspapers could now be nominated in the category of working journalists. Also, it was specified that not more than one person interested in any newspaper or group of newspapers under the same control, could be nominated from the categories of editors, other working journalists, proprietors and managers.

The Nominating Committee was empowered to review any nomination on a representation made to it by any notified association or by any person aggrieved by it or otherwise. The amended Act also barred renomination of a retiring member for more than one term. Where any association failed to submit a panel of names when invited to do so, the Nominating Committee could ask for panels from other associations or persons of the category concerned or nominate members after consultation with such other such individuals or interests concerned as it thought fit. Under the original Act, the Chairman was nominated by the Chief Justice of India. But, after this amendment, nomination of the Chairman was also left to the Nominating Committee.

The Council set up under the Act of 1965 functioned till December 1975. During the Internal Emergency, the Act was repealed and the Council abolished *w.e.f.* 1/1/1976.

PRESS COUNCIL OF 1979

A fresh legislation providing for the establishment of the Council was enacted in 1978 and the institution came to be reviewed in the year 1979 with the very same object of preserving the freedom of the press and of maintaining and improving the standards of Press in India. The present Council is a body corporate having perpetual succession. It consists of a Chairman and 28 other members. Of the 28 members, 13 represent the working journalists. Of whom 6 are to be editors of newspapers and remaining 7 are to be working journalists other than editors. 6 are to be from among persons who own or carry on the business of management of newspapers. One is to be from among the persons who manage news agencies. Three are to be persons having special knowledge or practical experience in respect of education and science, law and literature and culture. The remaining five are to Members of Parliament: three from Lok Sabha, and two from Rajya Sabha.

The new Act provides for selection of the Chairman by a Committee consisting of the Chairman of the Rajya Sabha, the Speaker of Lok Sabha and a person elected by the members of the Council from among themselves. The twenty representatives of the Press are nominated by the associations of aforesaid categories of the newspapers and news agencies notified for the purpose by the Council in the each category. One member each is nominated by the University Grants Commission, the Bar Council of India and the Sahitya Academy. Of the five Members of Parliament, three are nominated by the Speaker of the Lok Sabha and two by the Chairman of the Rajya Sabha. The term of the Chairman and the members of the Council is three years. A retiring member is eligible for renomination for not more than one term.

An extremely healthy feature of the Indian Press Council is the scheme and procedure of the nomination of its Chairman and other members, following a long search based on the experience of several years of functioning of the Council. Despite being a statutory body, the Government and its authorities have been completely kept out of the nomination process except for publishing the notification in the official gazette of the names of the members nominated. Nor has it been left to any individual to decide, however eminent or highly placed he may be. A totally non-subjective procedure which leaves no scope for the interference or influence by Government or any other agency was evolved with remarkable ingenuity. The scheme is in force since the enactment of the Press Council Act of 1978 under which the revived Press Council was set up in 1979.

OBJECTS AND FUNCTIONS OF THE COUNCIL

The objects of present Press Council are substantially the same as were laid down under the Act of 1965 and it is not necessary to repeat them here. But the functions have undergone some change in that the three of the functions listed in the earlier Act were not included in the 1978 Act as they were considered to be burdensome for the Council to perform. These related to: (a) promoting the establishment of such common services for the supply and dissemination of news to newspapers as may, from time to time, appear to it to be desirable; (b) providing facilities for proper education and training of persons in the profession of journalism; and (c) promoting technical or other research.

In addition, the Act of 1978 lists two new functions of the Council: (i) to undertake studies of foreign newspapers, including those brought out by any embassy or any other representative in India of a foreign State, their circulation and impact; and, (ii) to undertake such studies as may be entrusted to the Council and to express its opinion in regard to any matter referred to it by the Central Government.

The other functions remain the same as enumerated in the Act of 1965.

POWERS OF THE COUNCIL

The powers of the Press Council are provided in Section 14 and 15 of the Act as under:

Power to Censure

Where, on receipt of a complaint made to it or otherwise, the Council has reason to believe that a newspaper or news agency has offended against the standards of journalistic ethics or public taste or that an editor or a working journalist has committed any professional misconduct, the Council may, after giving the newspaper, or news agency, the editor or journalist concerned an opportunity of being heard, hold an inquiry in such manner as may be provided by the regulations made under this Act and, if it is satisfied that it is necessary to do, it may, for reasons to be recorded in writing, warn, admonish or censure the newspaper, the news agency, the editor or the journalist, as the case may be:

Provided that the Council may not take cognisance of a complaint if in the opinion of the Chairman, there is no sufficient ground for holding an inquiry.

- If the Council is of the opinion that it is necessary or expedient in public interest so to do, it may require any newspaper to publish therein in such manner as the Council thinks fit, any particulars relating to any inquiry under this section against a newspaper or news agency, an editor or a journalist working therein, including the name of such newspaper, news agency, editor or journalist.

- Nothing in sub-section (1) shall be deemed to empower the Council to hold an inquiry into any matter in respect of which any proceeding is pending in a court of law.
- The decision of the Council under sub-section (1), or sub-section (2), as the case may be, shall be final and shall not be questioned in any court of law.

GENERAL POWERS OF THE COUNCIL

For the purpose of performing its functions or holding any inquiry under this Act, the Council shall have the same powers throughout India as are vested in a civil court while trying a suit under the Code of Civil Procedure, 1908, in respect of the following matters namely:-

- Summoning and enforcing the attendance of persons and examining them on oath;
- requiring the discovery and inspection of documents;
- receiving evidence on affidavits;
- requisitioning any public record or copies thereof from any court or office;
- issuing commissions for the examination of witnesses or documents; and
- any other matter, which may be prescribed.

  (2) Nothing in sub-section (1) shall be deemed to compel any newspaper, news agency, editor or journalist to disclose the source of any news or information published by that newspaper or received or reported by that news agency, editor or journalist.

  (3) Every inquiry held by the Council shall be deemed to be a judicial proceeding within the meaning of sections 193 and 228 of the Indian Penal Code.

- The Council may, if it considers it considers it necessary for the purpose of carrying out its objects or for the performance of any of its functions under this Act, make such observations, as it may think fit, in any of its decisions or reports, respecting the conduct of any authority, including Government.

FUNDINGS OF THE COUNCIL

The Act provides that the Council may, for the purpose of performing its functions under the Act, levy fee at the prescribed rates from registered newspapers and news agencies. Apart from this, the Central Government has been enjoined to pay the Council by way of grant such sums of money as the Central Government may consider necessary, for the performance of its functions.

EMINENT PERSONALITIES

The Council has been adorned by a galaxy of distinguished judges, eminent editors, leading newspaper owners and managers, well-known working journalists and leaders of journalistic movement and renowned litterateurs, lawyers and educationists. Shri Justice J R Mudholkar, a sitting judge of the Supreme Court was the first Chairman who presided over the Council from November 16, 1966 to March 1, 1968. He was followed by Shri Justice N Rajagopala Ayyangar (May 4, 1968 to January 1,1976), Shri Justice A N Grover (April 3, 1979 to October 9, 1985), Shri Justice A N Sen (October 10, 1985 to January 18,1989) and Shri Justice R S Sarkaria (January 19, 1989 to July 24, 1995) and Shri Justice P B Sawant(July 24, 1995 till date). They were retired Judges of the Supreme Court. All of them led the Council with a deep commitment to its philosophy and objects. The Council got its direction from them and amply benefited from their vast knowledge and wisdom. Some of the many eminent persons who have, till 1998, served the Council as members are:

Editors: Sarvshri Frank Morraes, Akshay Kumar Jain, B G Verghese, Prem Bhatia, Arun Shourie, Kuldip Nayar, Cho Ramaswamy, A N Sivaraman, Dr Dharmvir Bharati, Dr N K Trikha (who also served for one term in the category of working journalists other than editors), V N Narayanan, Shri Ramu Patel and Narla Venkateswar Rao, Shri Nikhil Chakravorty, Shri Mammen Mathew.

Working Journalists other than editors: Sarvshri Durga Das (who was also a member in the category of owners for one term), Sailen Chatterji, Prithvis Chakravarti, K Vikram Rao, S Viswam, G N Aharya, Gour Kishore Gosh, A Raghavan,

P. Raman and Arun Bagchi, Nitish Chakravarty, Brij Bhardwaj. Proprietors and managers: Sarvshri G Narshimhan, K M Mathew, C R Irani, Dr N B Parulekar, A G Sheerey, A R Bhat, Narendra Tiwari, Raj MohanGandhi, Yadunath Thatte, Basudev Ray Chowdhury, N R Chandran and G G Mirchandani, Naresh Mohan, V B Gupta.

Literateurs: Dr Uma Shankar Joshi, Dr Birendra Kumar Bhattacharya, Prof. K K Srinivasa Iyengar, Prof. U R Anantha Murthy, Prof. Indira Nath Choudhary.

Lawyers: Shri Ram Jethmalani, Shri Ranjit Mohanty, Shri P Vishwanath Shetty.

Educationists: Dr (Miss) Alu Dastur, Dr (Miss) Usha Mehta, Dr (Mrs) Madhuri Shah, Prof. Tapas Mazumdar, Dr M V Pylee, Prof K Satchidanandan Murthy.

Members of Parliament: Sarvshri H V Kamath, Ganga Sharan Sinha, Piloo Mody, Rafiq Zakaria, S N Dwivedi, C L Chandrakar, George Fernandes, L K Advani, H K L Bhagat, M S Gurupadaswamy, V N Gadgil, Arun Nehru, Eduardo Falerio, R K Karanjia, Smt Geeta Mukherjee, M C Bhandare, Brij Mohan Mohanty, D P Yadav, M J Akbar, K L Sharma, P C Chacko. Of these Sarvshri L K Advani, V N Gadgil and Shri H K L Bhagat have had the distinction of being Union Ministers of Information and Broadcasting either before or after becoming members of the Council. Many others have been Union Ministers with other portfolios.

Shri B Siva Rao, journalist and member of the Constituent Assembly and Shri K Ishwara Dutt, journalist and author had been nominated to the first Council in the category of eminent persons along with Shrimati Deena Ahmadullah.

FUNCTIONING OF THE COUNCIL

The Council discharges its functions primarily through the medium of its Inquiry Committees, adjudicating on complaint cases received by it against the Press for violation of the norms of journalism or by the Press for interference with its freedom by the authorities. There is a set procedure for lodging a complaint with the Council.

A complainant is required essentially to write to the editor of the respondent newspaper, drawing his attention to what the complainant considers to be in breach of journalistic ethics or an offence against public taste. Apart from furnishing to the Council a cutting of the matter complained against, it is incumbent on the complainant to make and subscribe to a declaration that to the best of his knowledge and belief he has placed all the relevant facts before the Council and that no proceedings are pending in any court of law in respect of any matter alleged in the complaint; and that he shall inform the Council forthwith if during the pendency of the inquiry before the Council any matter alleged in the complaint becomes the subject matter of any proceedings in a court of law. The reason for this declaration is that in view of Section 14(3) of the Act, the Council cannot deal with any matter which is sub judice.

If the Chairman finds that there are no sufficient grounds for inquiry, he may dismiss the complaint and report it to the Council; otherwise, the Editor of the newspaper or the journalist concerned is asked to show cause why action should not be taken against him. On receipt of the written statement and other relevant material from the editor or the journalist, the Secretariat of the Council places the matter before the Inquiry Committee. The Inquiry Committee screens and examines the complaint in necessary details. If necessary, it also calls for further particulars or documents from the parties. The parties are given opportunity to adduce evidence before the Inquiry Committee by appearing personally or through their authorised representative including legal practitioners.

On the basis of the facts on record and affidavits or the oral evidence adduced before it, the Committee formulates its findings and recommendations and forwards them to the Council, which may or may not accept them. Where the Council is satisfied that a newspaper or news agency has offended against the standards of journalistic ethics or public taste or that an editor or working journalist has committed professional misconduct, the Council may warn, admonish or censure the newspaper, the news agency, the editor or journalist, or disapprove the conduct thereof, as the case may be. In the complaints lodged by the Press against the authorities, the

Council is empowered to make such observations as it may think fit in respect of the conduct of any authority including government. The decisions of the Council are final and cannot be questioned in any court of law. It will thus be seen that the Council wields a lot of moral authority although it has no legally enforceable punitive powers.

The Inquiry Regulations framed by the Council empower the Chairman to take suo motu action and issue notices to any party in respect of any matter falling within the scope of Press Council Act. The procedure for holding a suo motu inquiry is substantially the same as in the case of a normal inquiry except that for any normal inquiry a complaint is required to be lodged with the Council by a complainant. For the purpose of performing its functions or holding an inquiry under the Act the Council exercises some of the powers vested in a Civil Court trying a suit under the Code of Civil Procedure, 1908, in respect of the following matters, namely:-

- Summoning and enforcing the attendance of persons and examining them on oath;
- requiring the discovery and inspection of documents;
- receiving evidence on affidavits;
- requisitioning any public record or copies thereof from any court or office;
- issuing commissions for the examination of witnesses or documents; and
- any other matter, which may be prescribed.

The Council expects the parties to cooperate with it in the conduct of its business. At least in two cases where the Council noticed that the parties were literally uncooperative or adamant, it exercised, its authority under Section 15 of the Act to compel them to appear before it and/or to furnish record etc. In the complaint of some Chandigarh journalists against the Chief Minister and the Government of Haryana, the erstwhile Council had to warn the authorities about the use of Council's coercive powers if they failed to respond to the notices sent by the Council. Similarly, in the famous case of B G Verghese against The Hindustan Times, the Birlas were directed to provide complete correspondence exchanged between Shri Verghese and Shri K K Birla. The Council, in 1980 had proposed amendment of the Act, for empowering the Council to recommend to the authorities concerned, denial of certain facilities and concessions in the form of accreditation, advertisements, allocation of newsprint or concessional rates of postage for a certain period in the case of a newspaper which was censured thrice by the Council. Acceptance of the Council's recommendations on the part of the authorities was sought to be made obligatory. The Council was further of the view that, as in the case of newspapers, the power vested in it under Section 15(4) of the Press Council Act, 1978, to make such observations as it may think fit, in any of its decisions or reports, respecting the conduct of any authority including government, should expressly include the power to warn, admonish or censure such authorities and that the observations of the Council in this behalf should be placed on the Table of both the Houses of Parliament and/or of the Legislature of the State concerned. In the year 1987, the Council reconsidered the matter and after detailed deliberations, decided to withdraw its proposal for penal powers because it was of the reconsidered opinion that in the prevalent conditions these powers could tend to be misused by the authorities to curb the freedom of the Press.

Since then, time and again, suggestions/references have been made to the Council that it should have penal powers to punish the delinquent newspapers/journalists. In response, the Council has consistently taken the view that the moral sanctions provided to it under the existing scheme of the Act are adequate. The suggestion was repeated by the Union Minister for Information and Broadcasting in his inaugural address to the International Conference of Press Councils held in New Delhi in October, 1992, but the Council unanimously rejected it with the following reasoning:-

"Were the Council to be endowed with the power to impose sanctions/penalties, it would be equitable that the power to impose sanctions applies also when complaints are made by the Press against the Government and its authorities. A power to impose meaningful sanctions raises a number of issues, including, (a) the onus of proof; (b) the standard of proof; (c) the right to and cost of legal representation; and (d) whether review and/or appeal would be available. The effect of any or all of these issues may militate against the basic premise, that the Press Council's provide a democratic and efficient and inexpensive facility for hearing of the complaints, and that the consequent inevitability would, in effect, become courts, excercising judicial power and well known problems of access, cost, formality and delay would equally apply, thus defeating the basic purpose of the Press Council."

In December 1992 the Council received a reference from the Central Government soliciting its views on "whether a procedure can be laid down to ensure that newspapers/ magazines censured by the Press Council for breach of guidelines in connection with communal writings, can be deprived of incentives from government, such as advertisements etcetera, and whether the Press Council would be in a position to suggest what action should be taken when it holds a newspaper/ magazine guilty of breach of guidelines." The Council considered the matter in the meeting held in June 1993 in the light of the stand adopted by it in the past against arming the Council with punitive powers. Having considered the matter in depth, the Council felt that the moral authority presently exercised by the Council is quite effective and the Council does not need any punitive powers in showing the Press the path of self-regulation. The Council, however, decided that if the newspaper is censured twice for any type of unethical writings within a period of three years, copies of such decisions should be forwarded to the Cabinet Secretary to the Government of India and to the Chief Secretary of the concerned State Government for information and such action, as may, in exercise of their discretion, be deemed to be appropriate in the circumstances of the case. The Council decided that the period of three years will be taken as preceeding three years counted backwards from the date of the second censure.

SOME OF THE IMPORTANT ADJUDICATIONS RENDERED AND GUIDELINES ISSUED BY THE COUNCIL

Since its establishment in 1966, the Council has rendered several momentous adjudications and issued guidelines which may have a lasting impact on the press in the country. The following are some of the important cases in which adjudications have been pronounced. The details are given at annexure A1-40.

Communal Writings:

- Government of Orissa Vs. Desh, Calcutta Weekly (1968 A.R. 25-27) (A-1)
- Government of Mysore Vs. Zam Zam, Urdu Weekly of Bangalore (1969 A R 56-57) (A2)
- The Council initiated suo-motu action against the following papers and after due enquiry, while dropping the cases, it observed that restraint by the Press is necessary during the period when the country is passing through a tense phase resulting from conflict over such sensitive issues as communal riots: (1980 A R 131-146) (A-3)
- Dainik Jagran
- Asli Bharat
- Current
- Free Press Journal
- Shri Varsha
- Malayala Manorama
- Northern Indian Patrika

Dy. Commissioner, Hazaribagh Vs Ranchi Express (A R 86-87):

- Shri Shopat Singh Makkasor Vs. Rajasthan Patrika 18 th A R (231-232)
- Shri Zile Singh Chahal, General Secretary, All India Jat Maha Sabha, Rohtak versus Vishwa Mail Evening Daily, Kota. 18 th AR (234-235)

Defamation:

- Government of Goa, Daman and Diu versus Blade (1969 A R 12-14) (A-4)
- P.K. Bansal Versus Surya India (12th AR 218-222) (A5)

- Madhu Limaye Versus Indian Express (13th AR 139-158) (A-6)
- Harikishan Singh Surjeet Vs Indian Express (13th AR 125-139) (A-7)
- Vasant Sathe Vs The Independent (12th AR 242-252) (A-8)
- Sh H N Kumar, Municipal Councillor as representative of the Municipal Committee, Madikheri Vs Editor 'Shakti', Kannada Daily, Madikheri. AR 1994 (A9)
- Sh Vatal Nagaraj, MLA, Karnataka Legislative Assembly, Bangalore Vs. Lankesh Patrika (111-112) 17th AR
- Complaints of Mrs Phanali Singhal versus Independent & The Hindustan Times (16th AR Page 123,128,129-132)

Investigative Reporting

- R C Bhargava, Chairman, Maruti Udyog Ltd. Vs The Statesman 15 th AR (130-142) (A-10).

Obscenity and Bad Taste

- Delhi Adminstration Vs Confidential Advisor (1969 AR 50-52) (A-11)
- Sh Dinesh Bhai Trivedi, MP Rajya Sabha Vs. The Sunday Statesman Miscellany (14th AR 531-536) (A-12)

Right to Privacy

- Sr. Cyrilla-Superior Franciscans of St. Mary of Angles/ Fr. Placido Fonseco Vs. The Indian Express, Free Press Journal, Times of India and Samna (13th AR 92-110) (A-13)
- Dr Vasudha Dhagamwar, Executive Director, MARG Vs India Today AR 1993 (A-14)

Right to Reply

- Shri T K Mahadevan Vs The Illustrated Weekly of India (1981 AR 130-135) (A-15)
- Dr Walter Fernandes Vs Surya India (11th AR 233-235) (A-16)
- P K Bansal Vs Surya India (12 th AR 218-222) (A-5)

- Madhu Limaye/Harkishan Singh Surjeet Vs Indian Express (13th AR 139-158) (A-6)

Pre-Publication Verification

- Government of Assam Vs Dainik Asom (1982 AR 82-85) (A-17)
- D N Saikia, Deputy Secretary, Government of Assam Vs. The Press Trust of India and The Statesman (12th AR 140-142) (A-18)
  - (i) Government of Goa, Daman and Diu Vs Blade (1969 AR Pg 12-14) (A-4)
  - (ii) P K Bansal Vs Surya India (12th AR 218-222) (A5)
  - (iii) Madhu Limaye Vs Indian Express (13th AR 139-158) (A-6).
  - (iv) Harkishan Singh Surjeet Vs Indian Express (13th AR 125-139) (A-7)
  - (v) Vasant Sathe Vs The Independent (12 th AR 242-252) (A-8)

Deepak Vohra Vs Sunday Mail (PCI Review July 1994 59-71) (A-19) 16th AR 133-144

Right of the Press to use its own column

- Shri Ashok Mehta, DUJ, IUJ, PUCL Vs Times of India (Aug. 4-5, 1998)

Threats to Press Freedom

- Malayala Manorama Versus Government of Kerala (PCI Review, January 1983 Page 62) (A-20)
- Malayala Manorama Versus various State Governments. (PCI Annual Report 1968, Page 38) (A-21).
- Blitz Versus District Administration of Dehradun (PCI review April 1984, Page 30) (A-22).
- Mahajati Versus Government of Assam (PCI Review, October 1983, page 55) (A-23).
- Suo Motu action by Press Council of India against the Government of Karnataka (PCI Review April 1982, page 36) (A-24)

- Madhya Pradesh Small Newspapers Association Versus Municipal Commissioner. (PCI Annual Report, 1972, page 66) (A-25).
- Searchlight Versus Deputy Commissioner of Ranchi. (PCI Annual Report 1972, page 65) (A-26).
- Dainik Janambhumi Versus Government of Assam. (PCI Annual Report 1980, page 56) (A-27)
- Chandigarh Union of Journalists Versus Government of Haryana. (PCI Annual Report 1974, page 68) (A-28)
- U.P. Small & Medium Newspapers Editors Council Versus District Magistrate, Hardoi. (PCI Review January 1983, page 58) (A-29)
- Suo Motu action by Press Council of India (Annual Report 1983, page 37) (A-30)
- Sarita Mukta Versus Government of Madhya Pradesh (PCI Annual Report 1981, page 60) (A-31)
- Suo motu action-attacks on Gujarat Samachar (Annual Report 1986, page 44) (A-32)
- Shri Rama Shanker Prasad, Bihar Vs S.P. Nalanda 15 th AR page 24-25

Advertisement and Press Freedom

- Tribune Versus Government of Haryana (PCI Annual Report 1979, page 45) (A-33)
- Saptahik Mujahid Versus Government of Assam. (PCI Review July 1983 page 44) (A-34)
- Searchlight and Pradeep Vs Government of Bihar (PCI Annual Report 1974, Page 11) (A-35)

Amar Ujala (Bareilly & Meerut Editions) Vs Distt. Admn, UP 15 th AR 66-67

Impropriety and Press Freedom

- Arjun Baan Versus Pargana Officer of Tehsil Briswa, UP (PCI Annual Report, 1983, Page 40)(A-36)
- Press Correspondent, Hind Samachar Versus Government of Punjab (PCI Annual Report 1973, page 27) (A-37)

- Vishwa Manav Versus S.P., Badayun (PCI Review October 1983, page 52) (A-38)
- Ex Member of ParliamentVersus Government of Andhra Pradesh (PCI Annual Report 1972, Page 7) (A-39)
- Complaint of P Rajan Vesrsus Mathrubhumi (AR 1989-90 page 72)(A-40)
- Atul Maheshwari, Editor, Amar Ujala, Hindi Daily, Meerut Vs ECI (17 th AR Page 45)

Shri Ritendra Mathur, Panchjanya Versus PRO, MP Legislative Assembly (June 98)

A study of these adjudications would show that the Council has been unquestionably successful in its efforts towards achieving the objects set before it of not only preserving the freedom of the press but also ensuring that the standards of journalism are maintained and improved. While the authorities, after Press Council's intervention, have been seen to be generally refraining from indulging in putting undue pressure on the Press, the press-persons too have tended to restrain themselves from the kind of journalism that could undermine the standards expected of them. The moral impact of the Council has come to be widely recognised.

The tremendous increase in the number of complaints from 80 in 1979 to 1075 in 1997 is ample proof of the faith expressed by mediamen and the public alike, in the working, importance and need for a body like the Council at the helm of the fourth estate.

CODE OF CONDUCT

Section 13 (2) (b) of the Press Council Act, 1978, enjoins the Council to build up a Code of Conduct for newspapers, news agencies and journalists in accordance with the high professional standards to help and guide the newsmen. Building of such a Code is a dynamic process which has to keep pace with time and events. The expression "build up" indicates that the code may be evolved by the Press Council on case by case basis through its adjudications. A compendium of broad principles evolved by the Press Council through its adjudications/guidelines was first published in the year 1984 by the Council in collaboration with the Indian Law Institute under the title " VIOLATION OF JOURNALISTIC ETHICS AND PUBLIC TASTE" This compilation of principles is sorted out from the decisions or adjudications of the Council or the guidelines issued by it or its Chairman. In 1986, the second part of the compendium entitled "VIOLATION OF FREEDOM OF THE PRESS" relating to adjudications and principles in matters or complaints against the government and its authorities which were of important and far reaching nature and which involved observations respecting the conduct of any authority including government was published.

Since 1986 there has been a continuous increase in the institution of complaints and their disposal by the Press Council with consequent acceleration of the process of building up the code. In 1992, the Council brought out " A Guide to Journalistic Ethics" containing principles of journalistic ethics culled out from the adjudications of the Council and the guidelines issued by it in their wake.

As several more decisions of far reaching importance relating to the rights and responsibilities of the press have been rendered since then by the Council, a 162 page elaborate and comprehensive second edition of the guide has been issued. It also deals with the concept of right to privacy and lays down the guidelines to be followed in this behalf. The law of defamation has also been dealt with in some of its aspects for the guidance of the press, public servants and public figures.

The Council has in an important adjudication respecting alleged defamation of public officials of a Municipal Committee held that the remedy of action for damages against the Press or the media is simply not available to public officials with respect to their acts and conduct relevant to the discharge of their official duties, even if the publication is based on facts and statements which are not true, unless the official establishes that the publication was made with reckless disregard for the truth. In such a case it will be enough for the defendant (member of the press or media) to prove that he acted after a reasonable verification of the facts; it is not necessary for him to prove that what he has written is true. But where the publication is proved to be false and actuated by malice or personal animosity, the defendant would have no defence and would be liable for the damages. However, a public official enjoys the same protection as any other citizen in matters not relevant to the discharge of his duties. Of course, judiciary and Parliament and State Legislatures represent exception to this rule as the former is protected by the power to punish for its contempt and the latter by their privileges under Articles 105 and 194 respectively of the Constitution. The Council has further held that this does not mean that the Official Secrets Act, 1923 or any similar enactment or provision having the force of law does not bind the press or media. It has also been held that there is no law empowering the State or its officials to prohibit or to impose a prior restraint upon the press/media.

In regard to public official's claim to privacy, the Council has laid down that if there is a clash between the public official's privacy and the public's right to know about his personal conduct, habits, personal affairs and traits of character impinging upon or having a bearing on the due discharge of his official duties, the former must yield to the latter. However, in matters of personal privacy which are not relevant to discharge of his official duties, the public official enjoys the same protection as any other citizen.

This Guide as a whole suggests a way of steering safely and responsibly through the mine-field of legal, moral and ethical problems which confront the editors, journalists and owners of newspapers everyday. The Guide is not a compilation of cast-iron principles but contains broad general principles, which, if applied with due discernment and adaptation to varying circumstances of each case, will help the journalists to self-regulate the conduct of their profession along the path of professional rectitude. These are by no means exhaustive nor are they meant to obtain a rigidity which could hinder the unfettered working of the Press.

BROAD PRINCIPLES EVOLVED

Some of the broad principles evolved by the Council in course of its adjudication on various subjects both in respect of standards of journalism and the freedom of the Press are summarised as under:

JOURNALISTIC STANDARDS–

Communal Writings

Scurrilous and inflammatory attacks should not be made on communities and individuals. Any news on communal events based on rumours will be violative of the journalistic ethics. Similarly, distorted reporting making important omissions will not be correct. While it is the legitimate function of the Press to draw attention to the genuine grievance of any community with a view to seeking redress in a peaceful and legal manner, there should be no invention or exaggeration of grievances, particularly those which tend to promote communal discord.

It will be highly conducive to the creation of a healthy and peaceful atmosphere if sensational, provocative and alarming headlines are avoided, and acts of violence or vandalism are reported in such a manner as may not undermine people's confidence in law and order machinery of the State and may at the same time have the effect of discouraging and condemning such activities.

Defaming a community is a serious matter and ascribing to it a vile, anti-national activity is reprehensible and amounts to journalistic impropriety.

There is no impropriety in publishing historical facts in order to warn the present generation against repetition of past mistakes even though these mistakes may not be palatable to a particular community.

There is no objection in making statements about religious communities if they are couched in temperate language and are not exaggerated or incorrect.

Journalistic Impropriety

Some of the principles evolved by the Council through its adjudications in respect of journalistic impropriety are:

Any matter discussed or disclosed in confidence ought not to be published without obtaining the consent of the source. If the editor finds that the publication is in the public interest, he should clarify it in an appropriate footnote that the statement or discussion in question was being published although it had been made "off the record". An advertisement containing anything unlawful or illegal, or the one which is contrary to good taste or journalistic ethics or propriety should not be published.

Proper care should be taken by newspapers in maintaining accuracy in respect of quotations.

Where a newspaper is charged with violation of journalistic ethics, a plea that it has ceased publication will afford the editor no defence, since it is his conduct which is subject of the complaint.

Obscenity and Bad Taste

The meaning of taste varies according to the context. For a journalist it implies that "which on grounds of decency or propriety he should not publish". Where a matter has "a tendency to stimulate sex feelings" its publication in a journal meant for the lay public, young or old, undesirable. Exploitation of sex falls short good taste. Public taste is to be judged in relation to the environment, milieu as well notions of taste prevailing in contemporary society.

The basic test of obscenity is whether the matter is so gross or vulgar that it is likely to deprave or corrupt. Another test is whether depiction of the scene and language used can be regarded as filthy, repulsive, dirty or lewd.

Whether a story is obscene or not, will depend on such factors as literary or cultural nature of the magazine, and the social theme of the story. The relevancy of a picture to the subject matter of a magazine or a paper has a bearing on the question whether the matter published falls below the standards of public taste. One of the relevant factors for judging whether the picture falls below the standard of public taste will be the purpose or nature of the magazine-whether it relates to art, painting, medicine, research or reform of sex.

The Press Council expressed concern over the increasing instances of obscene advertisements in the print media. It was opposed to censorship but favoured preventive steps to check any obscene material at pre-publication stage. Since most of such advertisements are routed through advertising agencies, the Council felt that this task should not be difficult if these agencies were to exercise more caution and restrain in preparing and releasing the advertisements that may be considered objectionable to family viewing by an average citizen. It felt that the Association of Advertising Agencies of India as an Umbrella organisation of all these advertising agencies could play a very meaningful and positive role in the matter and sought its cooperation to contain advertisements that are likely to damage the socio-cultural ethos of the country in the longer run. The Council appealed to the newspapers also to carefully scrutinize the advertisements received by them either directly from the advertisers or through the advertising agencies and exercise a self-restraint by rejecting such advertisements as may be considered obscene and objectionable. It has also reiterated the following guidelines framed by it to counter against obscene publication.

"Newspapers shall not display advertisements which are vulgar or which through depiction of a woman in nude or lewd posture, provoke lecherous attention of males as if she herself was commercial commodity for sale".

Whether a picture is obscene or not, is to be judged in relation to three tests; namely:

(i) Is it vulgar and indecent?

(ii) Is it a piece of mere pornography?

(iii) Is its publication meant merely to make money by titillating the sex feeling of adolescents and among whom it is intended to circulate? In other words, does it constitute an unwholesome exploitation for commercial gain.

Other relevant considerations are whether the picture is relevant to the subject matter of the magazine. That is to say, whether its publication serves any preponderating social or public purpose, in relation to art, painting, medicine, research or reform of sex.

Right of Reply

The prime principle that emanates from the various adjudications on this subject upholds the editors discretion in publication of letters. He would, however, be expected to voluntarily rectify an incorrect statement or report on a matter of public nature; the general reader can claim a locus standi on the basis of the public right to know. Besides, any person who has been specifically referred to in a publication can claim an automatic right to reply in the columns of the paper. Though the Council does not have the power to force a newspaper to publish, a rejoinder it may direct it to publish the particulars of the inquiry against it.

Pre-verification of News

Verification of news is necessary before publication, especially when the report has slanderous or libellous overtones or could lead to communal tension; nor can the publication of rumours as views of a cross-section of people be justified under any circumstances. The editor shall make necessary amends when any false or distorted publication is brought to his notice.

Defamation-Scurrilous Writings

Under the second exception to Section 499 of the Indian Penal Code it is not defamation to express in good faith any opinion whatever respecting the conduct of a public servant in the discharge of his public functions, or respecting his character, so far as his character appears in that conduct, and no further. The Council has accordingly held the opinion that fair comments on the public life cannot be held to be improper. But if any factual statements are made, they must be true and correct. In case a defamatory element is involved, more good faith will not be a defence in any civil action for damages.

Right to Privacy Vs. Public Figures

The Press Council of India formulated guidelines to achieve a balance between the right to privacy of the public persons and the right of the press to have access to information of public interest and importance. The issue under heated debate at both national and international level and the international conference of the World Association of Press Councils (WAPC) held in April 1998 in Delhi, stressed that there is a need for reconciliation between three competing constitutional values at play on this count, viz: (a) an individual's right to privacy, (b) freedom of the press, and (c) the people's right to know about public figures in public interest. The Council has prepared a report on the issue and framed the guidelines as follows:-

"Right to privacy is an inviolable human right. However, the degree of privacy differs from person to person and from situation to situation. The public person who functions under public gaze as an emissary/representative of the public cannot expect to be afforded the same degree of privacy as a private person. His acts and conduct are of public interest ('public interest' being distinct and separate from 'of interest to the public') even if conducted in private may be brought to public knowledge through the medium of the press. The press has, however, a corresponding duty to ensure that the informations about such acts and conduct of public interest of the public person is obtained through fair means, is properly verified and then reported accurately. For obtaining the information in respect of acts done or conducted away from public gaze, the press is not expected to use surveil devices. For obtaining information about private talks and discussions, while the press is expected not to badger the public persons, the public persons are also expected to bring more openness in their functioning and co-operate with the press in its duty of informing the public about the acts of their representatives".

FREEDOM OF THE PRESS

Threats to Press Freedom

An attack on a paper or those connected with it editorially or in management with a view to pressurising or intimidating them for the opinion expressed in the paper, constitutes a gross interference with the freedom of the Press (case of Malayala Manorama, PCI Review, Jan 1983 p. 62).

Tendencies to coerce newspapers to desist from publishing facts or toe a particular line are matters of concern. (Case of Malayala Manorama, PCI Annual Report 1968, p. 38).

The local administration is expected to help the journalist to perform his duties without being under duress or pressure (case of Blitz, PCI Review April 1984, p. 30).

Implication of an editor of a newspaper in a fabricated case by the police authorities with a view to harassing him for his treatment of the news or critical writings amounts to interference in the freedom of the Press. (Case of Mahajati, PCI Review October 1983, p. 55)

Groups raids on newspaper offices by unruly mobs interferes with the freedom of the Press. Suitable precautionary protective measures ought to be taken by the police. The same applies to blockade of newspapers offices. (Suo motu action by the Press Council against the Government of Karnataka, PCI Review April 1982, p. 36)

Harassment and victimization of journalists by police is a direct attack on the freedom of the Press. (Case of Madhya Pradesh Small Newspapers' Association, PCI Annual Report 1972, p. 66)

Seizure of camera and removal of film by police from a Press Photographer while covering the news would amount to preventing the journalist from performing his duties and is a matter to be viewed seriously. (Case of Searchlight, PCI Annual Report 1972, p. 65)

Filing of motivated frivolous cases against a journalist would amount to interfering with his functions. (Case of Malayala Manorama, PCI Annual Report, 1968, p. 38 and PCI Annual Report 1967, p. 52-58)

Any attempt by a minister to browbeat a reporter into toeing his line in the matter of reporting would be inconsistent with maintaining the proper standards of ministerial conduct towards the Press. (Case of Dainik Janambhumi, PCI Annual Report 1980, p. 56)

Disaccreditation and withdrawal of housing facilities from a newspaper correspondent because of articles/news items written by him would amount to an attempt to pressurise the correspondent and, therefore, the Press. (Case of Chandigarh Union of Journalists, PCI Annual Report, 1974, p. 68)

The Press and Registration of Books Act, 1867, does not empower the District Magistrate to obtain "Assurance Letters" from prospective editors before granting or refusing a declaration. (Case of U.P. Small and Medium Newspapers Editors' Council, PCI Review, Jan. 1983, p. 58)

Declaration of newspapers under the Press and Registration of Books Act, 1867, cannot be cancelled on the ground that the newspapers concerned were indulging in yellow journalism. Any complaint in regard to yellow journalism should be filed with the Press Council (Suo Motu action by the Press Council, PCI Annual Report 1983, p. 37)

Closeness of the date of appearance of a critical article and the date of disaccreditation would be material factors determining whether the disaccreditation was on account of that article. (Case of Sarita, Mukta etc., PCI Annual Report 1981 p. 60)

Advertisement and Press Freedom

The giving or withholding of advertisements, whether by individuals or by the government as a lever to influence the editorial policy constitutes a threat to and jeopardises the liberty of the Press, meaning in this context the freedom of the editor. This is especially so in case of the government since it is the trustee of public funds and, therefore, bound to utilise them without discrimination. (Case of Tribune, PCI Annual Report 1970, p. 45)

Advertisements, from any party including the government cannot be claimed as a matter of right by a newspaper. Government can frame its policy of placing advertisements based on objective criteria. But this should be based upon publicly stated principles without taking into consideration the editorial policy of the paper. (Cases of Saptahik Mujahid, PCI Review July 1983, p. 44, and Tribune, PCI Annual Report 1970, p. 45)

If an editor is guilty of an action or an impropriety of his paper, he can be proceeded against personally but this would not justify denial of advertisements to the paper of which he happens to be the editor. This applies to an employee or even the proprietor of a newspaper. (Case of Searchlight and Pradeep, PCI Annual Report 1974, p. 11)

The outside activities of the editor or other journalists might throw light on what he wrote for the paper, and in the event of such writings being improper, action against the paper is justified. However, this is for improper publication and for the employees' activities de hors the paper. (Ibid)

Impropriety and Press Freedom

It is improper to offer an inducement to a journalist to adopt a particular line of comment, and for the journalist to accept such an inducement. In the event of improper inducement being offered by the government the situation would be worse, since, then the media would become an arm of law enforcement. (Ibid).

It is improper for a journalist to accept an assignment which would be incompatible with the integrity and dignity of his profession or exploitation of his status as journalist. (Ibid)

The editor of a newspaper cannot be asked to divulge the source of information of a letter published in his paper. (Case of Arjun Baan, PCI Review, July 1983, p. 53)

Asking a journalist to divulge his personal and confidential source of information amounts to violation of his obligation to report on events of public interest and constitutes a threat to Press freedom. (Case of Press Correspondent, Hind Samachar, PCI Annual Report 1973, p. 27)

The editor of a newspaper cannot be directed by the police to alert his correspondent against the publication of a news item relating to the acts of the police, as it would be against the fundamental right of the Press. (Case of Vishwa Manav, PCI Review, October 1983, p. 52)

The motivated stoppage of subscription of teleprinter service of a news agency due to the feeling that reportage of a certain situation was exaggerated and to pressurize the agency would amount a threat to the freedom of the press. (Case of ex-Member of Parliament, PCI Annual Report 1972, p. 7)

Singling out news despatches to a newspaper and arrest of editors for activities in discharge of their professional duties and issue of warning letter from the government to newspapers to desist from publishing anything relating to certain activities of some groups, could legitimately give rise to an apprehension of threat to the freedom of the Press. (Suo motu action by the Press Council, PCI Review April 1983, p. 52)

GUIDELINES AND POLICY FORMULATIONS

The Council has issued guidelines and recommended policy framework on various matters concerning the Press and the people. In addition, the Chairmen of the Council have been guiding the Press through statements whenever a serious situation arose in which the Press was expected to work with restraint and circumspection. They also reacted sharply through such statements whenever organised major offensives were made against the Press.

In 1969, the Council issued a 10-point guidelines laying down norms and standards in reporting and commenting on matters which bear on communal relations. Without being exhaustive the guidelines listed and explained what would be offending against journalistic propriety and ethics, and should, therefore, be avoided (Annexure B-1).

Again, in the wake of the happenings in Ayodhya in 1990, the Council while reiterating the 1969 guidelines, issued another 12-point guidelines in the light of the new experience. The Council said that the principles outlined in it should be inculcated at every level of the media from training stage upwards and made a standard of external accountability. These principles (Annexure B-2) laid down certain 'dos' and don'ts for both the Press and the State.

The Council has over the years formulated policy framework in respect of such subjects as rules of accreditation, newsprint, advertisements, selection of journalists for accompanying the President, the Prime Minister etc., on their foreign tours.

As stated earlier, the Council has, following a decision taken in its meeting in October 1982, published two compendiums of its adjudication; one each on violation of journalistic ethics and violation of freedom of the Press, giving at the end of a similar set of cases the principles underlying the adjudications.

SPECIAL INQUIRIES

Apart from inquiring into the regular complaints, the Council has held a number of special inquiries, mostly suo motu, but sometimes on complaints into incidents and matters concerning the Press.

Report on Deshar Katha, Tripura 1990

Following a complaint by Shri Gautam Das, Editor, Daily Deshar Katha, a Bengali newspaper of Agartala, Tripura, regarding frequent violent attacks on the employees and hawkers of his newspapers by Congress (I) workers, the Press Council set up a Special Committee to make a thorough on-the-spot inquiry. The Committee visited Agartala and heard the representatives of the Government of Tripura and the complainant. As a result the Government of Tripura assured that they would take all necessary steps to prevent recurrence of such incidents and provide full security to Deshar Katha.

AYODHYA REPORT 1990

A special inquiry was set up on the Ayodhya happenings in 1990 and another in 1992. Their reports were made public in 1991 and 1993 respectively. In the first inquiry, the Council found four Uttar Pradesh dailies Jagran, Aj, Swatantra Bharat and Swatantra Chetna, guilty of publishing reports which constituted a grave violation of norms of journalistic ethics. The Council censured* these newspapers for violation of the norms. The Council also criticised the Uttar Pradesh Government for its many lapses in dealing with the situation and its behaviour towards the Press. It expressed serious concern over the authorities taking recourse to punitive and preventive action in excess of the demand of the situation and deplored invoking provisions of non-existent Press (Objectionable Matters) Act, 1951, and misapplying the provisions of the Press and Registration of Books Act, 1867.

Ayodhya Report 1993

In the wake of the demolition of the disputed shrine at Ayodhya on 6.12.1992 came the reports of numerous attack on journalists/press media photographers/cameramen who were covering the happenings at Ayodhya on 6.12.1992 and thereabout. As the matter was of great urgency and concern, a Special Inquiry Committee headed by the Chairman of the Council was set up to inquire into the matter. Prior to this the Chairman had already issued an appeal urging restraint and moderation on the part of the press while reporting events and presenting comments bearing on communal relations. Simultaneously, he expressed concern on the incidents of assaults on journalists when, they in discharge of their professional duties, were trying to cover the events. He also appealed to the authorities to ensure that the press is allowed to function freely and fearlessly to disseminate information on matters of public importance.

The Special Committee set up vide order dated 14.12.1992 collected oral and written evidence at its sittings at Ayodhya, Faizabad, Lucknow and Delhi and submitted its report to the full Council on 7.1.1993. The report as adopted by Council was released on 8.1.1993.

Punjab Report 1991

An inquiry was held into the pressures and problems confronting the Press and its personnel during acts of terrorism in Punjab. Adopting the report of the Special Committee, captioned 'Overcoming Fear' the Council extended its full support to the Punjab Press in its efforts to inform the people truthfully and impartially of the events and circumstances in the State and in resisting any code or norm sought to be imposed on it through force or intimidation by any extraneous authority or organisation.

J&K Report 1991

Similarly, a special inquiry was held on the problems faced by the Press in Jammu and Kashmir. Adopting the report of this committee in July 1991, the Council said the critical importance of information and communication in the complex and difficult situation in Kashmir had not been adequately realised either by the government or by the media itself. It suggested a series of measures to respond effectively to the various aspects of the situation. The full report was later published under the caption 'Crisis and Credibility'.

Bihar Report 1993

The report on increasing incidents of assaults on journalists and the pressures/impediments in the way of free functioning of the Press in the State of Bihar adopted by the Council on March 31, 1993 advised the Press and the authorities to put their relations on more healthy footings.

Report on AIDS and the Media 1993

The report on 'AIDS AND THE MEDIA' laid down certain do's and don'ts for the media advising them that from sporadic news AIDS must become campaign target. At the same time, the Press should bear in mind that the 'public interest' which may justify publication of a matter within the preserve of personal privacy, must be a 'legitimate interest' and not prurient or morbid curiosity.

Defence Report 1993

Yet another report of June 1993 captioned 'Pen and Sword' advocated an attitude of greater openness in Defence related information.

J & K Report 1994

The Council's latest report of 1994 on "Threats to the media from militant organisation in J & K" has recommended prompt dissemination of information at government level to counter militant propaganda. The report has also advised the Government to provide institutional and area security to the media personnel who face threats from the militants for taking independent stand.

The Model Advertisement Policy 1994

In the year 1994 the Council formulated uniform Advertisement Policy for application throughout India. It provides a succinct criteria for approval of newspapers for empanelment by the authorities for advertisements.

Guidelines on 'Pre-poll' and 'Exit-polls' Survey: The Press Council of India having considered the question of desirability or otherwise of publication of findings of pre-poll surveys and the purpose served by them, is of the view that the newspapers should not allow their forum to be used for distortions and manipulations of the elections and should not allow themselves to be exploited by the interested parties.

The Press Council, therefore, advises that in view of the crucial position occupied by the electoral process in a representative democracy like ours, the newspapers should be on guard against their precious forum being used for distortions and manipulations of the elections.

This has become necessary to emphasize today since the print media is sought to be increasingly exploited by the interested individuals and groups to misguide and mislead the unwary voters by subtle and not so subtle propaganda on casteist, religious and ethnic basis as well as by the use of sophisticated means like the alleged pre-poll surveys. While the communal and seditious propaganda is not difficult to detect in many cases, the interested use of the pre-poll survey, sometimes deliberately planted, is not so easy to uncover.

The Press Council, therefore, suggests that whenever the newspapers publish pre-poll surveys, they should take care to preface them conspicuously by indicating the institutions which have carried such surveys, the individuals and organisations which have commissioned the surveys, the size and nature of sample selected, the method of selection of the sample for the findings and the possible margin of error in the findings.

Further in the event of staggered poll dates, the media is seen to carry exit-poll surveys of the polls already held. This is likely to influence the voters where the polling is yet to commence. With a view to ensure that the electoral process is kept pure and the voters' minds are not influenced by any external factors, it is necessary that the media does not publish the exit-poll surveys till the last polls is held. The Press Council, therefore, request the Press to abide by the following guideline in respect of the exit-polls:

Guideline: No newspaper shall publish exit-poll surveys, however, genuine they may be, till last of the polls is over.

Press Council of India Frames Guidelines for Financial Journalists

The Press Council of India counselled reporters/financial journalists/newspaper establishments to refrain from receiving any gift/grants/concessions/facilities, etc., either in cash or kind which are likely to compromise free and unbiased reporting on financial matters.

The Council in its Report observed that the financial journalists today enjoy considerable influence over readers' minds and, therefore, they owe it to them to present a balanced and objective view of the financial dealings, status and prospects of a company. It observed that some companies are given excessive news coverage in the newspapers/magazines because they have issued advertisements to that print media. Sometimes, adverse reports are published of those companies which do not give advertisements to the newspapers or magazines. Again, when a media is not happy with any company/management for whatever reason, the negative aspects of the company are highlighted, while in the reverse situation, no negative aspects are brought to light. Some companies are also known to give gifts, loans, discounts, preferential shares, etc., to certain financial journalists to receive favourable and positive reports of the companies. At the same time, there is no mechanism for investors' education or for raising public opinion against such unhealthy practices.

The Council feeling concerned over the malpractice in the Corporate Sector and after holding detailed deliberations and discussions with the representatives financial institutions and journalists, has recommended the guidelines enumerated below for observance by the financial journalists:

1. The financial journalists should not accept gifts, loans, trips, discounts, preferential shares or other considerations which compromise or are likely to compromise his position.
2. It should be mentioned prominently in the report about any company that the report is based on information given by the company or the financial sponsors of the company.

3. When the trips are sponsored for visiting establishments of a company, the author of the report who has availed of the trip must state invariably that the visit was sponsored by the company concerned and that it had also extended the hospitality as the case may be.
4. No matter related to the company should be published without verifying the facts from the company and the source of such report should also be disclosed.
5. A reporter who exposes a scam or brings out a report for promotion of a good project, should be encouraged and awarded.
6. A journalist who has financial interests such as share holdings, stock holdings, etc., in a company, should not report on that company.
7. The journalist should not use for his own benefit of his relations and friends, information received by him in advance for publication.
8. No newspaper owner, editor or anybody connected with a newspaper should use his relations with the newspaper to promote his other business interests.
9. Whenever there is an indictment of a particular advertising agency or advertiser by the Advertising Council of India, the newspaper in which the advertisement was published must publish the news of indictment prominently.

PORTRAYAL OF WOMEN IN MEDIA (1996)

The Central Government in February 1995 forwarded to the Press Council for its views, the recommendations of Maharashtra Government on the possible role of audio-visual and print media in the advancement of the cause of women. A Sub-Committee of the Council interacted with prominent film/media personalities and other eminent persons. Its report was adopted by the Council on January 8, 1996.

While concurring with and endorsing the recommendations of Maharashtra Government's Policy for Women, the Council made seventeen more recommendations, prominent among them being (a) stories of atrocities on women should be published but without sensationalising them; (b) efforts of the media should be directed towards highlighting the positive achievements of women; (c) the downward slide in the moral ethos has to be checked by combating obscenity and vulgarity; (d) the Press Council of India on its part should accord priority to consideration of complaints brought before it on charges of denigrating women and build up further guidelines etc. In conclusion, it was emphasized that fructification of such a policy document will be possible only through the cohesive will of the people of all strata of society.

PROBLEMS OF SMALL AND MEDIUM NEWSPAPERS (1996)

A sub-committee of the members of the Council had been set up to go into the problems of small & medium newspapers in the country.

The sub-committee in its report to the Council, while identifying the problems faced by the small and medium newspapers, made some concrete long-term/short term recommendations in the matter: (a) a Small and Medium Newspaper Development Corporation should be set up as an autonomous body with a view to promote and ensure the development of small and medium papers or in the alternative they be encouraged to form cooperative society; (b) the government should devise a suitable advertisement policy in keeping with the guidelines framed by the Press Council of India; (c) the DAVP should display the list of those newspapers which are granted advertisements every quarter; (d) all advertisement bills of the papers should be settled by the Directorate of Audio-Visual Publicity and Directorate of Information and Public Relations within 45 days of the receipt thereof; (e) while printing paper be brought within the purview of newsprint and a specific quantity thereof be earmarked for small and medium newspapers; (f) 75% advertisements like those of biogas chulha, which do not concern the urban areas, should be given to the small and medium newspapers. These recommendations which were twenty-two in all were unanimously adopted by the Press Council.

CLOSURE OF NEWSPAPERS AND PROBLEMS OF URDU NEWSPAPERS

The Council had undertaken a study to gauge the reasons for increase in closure of newspapers over the past few years. The Committee of the Council had studied the situation in various regions all over the country. In the meantime the specific problems being faced by the Urdu papers were also brought to its attention. (Annual Report 1997-98-PCI Review October 1997).

FAVOUR TO JOURNALISTS

The public outcry in 1998 over the reported attempts to win over the media through gifts and favours had prompted the Press Council of India to undertake a comprehensive study of the issue with regard to all kinds of favours/benefits, either in cash or in kind in the form of concessions, gifts, lands, house facilities etc., extended to journalists (both editors and other than editors) news agencies, newspaper establishments and owners by various authorities during the 10 year period from 1985-95). The Committee in its report, as adopted by the Council on 22.1.1998, listed the undue favours as apart from these facilities for journalistic work and observed that ultimately the strength of the moral fabric of the press itself shall decide whether or not to be swayed by the inducements and enticements thrown its way by those in power.

LEGISLATIONS EXAMINED

The Council considered in depth the provisions of the Press and Registration of Books (Amendments) Bill, 1988, and held that it went beyond the statement of its objects. It did not implement properly the recommendations of the Second Press Commission relating to the subject. Though some of the provisions were of a positive nature, certain others were fraught with mischief leading to consequences perilous to the freedom of the Press. The Council suggested many radical changes in the Bill. The government later withdrew the Bill.

Similarly, the Council examined suo motu the Jammu & Kashmir Special Powers (Press) Bill, 1989. It also heard the State Ministers and representatives of various organisations of the Press on September 29, 1989 on the provisions of the Bill. After that the Council held that the J & K Government already had sufficient powers in its armoury in the form of existing State and Central legislations which could be effectively used to deal with cases of gross misconduct by the Press over the entire ground for which fresh powers were sought under the Bill.

The Council said that preventive laws with wide powers of pre-censorship and forfeiture would, by muzzling the Press, give free rein to rumours and destroy the credibility of the entire print and broadcast media within J & K and in the rest of the country. The Council was of the view that pre-censorship was inherently inimical to the freedom of the press. It recommended that the Bill be withdrawn. It also recommended revival of the Press Advisory Council in the State. The Bill was later withdrawn by the J & K Government in the State Assembly.

The Council also examined the Karnataka (Freedom of the Press) Bill, 1988, and the Karnataka Legislature (Powers, Privileges and Immunities) Bill, 1988, and gave various suggestions to make them more effective in respect of the freedom of the Press.

The Council made concrete and comprehensive recommendations regarding the repeal/amendment of the Official Secrets Act, 1923. It was first done in 1982 and again in 1990. In 1990, the Council said that the existing Act should be repealed in toto. It is no use amending a bad law. The Official Secrets Act is repugnant to open government and also militates against the ethos of the Constitutional guarantee of freedom of speech and expression enshrined in Article 19 (1) (a). A new legislation should be enacted which may be called "Freedom of Information Act." In event of this not being done, the Council suggested many amendments aimed at removing the deleterious affects of the various provisions of the Act on the Press.

The Council discussed Shri V.N. Gadgil's (MP) Right to Reply in the Press Bill, 1994 and considered it in all its ramifications in response to a reference made to it by the Union Government. It communicated its view that 'the proposed legislation is vulnerable from the stand-points of its necessity, propriety, viability, workability and above all, its constitutional validity'. The bill has since been withdrawn.

In response to another reference from the Central Government on publication of newspapers in India by foreign interests, the Council communicated its opinion on June 22, 1992, "that it does not favour publication of foreign newspapers/ news journals in India involving equity and management participation", adding that "the present arrangements could be reconsidered or reviewed after 3 to 5 years". After a Cabinet Sub-Committee headed by Shri N.K.P.Salve was set. up to make recommendation for any modifications in the policy decisions taken by Government on the subject in 1955-56, the matter was again referred to the Council for its comments. The Council has reiterated its views conveyed in June 1992.

STUDIES

The Press Council Act, 1978, empowers the Council to undertake studies in regard to matters concerning the Press. The Council in collaboration with the Indian Law Institute has conducted various studies viz., Official Secrets Act 1923, (recommendations since updated in 1990) Contempt of Courts Act, 1971, Parliamentary Privileges and Law of Defamation etc., in so far as they relate to the Press. This is a major accomplishment. These publications help the media persons understand the scope of their rights and the limits of their functioning.

PROTECTION OF CONFIDENTIAL SOURCES OF INFORMATION

In Contempt of Court proceedings the press usually makes the plea that it should not be forced to disclose Confidential source. "Such a plea for justification has been permitted on a limited basis. The Press's right to hold on to its sources of information has been balanced against other aspects of public interest. By way of tail piece, it has also been added that the press often demands the right to break confidence more than they plead the right to hold on to their own confidential sources. It is only fair that each claim should be balanced against other claims without conceding total primacy to the press in respect of its investigative and truth verification functions". In 1983, the Law Commission of India sent a questionnaire soliciting the views of the Press Council, inter alia, regarding disclosure of source of information by a journalist acquired by him in confidence for the purpose of his profession. In response to the Law Commission's question on the subject, the Press Council expressed as follows:

"In the opinion of the Council, the provision contained in Section 15 (2) of the Press Council Act, 1978 incorporates the latest trend and principles on the subject. Although under the above Act it is confined only to the proceedings under the Act it is strongly recommended that it should be made a part of the general law of the land."

"It is equally strongly felt that if any exception is to be made, it should be done in cases of extreme nature where disclosure is altogether unavoidable in the interest of the administration of justice. But the powers to order disclosure should be conferred only on competent court and that also in confidence to the presiding officer in the first instance, who may then, if satisfied that it is germane to the decision of the case, take such steps as may be necessary to make it a part of the evidence on record".

The Law Commission of India submitted its 93rd Report to the Government of India on 10th August, 1983 recommending for insertion of Section 132A in the Indian Evidence Act, 1872, as under:

"132A-No court shall require a person to disclose the source of information contained in a publication for which he is responsible, where such information has been obtained by him on the express agreement or implied understanding that the source will be kept confidential".

"Explanation: In this section-

(a) 'publication' means any speech, writing, broadcast or other communication in whatever form, which is addressed to the public at large or any section of the public.

(b) 'source' means the person from whom, or the means through which, the information was obtained".

It seems that the Government of India has not taken any step to get this recommendation of the Law Commission, implemented. The same can be said about the relatively moderate recommendations of the Press Commission/or of the Press Council of India, on this subject.

LECTURES BY THE CHAIRMAN OF THE COUNCIL AND OTHER ACTIVITIES

The successive Chairman of the Council have been invited to address seminars or deliver lectures arranged by various organisations and institutions where they have stressed the need for ensuring objective and factually correct reportage by the Press, the need to safeguard and strengthen Press freedom and to help in maintaining peace and harmony between different communities.

All earlier Chairmen have also been participating in such activities and spreading awareness about the need to preserve and protect Press freedom and to observe high ethical standards of journalism as also about the role and functioning of the Press Council in this behalf.

Students of journalism from various universities which impart instructions on the subject have been visiting the office of the Press Council and the Chairman have addressed them about the objects, functioning and working of the Council and the rights and responsibilities of the Press. The Press Council of India is also a member of World Association of Press Council which seeks to promote self regulation at international level. The present Chairman of the Council Justice P.B. Sawant is the current President of the body.

PRESS AND REGISTRATION APPELLATE BOARD

Section 27 of the Press Council Act, 1978, entrusts the Council with the functions of the Press and Registration Appellate Board, constituted under sub-section (1) of Section 8C of the Press & Registration of Books Act, 1867, to hear appeals against unlawful cancellation of declarations of newspapers or non-authentication thereof by the District Magistrate. The Board consists of the Chairman and another member to be nominated by the Press Council of India from amongst its members. The Board has rendered a number of important judgment since it was first constituted in 1979.

FREEDOM OF THE PRESS

Freedom of expression has always been emphasised as an essential basis for the democratic functioning of a society. The reasons for this are: the right of an individual to self-fulfillment, which right requires the communication of thought; the importance of constantly attempting to attaint he truth, an attempt which is frustrated if information is suppressed or comment blocked; the inherent democratic right to participate in decision-making, which obviously implies the freedom to obtain, communicate and discuss information,; and the practical importance of maintaining the precarious balance between healthy cleavage and the necessary consensus; "coercion of expression is likely to be ineffective (and).... Conceals the real problems confronting a society... It is likely to result in neglect of the grievances which are the actual basis of the unrest and thus prevent their correction".* Especially because we are compelled to operate our democracy indirectly, it is of great importance that the citizens should be enabled to know what is happening in different regions and different sectors of the functioning of the society, and to listen to different and alternative approaches and comments, so that they can effectively participate in the process of self-government. If facts cannot be freely presented and comments cannot be freely exchanged, there is no way in which the citizens can even attempt to hold the rulers to account.

A further dimensions to the freedom of expression is added by the existence of mass society in which communication among citizens can take place only through the use of media like the Press and broadcasting and not directly, except in a limited way. With State monopoly over broadcasting which prevails both technical and, in the Indian context, financial, the importance of the Press is even more crucial.

Our actual experience since Independence, and especially in the last decade or so, also suggests that a free and vigilant Press is vital to restrain corruption and injustice at least to the extent that public opinion can be roused as a result of press investigations and comments. Recently a number of injustices and wrong-doings have been uncovered as a result of the initiative taken by newspapers. Whether it is the question of various types of bonded labour in different parts of the country, the misuse of powers by A. R. Actually or the existence of smuggling rackets on the West Coast, newspapers have served a very useful purpose by exposing them. The fear that the Press will expose such wrong-doing is a major restraint on potential wrong-doers.

WHO THREATENS FREEDOM?

Owners Structure

Having accepted that the freedom of the Press is of vital importance especially in our contest, the question arises: is this freedom threatened and, if so, by whom?

It has been frequently alleged, especially in India, that the freedom of the Press is in danger because of the ownership of the newspaper industry and the predominance of some newspaper groups and chains. It is also suggested that the editors and journalists cannot have adequate freedom of collecting and disseminating facts and offering comments as they are under the pressure of the capitalist owners. It is further pointed out that free collection and dissemination of facts is not possible in the case of newspapers which depend to a large extent on revenue from advertisements as the advertising interests cannot but influence the presentation of news and comments. Unless this whole structure of ownership and control in the newspaper industry, and also the manner of the economic management of the Press, is changed, it is therefore suggested, the Press cannot be really free.

HOW FAR ARE THESE ARGUMENTS VALID?

It should be conceded at the outset that, like any large private sector industry, the newspaper industry cannot be influenced by the understanding and approach of those who control it. With modern technology, large newspaper organisations enjoy various economies of scale. Groups and chains of newspapers are therefore in a better position to provide richer fare in their newspapers are bound to be businessmen/capitalists, and their overall approach to the society and its problems cannot but be conditioned by this. That is why we inevitably find that the Press which is commercially organised-not run by political pro-business, pro-capitalist as well as usually a pro-Establishment viewpoint. Few newspapers will endorse a philosophy which goes against the established they would hardly raise their voice, or even offer investigative material, about the working of private trade and industry. When those who own or control newspapers are also involved in other lines of business, their stake in the stability of the system is so large that they would not encourage anything which is likely to create problems in the smooth functioning of the society. With maximum emphasis on stability, they would rather connive with oppression and injustice. Unorthodox and anti-establishment vies may not find much place in the columns of such newspapers, while national chauvinism-even jingoism-may come easily. The recent controversy in a country like the United Kingdom with a long democratic tradition about the somewhat subjective stances taken by the B.B.C. in the Falklands crisis shows how difficult it is for the Press or the media to maintain objectivity. The days that we can forget that appalling experience, when the freedom of the press as well as many other freedoms were seriously endangered in the U.S.A.

NO WORKABLE ALTERNATIVE

But what is the possible remedy? Public ownership of newspapers in effect meaning State ownership? Is that what will ensure the freedom of the Press?

The idea has merely to be put forward to see how suicidal such a solution can be. Cooperative ownership could be a possible alternative; but there are few examples anywhere in the world of successful cooperative management of large newspaper organisations, or of any large business establishments. A newspaper industry is an increasingly large, technically complex and managerially challenging industry. Unless we want the newspapers to be poorly produced as a result of continuous inefficiency in their management, we can not but permit good and vigorous managers to control major units in this industry. The choice is between having good newspapers even with the shortfalls inevitably arising out of the inadequacies mentioned earlier, or having poor quality newspapers. What our choice will be is obvious.

COMPETITION THE BEST POLICY

One should also point out that our experience in India is not that all those who own and manage the newspaper industry are taking a uniform approach on important issues relating to vital policy-making in the country. There are differences among them and some do take a significantly anti-establishment line. Though they may not necessarily support socialist or communist policies, they may permit a great deal of criticism of the existing system and encourage information as well as comment along critical lines. The degree of such criticism will vary. But our experience does not indicate that all capitalist owners of newspapers will collaborate and operate in some kind of a collusion. In fact, to the extent that there is competition for increasing circulation, a newspaper is bound to attempt to ensure that it is not found wanting in investigating events and giving information which competing newspapers may provide. The owners cannot therefore take an approach which will reduce the circulation by insisting that it reflect his personal viewpoint rather than attempting to present facts and other materials which the readers would be interested in. A capitalist owner may not necessarily be actuated by any lofty motives; but the possibility cannot be ignored that competing newspapers would forge ahead if the paper is allowed to be too sectional or partial. Experience both in India and abroad also suggests that only large newspaper organisations can resist powerful institutions and persons. A small newspaper would institutions and persons. A small newspaper would have found it difficult to face the wrath of a Nixon.

What is therefore of real importance is to ensure that a certain minimum degree of competition exists in the newspaper world. It is true, as mentioned earlier, that, as in many other industries, technology and other aspects give a significant advantage to large scale organisations in the press industry. It is no longer possible for the number of successful newspaper ventures to be very large. We can only have a limited degree of competition and not anything approaching perfect competition. But this is the difficulty in all modern industries. All that can and should be emphasised is that a reasonable degree of competition should be attempted to be maintained.

This can be done in two ways: Firstly, in any effective circulation area which forms a single market for newspapers, careful watch should be kept on dominant newspapers who control a large proportion of the circulation. In the case of such newspapers the normal provisions of the MRTP Act such as special permission being required for their major expansion or setting up of new papers by them etc. should apply. Careful watch should also be kept on the possibility of their indulging in monopolistic and unfair trade practices. It has been already held that the MRTP Act applies to the newspaper industry. What is necessary is to make sure that the provisions of the Act are streamlined and its instruments given adequate teeth so that the anti-monopoly provisions can effectively operate. This is necessary not only in the newspaper industry but in all industries. The difficulty is that throughout the last ten years since the MRTP Act was put on the statute book, the Government has not rally bothered to see that anti-monopoly provisions become effective. In fact, the tendency of Government has been in opposite direction, Viz, to favour the monopoly organisations.

As for large business houses controlling a number of industries and also newspapers, to the extent that such houses represent a significant degree of concentration of economic power, they would come within the purview of the break-up provisions under Section 27 of the MRTP Act. The government would therefore be in a position to have the possibility of such breakup examined by the MRTP Commission and, if such a break-up is advised in public interest, it can take steps in that direction. The difficulty is that the Government has made no use of this section. The Government appears to be merely wanting to have many powers with it so that it can threaten and intimidate those enterprises, including newspaper ones, which are not ready to toe its line. It is significant that the only instance where the Government thought worth looking at; it was only the Indian Express, because it was proving to be a paper not easily amenable to the wishes of those in power at that time. This inference is supported by the fact that, at the Government's instance, R. N. Goenka was replaced as chairman of the Indian Express group by K. K. Birla, and the Government preferred this arrangement in spite of latter's connections with both a large business empire, and with the Hindustan Times. In thinking of any special powers relating to the Press being given to Government, the very real possibility of the powers being mainly used for arm-twisting for partisan interests should not be overlooked.

POSITIVE ASSISTANCE TO INDEPENDENT PAPERS

At the same time, it is important that steps are taken positively to make it possible for independent papers to survive develop. Assistance to them should be provided through general institutions meant to help the growth of independent entrepreneurs, including small ones. The financial institutions as well as promoting organisations-such as the National Small Industries Corporation-can be used for this purpose. Facilities such as subsidised teleprinter services, and facilitating the setting up of small electronic presses, could be other steps in this direction. The assistance should be granted in a manner where no discrimination among individual papers can be easily made, and where the subsidised facility cannot be misused and encashed. For this reason making available a marketable commodity like newsprint at a specially cheaper price should not be supported.

The dependence of newspapers on advertisement revenue may go against the perspective of some puritan minds about an ideal society. But in a world where mass persuasion is becoming respectable even in communist countries like Hungary and Yugoslavia, we cannot think of advertisement as a tainted source of revenue. At a time when the costs of producing newspapers are rapidly raising, advertisement revenue is the only mechanism which can keep the newspaper prices within reasonable limits. Any attempt by Government to put a restriction to advertisement revenue has to be looked upon as an indirect method of upsetting the economy of newspapers and thus an act which would affect Press freedom adversely. To the extent that a newspaper has a large number of sources from which advertisement revenue flows in, it is less likely to be influenced in its coverage by the wishes of any one of them. A smaller newspaper is more likely to be subject to the wishes of an important advertiser, including the Government. It is therefore necessary to realise that larger appears are less likely to be influenced by advertisers. Further, to the extent that the MRTP Act is effectively used, the power of any one advertiser would be limited. Of course, if the Government chooses to continue to keep the MRTP Act should be available to Government to curb undue concentration and misuse of monopoly powers in the Press industry. It should also be obligatory for Government to consult the MRTP Commission before any action under that Act is taken.

STATE—THE MAIN THREAT

This insistence is necessary because experience all over the world, as well as our own experience since Independence, suggest that the State remains the source of the most potential.threat to Press freedom. It cannot be overlooked that, within a short time after passing the Constitution, those in power-who used to swear by Press freedom before Independence-put in provisos to Article 19 (1) of the Constitution so as to clothe Government with powers to curb Press freedom. This was defended on the ground that these powers were likely to be necessary on occasions when the security of the State was threatened; it was emphasised that the powers will not be normally used. But a special legislation called the Press (Prevention of Objectionable Matters) Act was put on the statute book soon thereafter in 1951. No steps were taken to remove the lacunae which gave Government powers to intercept material going to the Press through the Posts and Telegraphs. Some Chief Ministers thought it proper to take steps against newspapers whose policy they did not like, whether it was a Morarji Desai in Bombay or a Charan Singh in U. P.

A persistent attempt to curb Press freedom how ever really began only after 1969. Indira Gandhi felt that the Press was too critical of her ways and she sought to change its approach. Various threats were held out by Government and steps proposed to curb that section of the Press which was thought to be the most independent. With the aid of some native leftist organisations, a propaganda barrage was mounted against the Press as well as the judiciary both of which appeared to be not easily·amenable to the wishes of Government. Apparently the only reason why the idea of spreading the equity ownership of newspaper companies especially among the workers and the journalists employed therein was not pursued was the feeling that such a measure would give more power in the hands of trade unions who were opposed to the ruling party.

On the other hand, arm-twisting of capitalist owners, especially of those who had many other industrial interests and were not very much concerned with the freedom of the Press, was thought to be not so difficult. The antipathy to the Press however continued and got further intensified, especially as most of the important papers expressed their dislike of the acts of the ruling establishment, and many of them advised the Prime Minister to resign after the Allahabad High Court Judgement in 1975. The antipathy culminated in the pre-censorship imposed in the country for the first time during the internal Emergency. That the pre censorship was used for partisan ends is sufficiently exemplified by the data published as a result of the various enquiries made in 1977-78. The misuse of powers like pre-censorship was a adequately envisaged by the fact that these powers were even used to black out some unpleasant news about the criminal convictions of an actress, and of some businessmen.

The experience of the Emergency also provided enough evidence to show how weak-kneed a very large part of the Indian Press was when it felt really threatened. One would not have believed that, during the independence movement, a much larger proportion of newspapers had faced difficulties and shown courage. The poor morale of many editors and others concerned was aptly characterised by the Janata Government's Minster for Information and Broadcasting who told the Press that, when they were only asked to bend, they crawled! Nevertheless, there were brave exceptions; and it is important to note who they were. Two of the so-called monopoly papers resisted encroachment on their freedom and faced considerable risks. These were the Statesman and the Indian Express.

Of course even a more valiant attitude was shown by independent, small journals like Sadhana (Marathi), Bhoomiputra (Gujrati), Seminar (a monthly journal) and Opinion (a weekly sheet); but these were run by individuals or groups who had a commitment to certain values and where the overall financial stake, the number of employees etc., was not very large.

A very large proportion of the regular Press offered little resistance and gradually accepted a kind of self-censorship. That the ruling group was thinking of controls over the Press as a permanent measure was indicated by the putting on the statute book of the Prevention of Publication of Objectionable Matters Act in 1976.

It was also known that the spokesmen of Government were threatening newspapers about "consequences", after the censorship was lifted and general elections announced. These threats indicated what might have been in store for the Press in the Congress party had won the elections in March 1977.

The Press began to act with great vigour almost as a rebound after the Emergency was lifted in 1977, and especially after the change brought in as a result of the elections in March 1977. The Janata Government and the short-lived Lok Dal Government, felt the thrust of this vigorous assertion of independence by the Press. This was also the time when the Press specially developed new traditions of investigative journalism, which has now become a major feature of an increasing number of important newspapers.

Since January 1980, with the change of Government, the attitude of the Government of India toward the Press has reverted back to one of antipathy. Many of the new State Governments which came to power in the middle of 1980 have shown active hostility. Instances of threats to the free functioning of the Press are not uncommon.

There was the instance in Bangalore when, as a result of the publication of a press report which was disliked by the Chief Minister, there was a kind of gherao of important papers so as to prevent their publication on one day and the police practically pleaded helplessness to do anything about the matter.

There was another instance of a former Chief Minister who compared the Press to snakes and scorpions.

The Tamil Nadu Government, belonging to a different political party, has put special curbs on contacts between Government officials and the Press, and has stiffened the Cr. P. C. in a manner which would make "scurrilous" writing a nonbailable offence and also one where imprisonment on conviction is made obligatory as a punishment. The Prime Minister herself has indicated more than once her dislike of the manner in which what is called the National Press operates.

HOSTILE ATTITUDE OF THOSE IN POWER

The basic attitude of those who are in power has been one of wanting the Press to conform. This is specially clear from the official attitude to the manner in which the broadcasting media under direct Government control are to operate. The demand that broadcasting media be separated from the direct tutelage of Government, and the work be entrusted to an autonomous corporation, has been put forward for a long time. But this has been resisted by all those who have been in political power at the Centre.

The Government of India had appointed in the 60's a committee (the Chanda Committee) to go into this question and it recommended an autonomous set up for the All India Radio. But the Government continued to ignore this recommendation. In fact, during the Emergency, spokesmen of the Government continued to ignore this recommendation.

In fact, during the Emergency, spokesmen of the Government made it quite clear that they thought it quite right that the broadcasting media should propagate only the official viewpoint. The Prime Minister herself had clearly state in 1975 that All India Radio is "a Government organ, it is going to remain a Government organ... It is there to project Government policies and Government views.

It does not mean we do not give the views of other people, but primarily its function is there to give the views of the Government of India". The Prime Minister justified this by stating that "in no country in the world, in no developing country, do they even allow anybody else to appear or any other viewpoint to be projected'.

Though the Janata Government appointed a committee (B. G. Verghese Committee) to examine this question, and the Committee recommended the setting up of an autonomous body for taking charge of broadcasting, the Janata Government, and also the short-lived Lok Dal Government, took no steps to pursue this recommendation and to make All India Radio autonomous and largely free of Government control. This is an adequate indication of the battles that may always have to be fought, whichever party is in power, to ensure that media of mass communication are permitted to operate freely.

A more recent indication of the Government's indifference to the economic functioning of the Press is provided by the Government's imposing an import duty on newsprint at a time when various costs of the newspaper industry, including the newsprint prices in the major supplying countries, have been rapidly escalating.

To impose a duty on newsprint which would further enhance the costs of producing newspapers, in a country where the incomes of the common people are very low and where the circulation of newspapers is still very small, is hardly calculated to ensure wider circulation of newspapers. The proceeds of the wider circulation of newspapers. The proceeds of the import duty form such a minor part of the Central Government's revenue that if the duty was not imposed it would have meant no real difficulty for the Government. In spite of widespread demand in the Press, the Government continues the import duty for a second year, only making it specific instead of ad valorem.

STATE POWERFUL IN INDIA

A further point of importance in this context is that, because of the necessity to ensure planned development of our economy, considerable powers regarding various aspects of the economy have been conferred on Government. With the attitude of the Government of intolerance of criticism as indicated earlier, the possibility of the Government misusing these powers against the newspapers whom it considers hostile is very real. Not only that Government misusing these powers against the newspapers whom it considers hostile is very real. Not only that Government has considerable powers which can be used at its discretion under statutes like the IDRA and MRTP Act, but here are also other powers such as under import control, the grant of credit through banks the bulk of whom are in the public sector, and even services provided by public utilities like Posts and Telegraphs (including telephones), and power supply.

Normal credit facilities may be denied, power supply may be cut off or made irregular (ostensibly on technical grounds), or postal and Telegraphic facilities may be discriminatingly used, to harass newspapers whose policies are disliked by those in positions of political power. Government advertisements and advertisements by the large and expanding public sector business organisations may be denied or they may be used in such a discriminating manner as to favour or disfavour particular newspapers.

The overall powers of the State may be used to create difficulties for independent newspapers and news people. Even police protection may mysteriously disappear when well organised mobs gherao newspaper offices and threaten it with violence. Enough data are available to show that these are not merely theoretical possibilities but realities which face the Indian Press.

It is therefore clear that the main threat to press freedom in India arises from the executive power of the State, both at the Centre and in the States. What is likely is not so much a direct and overt act of nationalisation as what may be culled salami tactics of putting curbs in an increasing and steady manner through various obstructions and threats.

LEGISLATORS' ATTITUDES

It is also necessary not to ignore the fact that the traditions of democratic polity and essential freedoms have not had a very long innings in India. Intolerance of inconvenient speech or writing therefore comes easily to many people in the country.

Enough data are available even about happenings in recent years to illustrate this, Chhabirani episode in Orissa being one of the most notorious ones.

Investigative journalism, when it touches some vested interest or the other-whether it is in politics, castes, property rights, trade unions, or any other-is in special danger as a result of persistent threats of violence. It would not be wrong to say that the greater the distance of the journal or the journalists from metropolis the greater the risk, though it is not as if such danger is quite absent even in metropolitan areas.

The intolerance of critical references is further exemplified in the attitude shown by many legislators to the question of legislative privileges. Even though it is now more than 30 years since the Constitution was passed and the idea then was that the privileges of legislatures would be codified within a few years, no legislature in India has yet taken any steps in that direction and there appears to be almost a consensus among legislators to avoid such codification.

The result is that the possibility that a legislature may treat a particular reference as an infringement of legislative privilege is a kind of Damocles' sword on the heads of newspapers. It does not infrequently happen that legislators utter obscenities, trade in abuses and generally behave in an undignified manner.

If the presiding officer expunges such words, or decides that nothing will go on record, the idea is that publication of such part of the proceedings, even if it has taken place, is not to be reported; and if it is, is may be treated as a contempt of the legislature. This is strange logic indeed. What actually happens, is actually said, is treated as if it is wiped out by the decision of the presiding officer and is not to be reported. Unlike in some foreign legislatures such a sin the U.K., it is not an odd word here or there which is expunged but, frequently, whole passages.

A citizen who is present in the visitors' gallery is obviously a witness to what happens; but those who are not present are not expected to be informed through the Press of what actually happened. One does not understand by what logic such an approach is taken. On the other hand, it is only proper that the citizen should have the maximum access to information about what his representatives do, the manner in which they behave, or misbehave.

IMPORTANCE OF CONSTITUTIONAL AMENDMENT

All these difficulties in the way of ensuring that the Press can have the maximum freedom to carry out its function of collecting facts about different facets of national life, analysing them and commenting upon them so as to keep the general body of citizens in our young democracy well informed show that the Press requires some special protection. Many authorities have held that the Right to Freedom of Speech conferred by Article 19(1) of the Constitution is adequate to protect the freedom of the Press.

Judicial decisions have however made it clear that the Fundamental Rights are conferred only on citizens and not on associations of citizens. In the present times, no newspaper or other periodical can normally be brought out by individuals; it can only be brought out by corporate bodies. Moreover, it has also been held by Courts that, in view of the limitations put under Article 19 (2) etc., pre-censorship can be imposed on newspapers even when the country is not faced by an Emergency due to external aggression or internal rebellion or similar circumstances.

That governmental authorities can be tempted to use such powers purely for partisan purposes was adequately proved in 1975-76 and, more recently, in Assam. There is also some uncertainty about whether some provisions in the Indian Penal Code cannot be used as a coercive instrument against the Press. It appears therefore necessary that a specific Constitutional amendment so as to confer the right of Freedom on the Press in particular and on media of communication in general needs to be taken up in right earnest.

If the general body of citizens in a vast country like ours is to be kept adequately informed both about the actual events and about alternative approaches to meeting the country's problems, it is essential that the freedom of the communication media is protected by a specific Constitutional provision to that effect.

Such a specific provision will enable newspapers and journalists to obtain judicial protection from direct as well as indirect threats. It would not then be impossible for a newspaper which may receive unfair treatment from those in charge of functions like import control, power supply, bank credit or communication facilities to obtain judicial redress if it can be shown that the discrimination is due to its being a newspaper which is critical of those in power.

CODIFICATION OF LEGISLATIVE PRIVILEGES

A complementary measure will be to insist upon the codification of legislative privileges, with the proviso that where a breach of privilege is alleged, the legislature should only be permitted to file a complaint, the decision regarding whether contempt is proved and, if so, the punishment to be awarded being left to a Court of Law. The idea that the legislature should itself be both the accuser and the judge might have had a historical reason in England; but there is not reason for such a fundamentally unjust approach to be accepted in our context.

PRESS NEEDS TO IMPROVE

It may be asked: Would this be enough to ensure that the Press is left genuinely free to carry out the functions that it must perform? Would it not be necessary to think of some other, more positive, steps to ensure that the press does not remain a hand-maid of only the powerful in the country?

The inadequacies of the Indian Press need not be connived at. There is no doubt that private business-and those who control it-are treated by most newspapers with kid gloves. This partly because of the ownership of many newspapers and therefore the philosophy of those who are appointed to senior journalistic positions.

The trade union side of industrial disputes, the approach of the political parties on the left side of the political spectrum and the difficulties of the unprivileged and the dispossessed have received far less attention than other smaller but influential sections and vested interests in the vast bulk of our newspapers. It should, however, be said that the situation is changing for the better. Competition, and also the increasing influence of professional journalists, are making it difficult for newspapers to ignore these various aspects.

It is well known that the blindings at Bhagalpur, the treatment of workers as bonded servants by many landed interests, the exploitation of child labour in slate factories, or of female labour in bidi factories ore even of adult workers in asbestos factories have been brought to light not by small newspapers but by large ones which are many times dubbed by critics as belonging to the Monopoly or the Jute Press category. This tendency shows that to the extent that at least some degree of competition can be ensured in every circulation area chances are that there would be a fair degree of investigation of different types of events.

A part of the answer to the difficulties lies in making it possible for independent newspapers and especially periodicals to operate without too much handicap. But, even then, such newspapers may not be as successful as the large ones operated as capitalist undertakings.

Their workers, including journalists, may have to work at a sacrifice. But unless there are elements in the country which are ready to work with self sacrifice and zeal for causes in which they believe, new and unorthodox ideas cannot develop and new political groups cannot emerge. There have been examples of such efforts such as the daily Shramik Vichar run by some trade union groups in Pune. There was even an attempt at running a paper devoted to the requirements of the district of Pune which however did not continue for long. Real entrepreneurship in this field would consist of such efforts and, except for direct and discretionary subvention, various other steps can be taken to help the whole category of such newspapers and periodicals. This would make it possible for the larger newspapers to be kept on their toes.

Even though investigative journalism is fast developing in India, the quality of the Indian Press in many respects leaves much to be desired. Even though, as a result of various awards, the emoluments of journalists have considerably improved in the last few years, adequate talent is not still attracted to this field. There is also a great deal of lethargy which leads to large scale reproduction of speeches as well as gossip from the corridors of power instead of well organised news. The tendency even of some of our top newspapers to rely on articles from the foreign Press when dealing with world affairs shows a lack of initiative in developing Indian talent for analysing world problems from the Indian point of view.

With some exceptions, there has also not been enough effort to develop interest in news, other information and comments on aspects of life other than politics, crime and sports. Investigative news collection can be of great use in matters like the operation of Plan programmes and projects. In some newspapers, useful reports of investigations in sectors like power and irrigation have recently appeared. But this is still experimental and confined only to a few papers. Such inadequacies can be overcome only with better training, more competition and greater professionalisation. There are no short-cut remedies for this.

The most serious inadequacy relating to the Indian Press is to be found in newspapers published in Indian languages. Most of them are poorer in quality as compared to newspapers in English. This is so even in respect of Indian language papers belonging to same groups. This obviously happens because the managements of such groups continue to think that the prestige of the group depends more on the English language newspapers than on the Indian language ones. It is quite obvious that the number of those proficient in English will not expand as rapidly as that of the literate in various Indian languages.

The demand for Indian language newspapers is already expanding faster and this trend will be further accelerated in future. As the number of legislators who understand English declines, it is essential in public interest and for the proper functioning of our democracy that the quality of the more important Indian language newspapers improves rapidly. Special steps such as the development of teleprinter services in Indian languages and support to the adaptation of the best techniques for printing Indian language newspapers should be taken by the Government so as to help.

THE MAIN GOAL-GROWTH WITH FREEDOM

We have had a wrong set of priorities regarding the Press. Even the first Press Commission appeared to have been more worried about what are called chain newspapers rather than about the very inadequate circulation of all newspapers-chain and non-chain-in the country. Even the so-called chain papers still hardly boast of a circulation which would have any relevance to the numbers of people in our metropolitan and urban areas, leave alone in the countryside. It needs to be emphasised that the topmost priority in India should be to help all newspapers to develop both in terms of circulation and quality.

It will take all types-chain and non-chain, multi edition and single edition, group and non-group, large kind of Press that the largest democracy in the world requires and deserves. What should never be overlooked when thinking of the Press in the Indian context is that it is only a free Press which can help develop a body of citizens who are well informed both regarding current events and also about the problems facing the country; and the alternatives available for tackling them. It is only such a Press that can enable a young democracy like India to survive, and also help its development in a manner where social justice is ensured and the interests of the common people served.

4

Press Council and Indian Government

The Press Council of India has held that government accommodation, concessional land, free air tickets and company shares being given to journalists, news agencies and newspaper establishments and owners, are 'undue favours'.

The Council, which undertook a comprehensive study of the subject between 1985 and 1995, concluded that free and concessional bus, rail and other transport facilities given to journalists also fell in the category of favours. It observed that free air travel provided by companies, corporations and airlines was an inducement to write favourably about their products and services, and hence, marred independent reporting.

The Council noted that proprietors of newspapers, instead of journalists and editors, were accompanying the president, vice president, prime minister and the external affairs ministry officials, on their foreign trips. Newspapers, it recommended, should take care to nominate eligible persons for such trips.

The Commission also observed that indiscriminate disbursement of money from the discretionary funds of the chief ministers encouraged unfaithfulness to the mission of journalism and promoted corrupt practices. The following are the recommendations:

RECOMMENDATIONS

The Committee (of the Council on undue favours to journalists) came to the conclusion that the following facilities so far being extended by the government and the authorities, companies and corporations would amount to favours subject to the observations made here under:

Accommodation: Government Housing/flats/land

The Committee is of the view that it is the responsibility of the newspaper establishments to provide accommodation to its employees. The Committee noted that the Punjab and Haryana High Court in its judgement has held that journalists are not entitled to government accommodation as they are not employees of the government. The Court has said that there were no rules, regulations or guidelines governing such allotment with the Chandigarh administration. The Court observed that the existing rules were only meant for government servants and there was no question of bringing journalists in its ambit. The Committee further noted that the Central Government in its action taken report on the suggestions of the Second Press Commission to the effect that: no further housing facility should be provided to the journalists and the existing allotments of the government accommodation in the National Capital and the States should be charged for at non-subsidised rates and phased out as the present occupants leave-had recorded that no further housing facility would be provided to journalists and in respect of the existing allotments, rent would be charged at non subsidised rates. This decision was taken nearly a decade ago. However, the allotments continued.

The Committee also noted that the governments were giving prime land to the newspaper owners at nominal price. Some of the newspaper establishments had either rented out the entire premises after retaining a small portion for their own use or had converted the premises into a commercial complex thereby earning huge profits. In some of the cases, it was found that the newspapers with a view to get another allotment at some other place after renting out the entire building, were not even reporting on attacks on their own scribes for the simple reason that they wanted to remain in the good books of the government. Such newspapers were compromising with the fascist forces and the freedom of the press.

Allotment of Shares in Companies: The Committee was of the opinion that if shares were allotted at special prices or were given under any quota, this would amount to favour. The Press Council of India has already issued guidelines for the financial journalists.

Bus Travel/rail travel/transport: The Committee was of the opinion that this was a favour so for as big and medium newspapers are concerned. The journalists attached to newspapers which are in profit have no justification for availing free or concessional bus/rail/air transport facility. However, in case of small newspapers this constituted a facility as the Committee felt that there was justification for extending such a facility. The media persons working at the grassroot level, and work for small newspapers are paid the bare minimum recommended under the Wage Board Awards. The financial condition of most of the small newspapers is precarious and without such a facility they would be unable to cover all news which is necessary to be communicated to their readers.

Most of the news of the local level which appears in these newspapers were most times picked up by the medium and big newspapers. The reporters of the small newspapers and accredited free-lance journalists, who cannot afford it, must have the facility to travel as much as possible.

Foreign Travel: The companies, corporations and airlines extend the facility of air travel to journalists not only within the country but also abroad. The journalists avail of this happily. This is an inducement to write favourably about their products/ airlines. A propaganda is undertaken through such devices to commercially promote the products/airlines. This certainly interferes with independent reporting.

Before 1986, the president, vice president, prime minister and external affairs minister were accompanied by journalists during their foreign trips on the basis of pick and choose policy. But in 1987, Press Council of India framed guidelines on selection of journalists on PM's entourage and this was being generally followed. The Committee, however, noted that often the proprietors of the newspapers were accompanying the president/ prime minister on foreign tours in place of journalists and editors. The Committee recommended that the newspapers should take care to nominate eligible persons for the purpose.

Free Air Tickets: The Committee was of the opinion that this practice constituted an undue favour as it enticed journalists to write favourable reports to commercially promote the airline.

Cash Disbursement from CM'S Discretionary Fund: The Committee noted that there are guidelines as to how the discretionary fund at the disposal of the chief minister or any other functionary has to be spent. The guidelines should be followed strictly. Indiscriminate disbursement of money from the discretionary fund of the chief ministers encourages unfaithfulness to the mission of journalism and promotes corrupt practices.

Financial Assistance: The Committee was of the opinion that if financial assistance is given for medical treatment purposes, it still constitutes a favour, unless, medical aid is being given under the clear cut policy uniformly applicable to all those destitutes or sick persons who cannot afford the medical treatment in case the journalist incidentally happens to be one of those persons, there is nothing wrong in it.

In Delhi, all the journalists accredited to PIB are entitled to CGHS facility. The Committee feels that extending the CGHS facility to journalists is illogical since CGHS facility is available to government servants only. The provision of medical facilities to its employees is the responsibility of the newspaper establishments.

Funds for Media Centre and Grants to Journalists Associations: The Committee was of the opinion that this was a favour, unless it was given for promoting the journalistic skills.

Gift Cheque by Advertising Agencies for Publication of Press Note of their Clients: The Committee was of the opinion that this was a favour and deserved outright condemnation.

Other Gifts: The Committee was of the opinion that gifts in any form, irrespective of their value, are to be condemned.

Free Parking: The Committee was of the opinion that this was a favour if a journalist uses this facility for purposes other than his professional work.

Guest Hospitality: The Committee was of the opinion that working journalists as a rule should not be treated as State guests. In case an individual is treated as a State guest he ipso facto becomes entitled to many facilities without any payment thereof. However, when press teams are invited in discharge of their professional duties, making due arrangements for them should be an exception. The committee further noted that the stay in government guest houses by accredited journalists, is permissible if it is for discharging professional duties.

Import of Duty Free Cameras and Computers

The Committee was of the opinion it is the duty of the newspaper establishment to, provide cameras/computers to its personnel. An individual employee journalist is not required to buy camera/computer for his work. In the recent past, the Central government had allowed import of duty free cameras and computers to the journalists. The Committee felt that this concession amounted to a favour. However, the Committee was of the opinion that this facility should be permissible for accredited free-lance journalists, provided it is not misused.

Insurance Premium: The Committee was of the opinion that it is not for the government to pay for the premium towards the insurance of journalists. It is the duty of the newspaper establishments or the individual concerned to make such payment towards annual dues once the scheme has been introduced.

Job to Relatives: Giving jobs to journalist's relative/s not on merit, is an outright attempt at inducement.

Loans: The Committee was of the opinion that the grant of loans within the ambit of policy already laid down for all citizens is permissible. But when the loan is given only to the journalists or at reduced rate of interest or when the interest due or the principal amount is waived/written off/condoned, such a practice would amount to undue favour.

Nomination on Committees: The Committee was of the opinion that in some states, the journalists are nominated on some organisations and institutions like Public Service Commission and are also given the status of state minister or

Cabinet Minister, which was a wrong practice. Except for the nomination by the professional organisations on committees which have a quota to represent the various professionals, this practice constitutes favour.

PCO/FAX/Phone booth or Centre: The Committee was of the opinion that this is obviously a favour, if gifted. The fax and the phone facility given to all journalists is, however, to be distinguished from the allotment of such booths.

Pensionary Benefits: The Committee was of the opinion that since the Fourth Estate was not a part of the government, this benefit constituted a favour if the pensionary benefits were extended by the government. The role of the authorities should be limited to ensuring that the newspaper establishments implement the awards of the Wage Boards.

Press Clubs-donation of Funds: The Committee noted that this practice is prevalent all over the country and fund are being donated lavishly by chief ministers/ministers/leaders not only to genuine press clubs but also to the press clubs of dubious nature. It, therefore, constituted an attempt to induce the journalists to give favourable reports about the donors.

Prizes: The Committee felt that the practice of giving spurious awards has to be curbed. There were instances, not worth mentioning, of sale of awards and prizes by racketeers making money out of it. Not only the racketeers but awardees also were often contributing towards the value of the prizes.

Shops: Allotment of shops in their capacity as journalists is a clear cut favour.

Facilities: The Committee was of the opinion that the following constituted facilities, subject to the remarks given:

Accreditation: The pattern of the formation of the Central Press Accreditation Committee should be followed in all states and union territories. The CPAC at present has a good composition of representatives of journalists, owners, editors and non editors' organisations headed by Principal Information Officer of the Press Information Bureau, Government of India. Another officer, Director of External Publicity is also called to attend the meeting whenever the issue of foreign accreditation is considered. However, it be made mandatory that the accreditation committee should be constituted within a month of the expiry of the term of the earlier committee and committee should hold its meetings quarterly. A provisional accreditation, if given, must come up before the accreditation committee in its first meeting thereafter.

Government and Public Authority Advertisements

It is a mutually beneficial transaction when conducted in keeping with the parameters defined in an already laid down policy. However, when given to individual newspapers on ad hoc basis or for extraneous considerations or when they are not routed through centralised agency, they constitute favour.

In addition, governments and public authorities, including the railways, must publish in their annual reports etc., the information regarding advertisements and facilities given by them to journalists and their organisations etc., to ensure greater transparency in their working.

Election Facilities: The Committee was of the opinion that this was a must, so that journalists are able to cover the events relating to the most important electoral process. Access to all the places of information must be given to them, subject to reasonable restrictions imposed by the Election Commission of India.

Meeting Expenses for Journalistic Conventions, Seminars, etc.: The Committee was of the opinion that this was permissible so long as under its garb, cash grants are not given by the governments and public authorities and others.

Press Rooms

They are a facility required to be provided for due discharge of the professional duties by the journalists.

Inviting Press Parties: The Committee was of the opinion that as stated earlier, this was a facility extended by the authorities to provide the necessary information on matters of public interest to the public.

Publication Material during Press Conference: The Committee was of the opinion that this was a facility.

Training

The Committee was of the opinion that this was a facility and should be encouraged as this will improve the knowledge and efficiency of all those engaged in the profession of journalism. The Press Council of India further stated: The State governments/UTs which have not provided complete information on further queries of the Council are Andhra Pradesh, Chandigarh Administration, Gujarat, Haryana, Kerala, Madhya Pradesh, Maharashtra, Orissa, Punjab and Uttar Pradesh.

THE BROADCASTING BILL, 1997

The bill is to provide for an independent authority to be known as the Broadcasting Authority of India for the purpose of facilitating and regulating broadcasting services in India. The authority will have a perpetual succession and a common seal with powers to enter into a contract and can sue and can be sued in its name. It consists of a chairperson who will be appointed by the President of India on recommendation from the chairman of the states who will be the chairman of the committee, the information and broadcasting minister and the Press Council of India. It will also consist of a maximum of 11 part-time members to be appointed by the central government, a secretary to the government in charge of the department of telecommunications and a secretary general.

The chairperson will be a whole-time member and will hold office for a term of five years. He will be appointed from amongst the persons of eminence with more than 15 years of experience in administration, law, broadcasting and public relations. The functions of authority will be:

1. To carry out frequency planning of such frequencies or band of frequencies assigned to it by the wireless adviser to the government for the purpose of ING services.
2. To grant licences for broadcasting services.
3. To ensure that a wide range of broadcasting services are available throughout India.
4. To ensure services of high quality and offer a wide range of programmes to appeal to a variety of tastes and interests.

5. To determine the programme code and standard.
6. To take necessary action for violation of code, violation of condition of licence.
7. To set technical and other quality standards to ensure a reasonable quality of reception.

The authority can appoint a committee of experts to advise on:

1. Practices to be followed in connection with unjust and unfair treatment to any person in programmes, unwarranted infringement of privacy included in programmes.
2. Practices to be followed in connection to portrayal of violence, sexual conduct in the programmes i.e., to set standards of decency for programmes, with regard to the attitude of the public at large.

LICENCES

No person is entitled to provide broadcasting services without obtaining a licence, after commencement of this act. The authority can grant licences for the following broadcasting services, namely:

1. Terrestrial radio broadcasting
2. Terrestrial television broadcasting
3. Satellite radio broadcasting
4. Satellite television broadcasting
5. Direct-to-home broadcasting
6. Local delivery services
7. Such other services as may be prescribed.

The terrestrial broadcasting services can be further categorized into analogue and digital and also into national, regional, local, restricted local services or any other similar service for the purposes of the licences and prevention of their accumulation.

The licence shall be provided subject to following conditions:

1. The person granted the licence will ensure that nothing is included in the programmes of the licensee which is likely to encourage crime or lead to disorder or will be offensive to public feeling.
2. The licensee will ensure that news given in the programme will be presented with due accuracy and impartiality.
3. The licensee has to ensure that due impartiality is maintained with respect to social or political issues or matters relating to public policy.
4. The licensee will ensure that due responsibility is exercised with respect to religious programmes with a view to avoiding improper exploitation of religious susceptibilities and offence to the religious views and beliefs of those belonging to a particular religion.
5. The licensee will ensure that due emphasis is given to promote national integration, Indian culture in his programmes.
6. The licensee will have to ensure that time, determined by the authority, is earmarked for broadcasting of—children's programmes, educational programmes, programmes of Indian origin, a range of diversity of independent production.
7. The licensee will have to follow the programme codes and standards and codes set by the authority.
8. The licensee will pay the licence fees in the same manner as may be determined by the regulations.
9. The licensee will not carry out networking of local or regional broadcasting services without prior approval of the authority.
10. The conditions of the licence can be changed by the authority after giving to the licensee a reasonable opportunity of being heard.

The licence granted for direct-to-home service or local delivery service shall be subject to the following conditions in addition to the conditions:

1. The licensee will have to provide a tier basic service which may include a number and type of terrestrial broadcasting for every permitted service and also of the public service broadcaster.
2. The licensee will include only licensed services or permitted services in his delivery package for the purpose of distribution and also he will not use more than that number of channels as determined by the authority out of the total channel capacity of the system for providing his own programming.

The period of licence for each category will be for a period not exceeding 10 years. The licence is not transferable and it will lapse prior to its normal expiry in case of insolvency or death of the licensee. No person will be given the number of licences for a category of service. There are restrictions on cross media ownership between the newspaper and the broadcasting service. The government can modify any limit on interest or equity holding in the body corporate or companies by notification in the official gazette.

Grant of Licence for Satellite Broadcasting Services

1. Any person desirous of obtaining a satellite broadcasting licence will have to apply to the authority.
2. If the authority is satisfied that the applicant—(a) has acquired transponder on an Indian satellite system or on a foreign satellite system. (b) has obtained technical clearance for transponders from the wireless adviser. (c) has fulfilled all other conditions laid down in the act; the authority may grant a licence to such person on payment of fees; if the authority refuses to grant a licence it will have to give the applicant an opportunity to be heard. Provide further that such a person providing his broadcasting services immediately before the commencement of the act may continue to do so without a licence for a period of one month from such commencement.

Grant of Licence for Direct-to-home Service

The authority will invite bids for grant of licence and it will be granted to the highest bidder if he fulfils all the conditions for the grant of such licence. The authority grants such number of licences (not less than two) as may be prescribed.

Special Provisions for Satellite Broadcasting and Direct-to-home Services

The wireless adviser will give technical clearance for licensing (the clearance can be refused on technical or security reasons). In cases where operations of the services are permitted with foreign satellite system, while giving technical clearance for relicensing or renewal of such services, give priority for their operation with Indian satellite system. The licensee shall carry out the uplinking of satellite broadcasting services or direct-to-home will grant two licences for local delivery service for each telecom circle as identified by the central government. The authority will invite bids and licence will be granted to the highest bidder. The wireless adviser shall assign frequencies for MMDS for providing local delivery service, wherever it is required. The authority may exempt the non-commercial establishments under common ownership from obtaining a licence for the purpose of providing cable television services for the exclusive use of their members. The government can by notification confer upon the licensee of the local delivery services, such rights and obligations as it may consider necessary in respect of the placing and maintaining of his cable networks as available to the telegraph authority.

Enforcement of Licences

The authority can take any of the following actions in case of breach of any terms of the licence:

1. Direct licensing to correction or apology or not to repeat a programme;
2. To impose a penalty which may extend up to Rs 50 lakh.
3. Suspend the licence for a specified period.
4. Curtail the period of the licence.
5. Revoke the licence.

Any aggrieved person may prefer an appeal and action of the authority in the high court having jurisdiction within 30 days of such action. The proceeds of the licence fee will be credited to the consolidated fund of India. The authority will have its own fund and all receipts of the authority will be credited to the fund and all payments by the authority will be from them. The authority will submit a report at the end of each financial year to the central government.

OFFENCE AND PUNISHMENTS

A person who provides, distributes or receives any broadcasting service which is neither a licensed service nor a permitted service or abets or assists transmission of such service in any manner which may include collection of subscription for his principal, issuing of advertisements to such service, dealing in or distribution of decoders or dish antennas, shall be guilty of committing an offence of illegal broadcasting and on conviction, shall be punishable with imprisonment which may extend up to five years, or with fine which may extend up to Rs 10 lakh and in subsequent offence such fine may extend to rupees Rs 50 lakh, or with both.

Special Provisions for Certain Foreign Satellite Broadcasting Services

The authority after receiving a request in this regard, may grant permission for reception of an unlicensed foreign satellite broadcasting service in India, if such broadcasting is service—

1. Is free to air broadcasting service;
2. Does not carry any advertisements; or carries advertisements for the duration as may be fixed by the authority and the service is devoted solely to sports or international news and current affairs;
3. Fulfils the programme standard with respect to permitted service. Provided that the authority may revoke such permission, if it feels that the service has contravened any of the above conditions.

No licensee shall carry a live broadcast of any sporting or other event of national or international interest held in India, without the consent of the authority unless the public service broadcasters have also been given the broadcasting right for carrying the same.

Procedure and Powers of the Authority

1. The authority will be guided by principles of natural justice and subject to the other provisions of this act and of any rules, the authority will have powers to regulate its own procedure including the fixing of places and times of its inquiry.
2. The authority will have for the purpose of discharging its functions under this act, the same powers as are vested in a civil court under the code of civil procedure, while trying a suit, in respect of the following matters, namely:
   - (a) Summoning and enforcing the attendance of any person and examining him on oath;
   - (b) Receiving evidence on affidavits;
   - (c) Issuing commissions for the examination of witnesses or documents;
   - (d) Any other matter which may be prescribed.

In event of any war or a natural calamity of national magnitude, the central government may, in public interest, take over the control and management of any broadcasting service or any facility connected therewith, suspend its operation or entrust the public service broadcaster to manage it in the manner directed by the government for such period as it deems fit. The government, if it considers necessary or expedient to do so, may, in public interest, at any time require the authority to direct any licensee to:

1. Transmit in his broadcasting service such announcement in such a manner as may be considered necessary;
2. Stop any broadcasting service which is considered prejudicial to friendly relations with a foreign country, public order, security of state, or communal harmony. The central government may in public interest, issue such other directions, to the authority, from time to time as considered necessary.

Powers of the authority to seek information conduct enquires, take evidence, etc.

1. The licensee will have to start his service within the period specified by the authority and maintain documents, records and transmission schedules as may be specified and allow inspection of such records to the authority.
2. The authority can call for information from the licensee which it considers in the public interest and necessary for the transparency and ascertaining the true ownership of the licensee. The authority will have all the powers of an inspecting officer. If the licensee defaults with any conditions, the authority can cancel the licence. The application of this law is in addition to and not in derogation of the provisions of any other law.

Power to Make Rules

The central government can by notification make rules for carrying out provisions of this act. The rules will provide for all or any of the following matter:

1. Provide for circumstances for communication.
2. Salaries and allowances payable to the chairperson and other part-time members.
3. The functions to be performed by the authority.
4. Number of licences more than which can't be given.

Power to Make Regulations

The authority can make regulations and rules made their underby notification. The rules will provide for all or any of the following matter:

1. The time and place of the meetings, the procedure of transaction of business.
2. The manner of appointment of officers and employees and their salary.
3. The quality of reception and the programme code and standard.

4. The manner in which the licence fee should be paid by the licensee and the conditions of granting licence.
5. The minimum number and type of ING service of public service broadcaster and of terrestrial broadcasting services for every permitted service.
6. The number of channels to be used and the period of licence to the licensee.
7. The criteria subject to which the uplinking from outside India will be permitted in respect of these services for coverage of live events taking place outside India.
8. Restricted area under which permission may be granted.
9. Any sporting or other event of national or international interest of which live telecast shall be carried out without the authority's permission.

Every rule and regulation is to be laid before the parliament. The central government can make provisions in the act within three years of commencement of this bill and not after that, to remove any difficulties that arise.

Repeal and Saving

The Cable Television Networks (Regulation) Act 1995 is repealed. The cable operators registered under this act can make an application to the authority for grant of licence within six months of commencement of this act. The authority may grant or refuse the licence to the operator. No licence will be granted to any cable TV network which provides such service to more than 5000 households and from more than one location. No refusal can be made unless the applicant has a chance to present the case. The authority will authorise a district magistrate to look in to the complaints of the public, give notice to the operators, make enquiries and take necessary action.

Restrictions on the Holding of Licences

Part—I

A disqualification for holding of licences

The following persons will be disqualified for the purpose of grant of licence:

General disqualification:

(a) An individual who is not an Indian national.

(b) A partnership firm all of whose partners are not citizens of India.

(c) Companies not incorporated in India.

(d) Companies incorporated in India but with: (a) foreign equity in case of terrestrial broadcasting services. (b) foreign equity exceeding 49 per cent in case of other services not mentioned in (i) above and management control not with Indian shareholders.

(e) Governments and local authorities.

(f) Any person convicted of an offence under this act or convicted under the Representation of the Peoples Act or declared as insolvent.

(g) A body, which is controlled by a person, referred to in any of clause (a) to (e) above.

(h) A body corporate, in which a body referred to in clause (g) above, is a participant with more than five per cent interest.

Foreign equity for this part will be notified to the government from time to time.

Disqualification of Religious Bodies

1. A body which is or is controlled by, a body or controls a body whose objectives are wholly or mainly of a religious nature.
2. A body corporate in which the body referred to above is a participant with more than five per cent interest.
3. A person who is an officer of the body.

Disqualification of Political Bodies

1. A body which is or affiliated to or is a participant with more than five per cent interest to a body whose objects are or mainly of political nature.
2. An individual who is an officer of the body.

Disqualification of Publicly Funded Bodies

1. A body (other than a local authority) which has in its last financial year received more than half its income from public funds.
2. A body which is controlled or a corporate which has more than five per cent interest in the above mentioned body.

Disqualification of Advertising Agencies

An advertising agency, its associate or a body corporate having more than five per cent interest in an ad agency.

Part-II

Restriction to prevent accumulation of interest in licensed services.

1. A person will be allowed to hold licences in only one of the following category of services:
   [a] Terrestrial radio broadcasting
   [b] Terrestrial television broadcasting
   [c] Satellite television or radio broadcasting
   [d] Direct-to-home broadcasting
   [e] Local delivery services
   [f] Any other category of services which may be notified by the central government.
2. Any restriction on participation imposed as above on the holder of a licence shall apply to him as if he and every person connected with him were one person.

Part-III

Restrictions on controlling interest in both newspapers and licensed services:

1. No proprietor of a newspaper will either be a participant with more than 20 per cent interest in or control a body corporate which is the holder of a licence to provide a licensed service under this act.
2. No proprietor of a newspaper who is a participant with more than five per cent but less than 20 per cent interest

in a body corporate and not controlling such a body corporate, holding a licence will be a participant with more than five per cent interest in any other such body corporate.

3. No person who is the holder of a licence to provide licensed service under this act will be either a participant with more than 20 per cent interest in or control a body corporate which controls a newspaper.

4. No person who is the holder of a licence and is a participant with more than five per cent but less than 20 per cent interest in a body corporate and not controlling such a body corporate which runs a national newspaper, shall be a participant with more than five per cent interest in any other such corporate.

5. For the purpose of this part, a person controls a newspaper if—

   [a] He is the proprietor of such newspaper; or

   [b] He controls a body which is the proprietor of such newspaper.

6. Any restriction on participation imposed as above on the proprietor of any newspaper or on the holder of licence shall apply to him as of he and every person connected with him were one person.

Part-IV

1.(1) For the purpose of this schedule, 'Advertising agency' means an individual or a body corporate who carries on business as an advertising agent (whether alone or in partnership) or has control over any body corporate which carries on business as an advertising agent, and any reference to an advertising agency includes a reference to an advertising agency includes a reference to an individual who-

   (a) is a director or officer of any body corporate who carries on such a business, or

   (b) is employed by any person who carries on such a business.

'Associate'-

(a) in relation to a body corporate, means a director of that body corporate or a body corporate interconnected with that body corporate.

(b) in relation to the partner of the firm, means a relative of such partner and includes any other person of such firm;

(c) in relation to the trustee of a trust, means any other trustee of such trust; and

(d) in relation to an individual, shall be construed in accordance with subclause (3);

(e) where a person or a body corporate is an associate of another person or body corporate, the latter shall also be deemed to be an associate of the former.

'Control'-

(a) in relation to the body corporate, shall be construed in accordance with subclause (3); and

(b) in relation to any body other than a body corporate, means the power of a person to secure, by virtue of the rules regulating that or any other body, that the affairs of the first mentioned body are conducted in accordance with the wishes of that person, and would include control as a result of, or by means of, trusts, agreements, arrangements, understandings and practices, whether or not having legal or equitable force and whether or not based on legal or equitable rights.

'Newspaper' means as defined under the Press and Registration Act, 1867 (25 of 1867).

(2) For the purpose of determining the persons who are an individual's associates for the purposes of this schedule, the following persons shall be regarded as associates of each other, namely:

(a) any individual and that individual's husband or wife of a relative, of that individual or of that individual's husband or wife;

(b) any individual or any body corporate of which that individual is a director;

(c) any person in his capacity as trustee of a settlement and the settlor or grantor and any person associated with the settlor and grantor;

(d) persons carrying on business in partnership and the husband or wife and relatives of any of them;

(e) any two or more persons acting together to secure or exercise control of a body corporate or any other associates or to secure control of any enterprise or assets; and in this sub-paragraph 'relative' means as defined under the Companies Act, 1956.

(3) A person controls a body corporate if—

(a) he has a controlling interest in the body, or

(b) (although not having such an interest in the body) he is able, by virtue of the holding of shares or the possession of voting power in or in relation to the body or any other body corporate, to secure that the affairs of the body are conducted in accordance with his wishes, or

(c) he has the power, by virtue of any powers conferred by the articles of association or other document regulating the body or any other body corporate, to secure that the affairs of the body are so conducted, and for this purpose, in the absence of proof to the contrary, a person has a controlling interest in a body corporate if he holds, or is beneficially entitled to, more than 20 per cent, of the voting power in it.

(4) it is hereby declared that a person may be regarded as controlling a body corporate by virtue of clause (b) of sub-clause (3) despite the fact that—

(a) he does not have a controlling interest in any such other body corporate as is mentioned in that paragraph, or

(b) any such other body corporate does not have a controlling interest in the body in question, or

(c) he and any such body corporate together do not have a controlling interest in that body.

(5) For the purpose of any provision of this schedule which refers to a body controlled by two or more persons or bodies of any description taken together, the persons or bodies in question shall not be regarded as controlling the body by virtue of paragraph (b) and sub-paragraph (3) unless they are acting together in concert.

(6) In this schedule any reference to a participant with more than a five per cent, or, as the case may be, 20 per cent interest in a body corporate is a reference to a person who—

(a) holds or is beneficially entitled to more than five or, as the case may be, 20 per cent of the shares in that body or,

(b) possesses more than five or, as the case may be, 20 per cent of the voting power in that body, and, where any such reference has been amended by an order under this schedule varying the percentage in question, this sub-paragraph shall have effect in relation to its subject to the necessary modifications.

2. (1) Any reference in paragraph 1 to a person—

(a) holding or being entitled to shares, or any amount of the shares or equity share capital, in a body corporate, or

(b) possessing voting power, or any amount of the voting power, in a body corporate, is a reference to his doing so, or being so entitled, whether alone or jointly with one or more other persons and whether directly or through one or more nominees.

(2) 'Inter connected undertakings or corporate bodies' shall have the same meaning as assigned in the Monopolies and Restrictive Trade Practices Act, 1969 (54 of 1969).

3. For the purpose of this schedule, the following persons are connected with each other in relation to a particular licence, namely:

(a) the license holder;

(b) a person who controls the holder;

(c) an associate of the license holder or of a person referred to in clause (b), and

(d) a body which is controlled by the license holder or by an associate of the license holder.

Statement of Objects and Reasons

1. The broadcasting scenario, especially in the realm of satellite broadcasting, has undergone a revolution during the last few years. A large number of satellite television channels have been beaming their programmes through the Indian skies to our people. All these channels are foreign entities and their programmes are uplinked from outside the country without any regulation through the law of our land, while Indian entrepreneurs and Indian companies are not at present permitted to own either radio or television stations.
2. Concern has been voiced both inside parliament and outside about the implications of these unregulated television programmes and the denial of a level playing field to Indian entities. The only legal instrument available is the Indian Telegraph Act, 1885, which is considered totally inadequate to govern modern broadcasting media. All leading democratic countries have enacted laws specifically regarding the broadcasting media. The introduction of the broadcasting bill is a step in this direction.
3. It is felt that the public service broadcaster alone will not be able to meet the needs and urges of the people in terms of variety and plurality of programmes required in different regions by different sections of society in our vast country. Keeping in view our great democratic traditions, it is imperative that our citizens are all informed and given wider choice in matters of information, education and entertainment. This can be provided by facilitating private broadcasting in the country.
4. The bill needs to establish an autonomous broadcasting authority for the purposes of facilitating and regulating broadcasting services in India so that they become competitive in terms of quality of services, cost of services and use of new technologies, apart from becoming a

catalyst for social change, promotion of values of Indian culture and shaping of a modern vision. It will also curb monopolistic trends in this sensitive field, so that people are provided with a wide range of news and views.

THE CONTEMPT OF COURTS ACT, 1971

The origin of the law of contempt in India can be traced to the English law. In England, superior courts of record have from the earliest times exercised the power to commit for contempt those who scandalised the court or the judges. The right of the Indian high courts to punish for contempt was, in the first instance, recognised by the judicial committee of the Privy Council which observed that the offence of the contempt of court and the powers of the high courts to punish it are the same in such courts as in the Supreme Court in England.

Almost all the high courts in India, apart from the chartered high courts have exercised the jurisdiction inherent in a court of record from the very nature of the court itself. It has been judicially accepted throughout India that the jurisdiction was a special one, inherent in the very nature of the court. The first Indian statute on the Law of Contempt, i.e., the Contempt of Courts Act was passed in 1926.

It was enacted to define and limit the powers of certain courts in punishing contempt of courts. When the Contempt of Courts Act, 1926 (XII of 1926) was in existence in British India, various Indian states also had their corresponding enactment. These states were Hyderabad, Madhya Bharat, Mysore, Pepsu, Rajasthan, Travancore-Cochin and Saurashtra. State enactments of the Indian states and the Contempt of Courts Act, 1926 were replaced by the Contempt of Courts Act, 1952 (32 of 1952).

An attempt was made in April 1960 to introduce in the Lok Sabha a bill to consolidate and amend the law relating to contempt of courts. On an examination of the bill, the government appears to have felt that the law relating to contempt of courts was uncertain, undefined and unsatisfactory and that in the light of the constitutional changes which have taken place in the country, it would be advisable to have the entire law on the subject scrutinised by a special committee set up for the purpose. In pursuance of that decision, a committee was set up on July 29, 1961 and it submitted its report on February 28, 1963 to define and limit the powers of certain courts in punishing contempt of courts and to regulate their procedure in relation thereto. The Joint Select Committee of Parliament on Contempt of Courts examined the issue in detail and a new bill, the Contempt of Courts Bill, 1968 was prepared by the committee.

Statement of Objects and Reasons

It is generally felt that the existing law relating to contempt of courts is somewhat uncertain, undefined and unsatisfactory. The jurisdiction to punish for contempt touches upon two important fundamental rights of the citizens, namely, the right to personal liberty and the right to freedom of expression. It was, therefore, considered advisable to have the entire law on the subject scrutinised by a special committee.

In pursuance of this, a committee was set up in 1961 under the chairmanship of the late H N Sanyal, the then additional solicitor general. The committee made a comprehensive examination of the law and problems relating to contempt of court in the light of the position obtaining in our own country and various foreign countries. The recommendations which the committee made took note of the importance given to freedom of speech in the Constitution and of the need for safeguarding the status and dignity of courts and interests of administration of justice.

The recommendations of the committee have been generally accepted by the government after considering the view expressed on those recommendations by the state governments, union territory administrations, the Supreme Court, the high courts and the judicial commissioners. The bill seeks to give effect to the accepted recommendations of the Sanyal Committee.

ACT 70 OF 1971

The Contempt of Courts Act, 1971 (70 of 1971) was passed by the Parliament in December 1971 and it came into force w.e.f. December 24, 1971.

List of Amending Act.

The Contempt of Courts (Amendment) Act, 1976 (45 of 1976)

Preamble (December 24, 1971).

An Act to define and limit the powers of certain courts in punishing contempt of courts and to regulate their procedure in relation thereto

1. Short Title and Extent:

(1) This Act may be called the Contempt of Courts Act, 1971.

(2) It extends to the whole of India.

Provided that it shall not apply to the state of Jammu and Kashmir except to the extent to which the provisions of this Act relate to contempt of the Supreme Court.

Comments

(i) The law of contempt of courts is for keeping the administration of justice pure and undefiled. While the dignity of the court is to be maintained at all costs, the contempt jurisdiction, which is of a special nature, should be sparingly used; Shakuntala Sahadevram Tewari v. Hemchand M.Singhania, (1990) 3 Bom CR 82 (Bom).

(ii) Proceedings of contempt are summary in nature and also are sui generis; Golcha Advertising Agency vs The State of Maharashtra, (1990) 2 Bom CR 262 (Bom).

2. Definitions: In this Act, unless the context otherwise requires:

(a) 'Contempt of court' means civil contempt or criminal contempt.

(b) 'Civil contempt' means willful disobedience to any judgement, decree, direction, order, writ or other process of a court or willful breach of an undertaking given to a court.

(c) 'Criminal contempt' means the publication (whether by words, spoken or written, or by signs, or by visible representation, or otherwise) of any matter or the doing of any other act whatsoever which:

(i) Scandalises or tends to scandalise, or lowers or tends to lower the authority of, any court, or

(ii) Prejudices, or interferes or tends to interfere with the due course of any judicial proceeding, or

(iii) Interferes or tends to interfere with, or obstructs or tends to obstruct, the administration of justice in any other manner.

(a) 'High Court' means the high court for a state or a union territory and includes the court of the judicial commissioner in any union territory.

Comments

(i) There are three different sorts of contempt, viz., scandalising the court, abusing parties who are concerned in causes here and prejudicing mankind against persons before the case is heard; In re: St. James Evening Post, (1974) 2 ATK 469

(ii) Courts seek to punish acts or conduct calculated to interfere with the administration of justice; In re: P C Sen, AIR 1970 SC 1821.

(iii) Comment on pending case or abuse of a party may amount to contempt when the case is tried by a judge: Subhash Chand v S M Aggarwal, 1984 Crl LJ 481 (De.).

(iv) Judges by reason of their office are precluded from entering into any controversy in columns of the public press; The State v.Vikar Ahmed, AIR 1954 Hyd 175.

(v) There is no special principle attached to the press to comment, criticise or investigate the facts of any case of the prejudice of the trial of the case; Sukhdev Singh v Teja Singh, AIR 1954 SC 186.

(vi) No editor has a right to assume the role of investigator to try to prejudice the court against any person; The District Magistrate v M A Hamid Ali Gardish, AIR 1940 Oudh 137.

(vii) It is time to stem institutionalised procrastination, K V Venkatesh v. taluka executive magistrate, AIR 1990 Kant 86.

(viii) The law relating to contempt of court is well settled. Any act done or writing published which is calculated to bring a court or a judge into contempt, or to lower his authority, or to interfere with the due course of justice or the lawful process of the court, is a contempt of court; Q.R. v. Gray, 1900 (2) QBD 36 (40)

(ix) Contempt by speech or writing may be by scandalising the court itself, or by abusing parties to actions, or by prejudicing mankind in favour of or against a party before the cause is heard. It is incumbent upon courts of justice to preserve their proceedings from being misrepresented, for prejudicing the mind of the people against persons concerned as parties in causes before the cause is finally heard has pernicious consequences. Speech or writings misrepresenting the proceedings of the court or prejudicing the public for or against a party or involving reflections on parties to a proceeding amount to contempt. To make a speech tending to influence the result of a pending trial, whether civil or criminal is a grave contempt. Comments on pending proceedings, if emanating from the parties or their lawyers, are generally a more serious contempt than those coming from independent sources; State of Haryana v Ch Bhajanlal, AIR 1993 SC 1348.

(x) In contempt proceedings there are essentially two parties—the court and contemporary; Shakuntala Sahadevram Tiwari v. Hemachand M Singhania, (1990) 3 Bom CR 82 (Bom).

(xi) The law of contempt must be strictly interpreted and complied with before any person can be committed for contempt; Roshan S Boyce v B R Cotton Mills Ltd., AIR 1990 SC 1881.

(xii) Any willful disobedience to the orders of the court to do or abstain from doing any act or breach of any undertaking given to the court is prima-facie civil contempt; Vidya Sagar v IIIrd additional district judge, Dehradun, 1991 All CJ 586 (588); See also State of Assam v. V K Vishnoi, 1993 (23) ATC 581 (587-588); State of Orissa v. Bijaya Mohanty, (1993) 75 CLT 820 (830).

(xiii) Non caring of the warrant issued by the criminal court amounts to criminal contempt; E Venkaiah v. government of Andhra Pradesh, 1992 (3) ALT 193 (199).

3. Innocent Publication and Distribution of Matter not Contempt:

(1) A person shall not be guilty of contempt of court on the ground that he has published (whether by words, spoken or written, or by visible representations, or otherwise) any matter which interferes or tends to interfere with, or obstructs or tends to obstruct, the course of justice in connection with any civil or criminal proceeding pending at that time of publication, if at that time he had no reasonable grounds for believing that the proceeding was pending.

(2) Notwithstanding anything to the contrary contained in this Act or any other law for the time being in force, the publication of any such matter as is mentioned in sub section (1) in connection with any civil or criminal proceeding which is not pending at the time of publication shall not be deemed to constitute contempt of court.

(3) A person shall not be guilty of contempt of court on the ground that he has distributed a publication containing any such matter as is mentioned in sub section (1), if at the time of distribution he had no reasonable grounds for believing that it contained or was likely to contain any such matter as aforesaid.

Provided that this sub section shall not apply in respect of the distribution of:

(i) Any publication which is a book or paper printed or published otherwise than in conformity with the rules contained in section 3 of the Press and Registration of Books Act, 1867 (25 of 1867).

(ii) Any publication which is a newspaper published otherwise than in conformity with the rules contained in section 5 of the said Act.

Explanation

For the purposes of this section, a judicial proceeding—

(a) is said to be pending,

(b) in the case of a civil proceeding, when it is instituted by the filing of a plaint or otherwise,

(c) in the case of a criminal proceeding under the Code of Criminal Procedure, 1898 [5 of 1898 (Note: now see Code of Criminal Procedure, 1973 (2 of 1974)], or any other law-

(i) where it relates to the commission of the offence, when the charge-sheet or challan is filed, or when the court issues summons or warrant, as the case may be, against the accused, and

(ii) in any other case, when the court takes cognisance of the matter to which the proceeding relates, and

(iii) in the case of a civil or criminal proceeding, shall be deemed to continue to be pending until it is heard and finally decided, that is to say, in a case where an appeal or revision is competent, until the appeal or revision is heard and finally decided or, where no appeal or revision in preferred, until the period of limitation prescribed for such appeal or revision has expired,

(iv) Which has been heard and finally decided shall not be deemed to be pending merely by reason of the fact that proceedings for the execution of the decree, order or sentence passed therein are pending.

Comments

(i) The liberty of free expression is not to be compounded with a licence to make unfounded allegations of corruption against judiciary; M R Prashar v Dr Farooq Abdullah, (1984) 1 Cr LC 433.

(ii) The abuse of the liberty of free speech and expression carries the case nearer the law of contempt; M R Prashar v Dr Farooq Abdullah, (1984) 1 Cr. LC 433.

(iii) A defence of truth or justification is not available to the publisher of a newspaper in proceedings for contempt of court; managing director Vamin v O P Bansal, 1982 Cr. LJ 322 (Raj).

(iv) Publication of reports of proceedings before a court of law must be true, accurate and without malice; Wasuddeoraoji v A D Mani, AIR 1951 Nag. 26.

4. *Fair and Accurate Report of Judicial Proceeding not Contempt:* Subject to the provisions contained in section 7, a person shall not be guilty of contempt of court for publishing a fair and accurate report of a judicial proceeding or any state thereof.

Comments

(i) The words 'judicial proceeding' means day-to-day proceedings of the court. The media reports must represent a fair and accurate report of a judicial proceeding and not be a one-sided picture; Subhash Chand v S M Aggarwal, 1984 Cr LJ 481

(ii) While reproducing the court proceedings, no words may be added, omitted or substituted; E T Sen v E Narayanan, AIR 1969 Del 201.

(iii) Fair and accurate reporting of the judgment is essential for the healthy administration of justice. In re: Progressive Port and Dock Workers Union, 1984 Cr LJ 1061 (Ker).

5. *Fair Criticism of Judicial Act not Contempt:* A person shall not be guilty of contempt of court for publishing any fair comment on the merits of any case which has been heard and finally decided.

Comments

(i) The nature and circumstances under which allegations are made, the extent and the character of the publications and similar other considerations have to be taken into account in order to determine whether the act complained of amounts to contempt. No action is called for, if the criticism is reasonable and is offered for the public good; In re: Guljari Lal, 1968 MPLJ 725 (730-731).

(ii) Judgments are open to criticism that must be done without casting aspersions on the judges and the judges and the courts and without adverse comments amounting to scandalising the courts; advocate general v Abraham George, 1976 Cr. LJ 158 (161).

(iii) A fair comment on the judgment of a court could not constitute a contempt; state of Maharashtra v Chandrakant Tripathi, AIR 1936 PC 141.

(iv) The publication in newspaper of reports of proceedings before a court of law must be true; state v Bhavani Prasad, AIR 1954 Nag 36.

(v) The criticism of a judge must take the form of reasonable argument or exploitation; must be made in good faith and free from the imputation of improper motives; state of Uttar Pradesh v Brahma Prakash, AIR 1950 All 556.

6. *Complaint against Presiding Officers of Subordinate Courts when not Contempt :* A person shall not be guilty of contempt of court in respect of any statement made by him in good faith concerning the presiding officer or any subordinate court to-

(a) Any other subordinate court, or

(b) The high court to which it is subordinate.

Explanation: In this section, 'subordinate court' means any court subordinate to a high court.

Comments

(i) A complaint or report about a judicial officer of his dishonesty, partiality or other conduct unbecoming of a court, made to an authority to whom it is subordinate, is not contempt of court if all reasonable care is taken by the makers to keep it confidential; In re: Guljari Lal, 1968 MPLJ 725 (MP).

(ii) Immunity is provided to a citizen making a complaint to the high court against a presiding officer of a subordinate court so long as the complaint is made in good faith; In re: court on its own motion, 1973 Cr LJ 1106 (P & H).

7. Publication of Information relating to Proceeding in Chambers or in Camera not Contempt Except in Certain Cases:

(1) Notwithstanding anything contained in this Act, a person shall not be guilty of contempt of court for publishing a fair and accurate report of judicial proceedings before any court sitting in chambers or in camera except in the following cases, that is to say:

(a) Where the publication is contrary to the provisions of any enactment for the time being in force.

(b) Where the court, on grounds of public policy or in exercise of any power vested in it, expressly prohibits the publication of all information relating to the proceeding or of information of the description which is published.

(c) Where the court sits in chambers or in camera for reason connected with public order or the security of the state, the publication of information relating to those proceedings,

(d) Where the information relates to secret process, discovery or invention which is an issue in the proceedings.

(2) Without prejudice to the provisions contained in sub section (1) a person shall not be guilty of contempt of court for publishing the text or a fair and accurate summary of the whole, or any part, of an order made by a court sitting in chambers or in camera, unless the court has expressly prohibited the publication thereof on grounds of public policy, or for reasons connected with public order or the security of the state, or on the ground that it contains information relating to secret process, discovery or invention, or in exercise of any power vested on it.

8. *Other Defences not Affected :* Nothing contained in this Act shall be construed as implying that any other defence which would have been a valid defence in any proceedings for contempt of court has ceased to be available merely by reason of the provisions of this Act.

Comments

Since a proceeding in contempt is a quasi-judicial proceeding, the precise nature of contempt must be set out in the motion:

Nazamunnissa Shaukat Ali v Municipal Corporation of Greater Bombay, (1990) 1 Mah LR 329 (Bom).

9. *Act not to Imply Enlargement of Scope of Contempt:* Nothing contained in this Act shall be construed as implying that any disobedience, breach, publication or other act is punishable as contempt of court which not be so punishable apart from this Act.

Comments

The scope of contempt of courts has not been enlarged. What was not contempt so far is not contempt of court even now. The contempt of court should not be resorted to only for the purpose of enforcing interpretive rights; state of West Bengal v N N Bagchi, AIR 1966 SC 447.

10. *Power of High Court to Punish Contempts of Subordinate Courts :* Every high court shall have and exercise the same jurisdiction, powers and authority, in accordance with the same procedure and practice, in respect of contempts of courts subordinate to it and it has and exercise in respect of contempts of itself.

Provided that no high court shall take cognisance of a contempt alleged to have been committed in respect of a court subordinate to it where such contempt is an offence punishable under the Indian Penal Code (45 of 1860).

Comments

(i) The phrase 'courts subordinate to it' used in section 10 is wide enough to include all courts which are judicially subordinate to the high court even though administrative control over them under Article 235 of the constitution does not vest in the high court; S K Sarkar, member, board of revenue, U P Lucknow v Vinay Chandra Mishra, 1981 Cr LJ 283 (286).

(ii) The power of committal for contempt must be wielded with the greatest reluctance and the greatest anxiety and only with the object of seeing that the dignity and authority of the court are not imposed; E Chandra v member secretary, MMDA., (1990) 1 MLJR 537.

(iii) If the act is punishable by the Penal Code as contempt of court then that act cannot form the subject of contempt proceedings by the high court; the emperor V J P Swadhin, Air 1938 All 358.

(iv) The high court cannot take cognisance of 'contempt' which is punishable under the Indian Penal Code; N K Gupta v Umraomal Agarwalla, AIR 1951 Cal 489.

11. *Power of High Court to try Offences Committed or Offenders Found Outside Jurisdiction :* A high court shall have jurisdiction to inquire into or try a contempt of itself or of any court subordinate to it, whether the contempt is alleged to have been committed within or outside the local limits of its jurisdiction, and whether the person alleged to be guilty of contempt is within or outside such limits.

Comments

(i) This section provided for the extra-territorial jurisdiction of high courts of commit a person for contempt even though the act alleged was committed outside its territorial jurisdiction; state v V Adilakshmi Amma, 1954 Cr. LJ 988 (Ori).

(ii) This section expands the ambit of the authority beyond with was till then considered to be possible but it does not confer a new jurisdiction. It merely widens the scope of our existing jurisdiction of a very special kind; Sukhdev Singh v Teja Singh, AIR 1954 SC 186 (190); state of Uttar Pradesh v Radhey Shyam.

12. *Punishment for Contempt of Court:*

(1) Save as otherwise expressly provided in this Act or in any other law, a contempt of court may be punished with simple imprisonment for a term which may extend to six months, or with fine which may extend to two thousand rupees, or with both. Provided that the accused may be discharged or the punishment awarded may be remitted on apology being made to the satisfaction of the court.

Explanation: An apology shall not be rejected merely on the ground that it is qualified or conditional if the accused makes it bona fide.

(2) Notwithstanding anything contained in any law for the time being in force, no court shall impose a sentence in excess of that specified in sub section for any contempt either in respect of itself or of a court subordinate to it.

(3) Notwithstanding anything contained in this section, where a person is found guilty of a civil contempt, the court, if it considers that a fine will not meet the ends of justice and that a sentence of imprisonment is necessary shall, instead of sentencing him to simple imprisonment, direct that the he be detained in a civil prison for such period not exceeding six months as it may think fit.

(4) Where the person found guilty of contempt of court in respect of any undertaking given to a court is a company, every person who, at the time the contempt was committed, was in charge of, and was responsible to, the company for the conduct of business of the company, as well as the company, shall be deemed to be guilty of the contempt and the punishment may be enforced, with the leave of the court, by the detention in civil prison of each such person.

Provided that nothing contained in this sub section shall render any such person liable to such punishment if he proves that the contempt was committed without his knowledge or that he exercised all due diligence to prevent its commission.

(5) Notwithstanding anything contained in sub section (4) where the contempt of court referred to therein has been committed by a company and it is provided that the contempt has been committed with the consent or connivance of, or is attributable to any neglect on the part of, any director, manger, secretary or other officer of the company, such director, manager, secretary or other officer shall also be deemed to be guilty of the be contempt and the punishment may be enforced, with the leave of the court, by the detention in civil prison of such director, manager, secretary or other officer.

Explanation: For the purpose of sub sections (4) and (5):

(a) 'Company' means any body corporate and includes a firm or other association of individuals, and

(b) 'Director' in relation to a firm, means a partner in the firm.

Comments

Breach of an injunction, or breach of an undertaking given to a court by a person in a civil proceeding amounts to contempt; Noorali Babul Thanewala v K M M Shetty, AIR 1990 Sc 564.

(i) Committing the contemner to prison is always discretionary with the court; Shakuntala Sahadevram Tiwari v Hemchand M Singhania, (1990) 3 Bom CR 82 (Bom).

(ii) The power to fine and imprison for contempt is a necessary incident and attribute of a court; Watson v Williams, (33) 36 Mis 341.

(iii) An unreserved apology, in less serious cases, has the asset of taking the stringent of contempt; court on behalf of the state of Punjab v Radha Krishan Khanna, AIR 1961 Punj 113.

(iv) The contempt power should be kept sheathed; union of India v S C Sharma, (1980) 2 SCC 144.

(v) Apology is an act of contrition. Apology must not be shorn of penitence. Tendering of apology cannot be a panacea in every case of contempt. No apology could undo gross contempt and serious cases of contempt; state of Orissa v R N Patra, (1975) 41 Cut LT 329.

(vi) The court can, even when accepts the apology, commit an offender to prison or otherwise punish him; Rupert J Bamabas v N Bharani, 1990 LW (Crl) 27 (Mad).

(vii) A haulting, hesitating and vacillating apology deserves to be rejected; state of Uttar Pradesh v Krishna Madho, AIR 1952 All 86.

(viii) The court may or may not accept an apology goes to sentence and cannot, therefore, be accepted without a finding that contempt has been committed. However, apology, though not a weapon of defence forged always to purge the guilty, should be tendered out the earliest possible stage, unreservedly and unconditionally and it must be indicative of remorse and contrition as well as free, full, frank and manly confession of a wrong done; In re: Hirenn Bose, AIR 1969 Cal 1.

13. *Contempts not Punishable in Certain Cases:* Notwithstanding anything contained in any law for the time being in force, no court shall impose a sentence under this Act for a contempt of court unless it is satisfied that the contempt is of such a nature that it substantially interferes, or tends substantially to interfere with the due course of justice.

Comments

(i) Every infraction of the court's order does not amount to contempt of court; H S Butalia v Subhas Saxena, 1974 Cr LJ 828 (Cal).

(ii) Technical contempts are to be ignored; Baradakanta Mishra v the registrar, Orissa high court, AIR 1974 SC 710.

(iii) A party (or person) can be committed for contempt only owing to any willful or deliberate or reckless disobedience of the order of the court; Jiwani Kumari v Satyabrata Chakraborty, AIR 1991 SC 326.

(iv) Exemplary costs may be awarded instead of imposing a fine; Naamunnissa Shaukat Ali v Municipal Corporation of Greater Bombay, (1990) Mah LR 329 (Bom).

14. *Procedure where Contempt is in the Face of the Supreme Court or a High Court:*

(1) When it is alleged, or appears to the Supreme Court or the high court upon its own view, that a person has been guilty of contempt committed in its presence or hearing, the court may cause such person to be detained in custody, and, at any time before the rising of the court, on the same day, or as early as possible thereafter, shall:

(a) Cause him to be informed in writing of the contempt with which he is charged.

(b) Afford him an opportunity to make his defence to the charge,

(c) After taking such evidence as may be necessary or as may be offered by such person and after hearing him, proceed, either forthwith or after adjournment, to determine the matter of the charge, and

(d) Make such order for the punishment or discharge of such person as may be just.

(2) Notwithstanding anything contained in sub section (1) where a person charged with contempt under the sub section applies, whether orally or in writing, to have the charge against him tried by some judge other than the judge or judges in whose presence or hearing the offence is alleged to have been committed, and the court is of opinion that it is practicable to do so and that in that interest of proper administration of justice the application should be allowed, it shall cause the matter to be placed, together with a statement of the facts of the case, before the chief justice for such directions as he may think fit to issue as respects the trial thereof.

(3) Notwithstanding anything contained in any other law, in any trial of a person charged with contempt under sub section (1) which is held, in pursuance of a direction given under sub section (2), by a judge other than the judge or judges in whose presence or hearing the offence is alleged to have been committed, it shall not be necessary for the judge or judges in whose presence or hearing the offence is alleged to have been committed to appear as a witness and the statement placed before the chief justice under sub section (2) shall be treated as evidence in the case.

(4) Pending the determination of the charge, the court may direct that a person charged with contempt under this section shall be detained in such custody as it may specify.

Provided that he shall be released on bail, of a bond for such sum of money as the court thinks sufficient is executed with or without sureties conditioned that the person charged shall attend at the time and place mentioned in the bond and shall continue to so attend until otherwise directed by the court.

Provided further that the court may, if it thinks fit, instead of taking bail from such person, discharge him on his executing a bond without sureties for his attendance as aforesaid.

Comments

(i) Where contempt-

(a) It committed in the presence or hearing of the Supreme Court or the high court, or

(b) Is not committed in the presence or hearing of the Supreme Court or the high court, but a complaint is made immediately before the alleged contemner leaves the precincts of that court, then the procedure laid down in this section has to be adopted.

(ii) If the court did not take action under section 14 then the procedure of section 15 cannot be adopted later; Mansiha Mukherjee v Aashoke Chatterjee, 1985 Cr LJ 1224.

15. *Cognisance of Criminal Contempt in other Cases:*

(1) In the case of a criminal contempt, other than a contempt referred to in section 14, the Supreme Court or the high court may take action on its own motion or on a motion made by-

(a) The advocate-general, or

(b) Any other person, with the consent in writing of the advocate-general, (Note:-Ins. by Act 45 of 1976, sec.2)

(c) [(Note:-Ins. by Act 45 of 1976, sec.2)] In relation to the high court for the union territory of Delhi, such law officer as the central government may, by notification in the official gazette, specify in this behalf, or any other persons, with the consent in writing of such law officer.

(2) In the case of any criminal contempt of a subordinate court, the high court may take action on a reference made to it by the subordinate court or on a motion made by the advocate-general or, in relation to a union territory, by such law officer as the central government may, by notification in the official gazette, specify in this behalf.

(3) Every motion or reference made under this section shall specify the contempt of which the person charge is alleged to be guilty.

Explanation: In this section, the expression 'advocate-general' means-

(a) In relation to the Supreme Court, the attorney or the solicitor-general

(b) In relation to the high court, the advocate-general of the state or any of the states for which the high court has been established.

(c) In relation to the court of a judicial commissioner, such law officer as the central government may, by notification in the official gazette, specify in this behalf.

Comments

(i) The court can take action-

(a) On motion by the advocate-general himself; or

(b) On motion by anyone with the consent of the advocate-general; or

(c) On report by a subordinate court, in cases not covered by section 14 of the Act.

(ii) Procedure of making a reference cannot apply in a case when the presiding officer of a subordinate court himself is guilty of contempt of court; Berely v Xavier, 1988 Cr LJ 90.

(iii) It is always open the high court to take action suo motu in respect of a subordinate court; state of Orissa v R N Patra, 1976 Cr LJ 440 (Ori); see also A R Rao, 1981 Cr LJ 1322.

(iv) Absolute discretion is rested in the advocate-general in the matter of according consent; N Venkataramanappa v D K Naikar, AIR 1975 Kant 57.

(v) Nobody has a right to compel the subordinate court to make a reference to the high court; Jomon v the state of Kerala, (1987) IJ Reports 273 (Kerala).

(vi) A negative fact cannot be proved; V K Kanade v Mandho Godkari, (1990) I Mah LR 544 (Bom).

(vii) Contemner has no right to produce defence to establish the truth of his allegations; In re: K L Gauba, AIR 1942 Lah 105; see also In re: Ram Mohanlal, AIR 1935 All 38.

16. *Contempt by Judge, Magistrate or other Person Acting Judicially:*

(1) Subject to the provisions of any law for the time being in force, a judge, magistrate or other persons act in judicially shall also be liable for contempt of his own court or of any other court in the same manner as any other individual is liable and the provisions of this Act, so far as may be, apply accordingly.

(2) Notwithstanding in this section shall apply to any observations or remarks made by a judge, magistrate or other person act in judicially, regarding a subordinate court in an appeal or revision pending before such judge, magistrate or other person against the order or judgement of the subordinate court.

Comments

(i) Only a judge of a subordinate court can be said to have committed contempt of his own court i.e. the court in which such judge is presiding; Harish Chandra v S Ali Ahmed, 1987 Cr LJ 320 (Pat).

(ii) A judge can foul judicial administration by misdemeanors while engaged in the exercise of the functions of a judge; Baradakanta v the registrar, Orissa high court, AIR 1974 SC 710.

(iii) The magistrates should be conscious of their heavy responsibilities and should not act in a manner prejudicial to the litigants; B N Choudhary v S M Singh, 1967 Cr LJ 1141 (Pat).

(iv) When the president officer of a subordinate court is guilty of contempt of court, procedure of making a reference cannot apply under section 15 of the Act; Berely v Xavier, 1988 Cr LJ 90.

17. *Procedure after Cognisance:*

(1) Notice of every proceeding under section 15 shall be served personally on the person charged, unless the court for reasons to be recorded directs otherwise.

(2) The notice shall be accompanied-

(a) In the case of proceedings commenced on a motion, by a copy of the motion as also copies of the affidavits, if any, on which such motion is founded and,

(b) In case of proceedings commenced on a reference by a subordinate court, by a copy of the reference.

(3) The court may, if it is satisfied that a person charged under Section 15 is likely to abscond or keep out of the way to avoid service of the notice, order the attachment of his property of such value or amount as it may deem reasonable.

(4) Every attachment under sub section (3) shall be effected in the manner provided in the code of civil procedure, 1908 [5 of 1908 (Note: now see code of criminal procedure, 1973 (2 of 1974)], for the attachment of property in execution of a decree for payment of money, and if, after such attachment, the person charged appears and shows to the satisfaction of the court that he did not abscond or keep out of the way to avoid service of the notice, the court shall order the release of his property from attachment upon such terms as to costs or otherwise as it may think fit.

(5) Any person charged with contempt under Section 15 may file an affidavit in support of this defence, and the court may determine the matter of the charge either on the affidavits filed or after taking such further evidence as may be necessary, and pass such order as the justice of the case requires.

Comments

(i) The period of one year has to be reckoned from the date on which a notice under this section has been issued; K K R Nair v Mohan Das, 1990 Cr LJ 1641 (AP).

(ii) An order initiating proceeding for contempt by a notice issued under section 17 is not appealable under section 19 of the Act; the union of India v Mario Coural Sa. AIR 1982 SC 691.

(iii) Committal for contempt is always discretionary with the court; S C Nandy v G M Bhattacharjee, AIR 1951 Cal 507.

(iv) The position of a contemner is that of an accused person; M R Parashar v Dr Farooq Abdullah 1984 Cal LJ 337 (SC).

(v) Contempt proceedings are quasi criminal in nature; Sheoraj v A P Batra, AIR 1955 All 638.

(vi) Benefit of doubt is available to an accused; state of Orissa v Nityananda Mohopatra, AIR 1960 Ori 132.

(vii) Personal appearance, unless dispensed with, of a contemner is mandatory; B N Jaisimha v N T Prabhakar, (1985) 29 MLJC Crl 640.

18. *Hearing of Cases of Criminal Contempt to be by Benches:*

(1) Every case of criminal contempt under section 15 shall be heard and determined by a bench of not less than two judges.

(2) Sub section (1) shall not apply to the court of a judicial commissioner.

Comments

(i) The jurisdiction rests exclusively with a bench of not less than two judges of the high court; B R Karandikar v M Y Joshy, (1983) 2 Bom Cr 558 (Bom).

(ii) However, it was observed that a single judge can also deal with criminal contempts committed in facie curium; In re: court on its own motion, AIR 1980 P & H 72.

19. *Appeals:*

(1) An appeal shall lie as of right from any order to decision of high court in the exercise of its jurisdiction to punish for contempt-

(a) Where the order or decision is that of a single judge, to a bench of not less than two judges of the court.

(b) Where the order or decision is that of a bench, to the Supreme Court.

Provided that where the order or decision is that of the court of the judicial commissioner in any union territory, such appeal shall lie to the Supreme Court.

(2) Pending any appeal. The appellate court may order that-

(a) The execution of the punishment or order appealed against be suspended

(b) If the appellant is in confinement, he be released on bail, and

(c) The appeal be heard notwithstanding that the appellant has not purged his contempt.

(3) Where any person aggrieved by any order against which an appeal may be filed satisfied the high court that he intends to prefer an appeal, the high court may also exercise all or any of the powers conferred by sub section (2).

(4) An appeal under sub section (1) shall be filed-

(a) In the case of an appeal to a bench of the high court, within 30 days.

(b) In the case of an appeal to the Supreme Court, within 60 days, from the date of the order appealed against.

Comments

(a) When thee high court acquits the contemner, no appeal lies; Subhash Chandra v B R Kakkar, (1992) 2 Punj Lr 46 (P & H).

(i) If the order of committal for contempt of court is made

(b) By a single judge of the high court, an appeal lies to a division bench thereof; or

(c) By a division bench of the high court, an appeal lies to the Supreme Court, as of a statutory right; Mohammad Idris v R J Babuji, (1984) 2 Crimes 880 (SC).

(ii) It is not each and every order passed during the contempt proceedings that is appealable; S P Wahi v Surendra Singh, 1983 Cr LJ 1426.

(iii) An appeal does not automatically operate as a stay of the order appealed against; Hans Raj v state of Himachal Pradesh, 1985 Cr LJ 1030.

20. *Limitation for Actions for Contempt:* No court shall initiate any proceedings if contempt, either on its own motion or otherwise, after the expiry of a period of one year from the date on which the contempt is alleged to have been committed.

Comments

(i) Initiation of any proceedings for contempt is barred after the expiry of a period of one year from the date on which the contempt is alleged to have been committed; V M Kanade v Madhao Gadkari, (1990) 1 Mah LR 544 (Bom).

(ii) No intervening event or order stops the running of time specified in this section; Golcha Avertising Agency the state of Maharashtra, (1990) 2 Bom CR 262 (Bom).

(iii) The expression 'court' denotes a high court or the Supreme Court; the state of Bihar v Ambika Roy, 1991 Cr LJ 82 (Pat).

(iv) The provisions of the Limitation Act, 1963 do not apply; Krishnalal Chhoteylal, (1987) 13 ALR 44.

(v) Delay in initiating contempt proceedings cannot be condoned; T M A Abdul Hamed v S Radhakrishnan, 1989 LW (Crl) 237.

21. *Act not to Apply to Nyaya Panchayatas or other Village Courts:* Nothing contained in this Act shall apply in relation to contempt of nyaya panchayats or other village courts, by

whatever name known, for the administration of justice, established under any law.

22. *Act to be in Addition to, and not in Derogation of, other Laws Relating to Contempt:* The provisions of this Act shall be in addition to, and not in derogation of the provision of any other law relating to contempt of courts.

Comments

The provisions incorporated in the Act are supplemented to already existing law of contempt; Harish Chandra Misra v S Ali Ahmed, AIR 1986 Pat 65.

23. *Power of the Supreme Court and High Court to make Rules:* The Supreme Court or, a case may be, any high court, may make rules, not inconsistent with the provisions of this Act, providing for any matter relating to its procedure.

Comments

The court is guided by its own procedure to be followed in the facts and circumstances of each individual case and to see that the condemner is getting full opportunity to make his defence; Mohammed Vamin v O P Bansal, 1982 Cr LJ 322 (Raj).

24. *Repeal:* The Contempt of Courts Act, 1952 (32 of 1952) is hereby repealed.

Comments

(i) This section repealed the Contempt of Courts Act, 1952 (32 of 1952) with effect from 24-12-1991 which had already repealed the Contempt to Courts Act, 1926 (XII of 1926 w.e.f. 14-3-1952

(ii) For contempts committed prior to this Act, action could be taken under the Repealed Act (32 of 1952); see Ramniklal Nanalal v.Shah Pranlal Nahchand, AIR 1952 Kutch 74.

Rules to regulate proceedings for contempt to the Supreme Court, 1975 G.S.R. 142-In exercise of the powers under section 23 of the Contempt of Courts Act, 1971 read with article 145 of the Constitution of India and all other powers enabling it in this behalf, the Supreme Court hereby makes, with the approval of the President, the following rules-

1. (1) These rules may be called the rules to regulate proceedings for contempt of the Supreme Court, 1975.

   (2) They shall come into force on the date of their publication in the official gazette (Note: published in the gazette of India, dated February 1, 1975 and came into force from that date.

2. (1) Where contempt is committed in view or presence or hearing of the court, the contemnor may be punished by the court before which it is committed either forthwith or on such date as may be appointed by the court in that behalf.

   (2) Pending the determination of the charge, the court may direct that the contemnor shall be detained in such custody as it may specify.

   Provided that the contemnor may be released on bail on such terms as the court may direct.

3. In case of contempt other than the contempt referred to in rule 2, the court may take action.

   (a) Suo motu, or

   (b) On a petition made by attorney general, or solicitor general, or

   (c) On a petition made by any person, and in the case of a criminal contempt with the consent in writing of the attorney general or the solicitor general.

4.(a) Every petition under Rule 3 (b) or (c) shall contain:

   (i) The name, description and place of residence of the petitioner or petitioners and of the persons charged.

   (ii) Nature of the contempt alleged, and such material facts, including the date or dates of commission of the alleged contempt, as may be necessary for the proper determination of the case.

   (iii) If a petition has previously been made by him on the same facts, the petitioners shall give the details

of the petition previously made and shall also indicate the result thereof.

(b) The petition shall be supported by an affidavit.

(c) Whether the petitioner relies upon a document or documents in his possession or power, he shall file such document or documents or true copies thereof with the petition.

(d) No court-fee shall be payable on the petition, and on any documents filed in the proceedings.

5. Every petition under rule 3 (b) and (c) shall be posted before the court for preliminary hearing and for orders as to issue of notice. Upon such hearing, the court, if satisfied that no prima facie case has been made out for issue of notice, may dismiss the petition, and, if not so satisfied direct that notice of the petition be issued to the contemnor.

6. (1) Notice to the person charged shall be in Form 1. The person charged shall, unless otherwise ordered, appear in person before the court a directed on the date fixed for hearing of the proceeding, and shall continue to remain present during hearing till the proceeding is finally disposed of by order of the court

(2) When action is instituted on petition, a copy of the petition along with the annexure and affidavits shall be served upon the person charged.

7. The person charged may file his reply duly supported by an affidavit or affidavits.

8. No further affidavit or document shall be filed except with the leave of the court.

9. Unless otherwise ordered by the court, seven copies of the paper book shall be prepared in the registry, one for the petitioner, one for the opposite party and the remaining for the use of the court. The paper book in case shall be prepared at the expense of the central government and shall consist of the following documents:

(i) Petition and affidavits filed by the petitioner,

(ii) A copy of, or a statement relating to, the objectionable matter constituting the alleged contempt.

(iii) Replay and affidavits of the parties.

(iv) Documents filed by the parties.

(v) Any other document which the registrar may deem fit to include.

10. The court may direct the attorney-general or solicitor-general to appear and assist the court.

11. (1) The court may, if it has reason to believe, that the person charged is absconding or is otherwise evading service of notice, or if he fails to appear in person or to continue to remain present in person in pursuance of the notice, direct a warrant bailable or non-bailable for his arrest, addressed to one or more police officers or may order attachment of property. The warrant shall be issued under the signature of the registrar. The warrant shall be in Form II and shall be executed, as far as may be in the manner provided for execution of warrants under the code of criminal procedure.

(2) The warrant shall be execute by the officer to officers to whom it is directed, and may also be executed by any other police officer whose name is endorsed upon the warrant by the officer to whom it is directed or endorsed.

(3) Where a warrant is to be executed outside the union territory of Delhi, the court may instead of directing such warrant to police officer, forward it to the magistrate of the district or the superintendent of police or commissioner of police of the district within which the person charged is believed to be residing. The magistrate or the police officer to whom the warrant is forwarded shall endorse his name thereon, and cause it to be executed.

(4) Every person who is arrested and detained shall be produced before the nearest magistrate within a period of 24 hours of such arrest excluding the time necessary for the from the place of arrest to the

court of the magistrate, and no such person shall be detained in custody beyond the said period without the authority of a magistrate.

12. The court may, either suo motu, or on motion made for that purpose, order the attendance for cross-examination, for a person whose affidavit has been filed in the matter.
13. The court may make orders for the purpose of securing the attendance of any person to be examined as a witness and for discovery of production of any document.
14. The court may pass such orders as it thinks fit including orders as to costs which may recovered as if the order were a decree of the court.
15. Save as otherwise provided by the rules contained herein, the provisions of the Supreme Court Rules, 1966 shall, so far as may be, apply to proceedings in relation to proceedings in contempt under this part.
16. Where a person charged with contempt is adjusted guilty and is sentenced to suffer imprisonment, a warrant of commitment a d detention shall be made out in Form IV under the signature of the registrar. Every such warrant shall remain in force until it is cancelled by order of the court on until it is executed. The superintendent of the jail shall in pursuance of the order receive the person so adjusted and detain him in custody for the period specified therein, or until further orders.

MEDIA POLICY

Summary of the recommendations contained in the working paper on the national media policy submitted by the sub-committee of the consultative committee for the ministry of information and broadcasting under the chairmanship of Ram Vilas Paswan. (March, 1996)

- The broadcasting should observe a greater degree of responsibility and sensitivity to Indian culture and ethos and cater to the developmental requirement of the country. It should achieve an Indian personality in telecasting/broadcasting.

- There should be a regulatory body to oversee both public and private telecasting/broadcasting. In this connection, the sub-committee noted that the provisions of the Prasar Bharati Act, which was unanimously passed by parliament in 1990 should be kept in mind while framing the regulatory mechanism which should be an independent autonomous authority.

The sub-committee is of confirmed opinion that no recourse should be taken by the government to dilute the provision of the Prasar Bharati Act, 1990. This regulatory body may be set up to ensure adherence to the programmes/advertisement codes and other stipulations. This body or similar independent body may also develop an effective mechanism for public grievance redressal as well as implementation of its recommendations in respect of such grievances.

- Adequate care should be taken to enable the setting up of non-commercial broadcasting stations to be run by universities, educational institutions, panchayats/local bodies, state governments, etc.
- The sub-committee recognises that for public broadcasting, adequate funding in the form of state support is necessary. The content of programmes or software is often dictated by the funding and therefore the sub-committee strongly recommends that this aspect should receive the attention of the government and an institutionalised system be worked out.
- The national broadcasters-Akashvani and Doordarshan-should bear the responsibility to offer a high quality public service broadcasting that informs, educates and entertains the people and also provide coverage to national events like the Republic Day Parade. Taking into account the reach of the national broadcasters, primacy and exclusive responsibility should be provided to them in the matter of coverage of national events like the Republic Day Parade, Independence Day, the President's address to both the houses of parliament, etc.
- The rights/obligations and exclusivity of the national broadcasters should be codified through law.

- Whereas the broad policy approach should be the same for radio and television, minor variations/differences can be made in view of the difference in reach and impact of the two media. Programme/advertisement codes should be similar, if not, same. The viewer/listener interest should be kept in mind while spacing the advertisements. A new production style, which is people-oriented should be developed.
- In tune with the policy framework suggested here, the Indian private sector/state government/NGOs/local self government should be allowed to enter the field of broadcasting/telecasting.
- Appropriate provisions must be made to ensure that the control of private broadcasting does not fall into the hands of companies having a major stake in the print medium or vice-versa. Cross-media ownership restrictions must, therefore, be considered.
- Direct or indirect foreign equity participation in companies entering the field of private broadcasting should not be permitted.
- Access on the private channel should be available to the common man through appropriate provisions in the law.
- In view of the supreme court's judgement on airwaves, an independent authority must be set up to control and regulate the use of airwaves. The sub-committee felt that the integrity of the Indian skies is as important as her territorial integrity. This regulatory authority must be set up through a law enacted by the parliament at the earliest.
- The apex regulatory body should be an independent autonomous public authority representative of all sections and interests in the society and should control and regulate the use of air waves in the interests of the public and to prevent invasion of their rights.
- The foreign satellite channels must also be brought within the ambit of the said regulatory body in order to make them amenable to the Indian laws.

- The sub-committee felt that in the case of skywaves, efforts should be made to develop an international convention to forge multilateral/regional agreements with countries especially in regard to software.
- The sub-committee noted that it will be difficult to pre-censor programmes aired on television in view of the vast structure such a step would call for. By bringing in the private broadcasting/foreign channels within the purview of the Indian legal system, much of the laissez-faire that exists can be curbed.
- The sub-committee felt that the present programming in electronic media, especially television needs to be more decentralised to meet the regional/local aspirations. In this connection, the Verghese Committee recommendations regarding decentralised programming, programme autonomy and constitution of five zones for this purpose (viz. south, west, central, eastern and north) should be considered by the government.
- Care should be taken that no monopoly is developed by the private broadcasters, by restructuring the number of channels, especially 'several interest' channels owned by them.
- The sub-committee agrees with the broad objectives of national film policy set out by the working group on the national film policy. As a formal declaration of the national film policy would be useful, the sub-committee recommends that the government should formalise the same as early as possible.
- Since the estimates committee and the standing committee have examined in detail the working of the CBFC as mentioned above, we have nothing further to add except to reiterate their recommendations. These recommendations are discussed elsewhere the sub-committee wishes to add that the government should amend the guidelines for certification of films to curb the distortion of image of eminent leaders in films.
- The production of good short films, both by Films Division and independent producers, needs to be actively

encouraged. The Films Division should make efforts to improve the quality of its documentaries and make them more interesting. The sub-committee recommends that the government should encourage the growth of Indian documentary film movement. The sub-committee suggests in this regard that the Films Division should farm out more and more films to independent producers on its panel. Further, Doordarshan should commission the production of documentaries through the Films Division and other agencies.

- It has been stated that it would be very difficult to find sponsors for telecasting documentaries on Doordarshan. The sub-committee recommends that the Doordarshan should allot timeslots for at least half-an-hour everyday on prime time for documentaries even if there are no sponsors.
- The sub-committee also recommends that the feasibility of showing documentary films in various educational institutions, schools, colleges and universities should be examined. The ministry of human resource development should consider the allocation of funds for the purpose.
- With a view to encourage children's films, the sub-committee recommends that more infrastructural facilities should be developed for the production of animation films.
- The sub-committee also recommends that more avenues for the exhibition of children's films in each district of the country should be identified.
- During meetings, representatives of the film industry pointed out that though the government called for recommendations from the Film Federation of India for the Dadasaheb Phalke Award, it did not normally accept their recommendation. The sub-committee is informed that the government gets recommendations from all quarters including the film industry and the best person is selected at the highest level: in the ministry for the award. To give more credibility to the government's decision, the sub-committee would recommend that. A small committee consisting of eminent persons including

those from film world should be appointed by government to consider all names received and recommend the name of the person who should be honoured with the Dadasaheb Phalke Award.

- The National Film Awards were instituted in 1953 to provide for a special impetus to regional cinema and to encourage the production of films of aesthetic excellence and social relevance. The sub-committee also recommends that the award winning films should be screened at various state capitals and other large towns so that the people in the regional centres may get an opportunity to see them. The central government should provide funds to the state government to organise such festivals of award-winning films.
- A number of witnesses before the sub-committee represented for the full implementation of the recommendations of the high-powered committee (1990). The sub-committee would suggest that the matter should be taken up with the various state government/union territory administrations again.
- The sub-committee recommends that the state government/union territory administrations should be persuaded to rationalise the rates of entertainment tax to help the film industry.
- During discussions some of the film industry representatives represented to the sub-committee that a view of high cost of imported raw stock, the customs countervailing duty may be reduced if not abolished. The sub-committee recommends that the countervailing duty on raw stock may be abolished in view of the act that there are no facilities to manufacture the raw stock in the country.
- Some of the witnesses before the sub-committee expressed concern about the shortage of theatres as well as the closure of cinema houses due to the advent of television and video. To overcome the shortage of exhibition facilities, the sub-committee suggests that wherever cinema theatres are being converted into commercial complexes, the local authorities should

ensure that in the complex coming up at the site at least one mini theatre is provided in the complex. The sub-committee would also recommend that more multiplex theatrical complexes should be encouraged.

- The sub-committee recommends that the National Film Development Corporation and other agencies should encourage construction of theatres with 400 to 500 capacity instead of very large theatres.
- During meetings the representatives of the cine workers pleaded for the declaration of the film industry as an 'industry' so that the workers of the industry are not exploited by the producers. The sub-committee feels that introduction of labour welfare measures of film industry workers will go a long way in improving their conditions. The sub-committee, therefore, recommends that the film industry may be declared as an industry not only for the purpose of institutional finance but also for application of labour legislation relating to welfare of labour.
- The National Film Archive of India is charged with the responsibility of preservation of cinema. There have been press reports about the damage and loss of important films. The sub-committee suggests that the archive should take immediate steps to acquire all film classics and preserve them properly for posterity.
- The sub-committee also suggests that the National Film Archive of India should take over the old documentaries from the Films Division for restoration and preservation.
- Nowadays film appreciation courses have been started in various universities and new film societies are coming up. However, the government gives only Rs three lakh per year to the Federation of Film Societies of India for its activities. This is awfully inadequate. The sub-committee recommends that the government should encourage the film society movement by giving all facilities including finance. The grant-in-aid to the Federation of Film Societies of India should be augmented suitably.

- Some of the witnesses informed the sub-committee that Akashvani's royalty rates for film songs which broadcast is Rs two per song and was fixed a long time ago. Considering the time lapse and increase in the cost of picturising film songs, the sub-committee recommends that this should be suitably revised upwards by Akashvani.
- With respect to the suggestions regarding evolving a code of conduct for the journalists and for vesting the Press Council of India with more powers, the sub-committee felt that the matter may be left to the Press Council for suitable decisions. However, the Press Council should consider arming itself with adequate powers to deal with habitual offences with respect to communalism, threats to national security and other undesirable activities.
- The language press and the small and medium newspapers should continue to grow. Therefore, the sub-committee recommends that the government must endeavour to create a suitable environment by helping in the modernisation of these sections of the press.
- Though the financial viability of a newspaper depends to a larger extent on the advertisement revenue which it is able to attract, the government's advertising policy and rates structure should be rational and uniform, evolved with a view to eliminate the possible use of advertisements as a lever to influence the press and thereby affecting its freedom.
- Even though the import of newsprint has been put under OGL, there is a need for a nodal agency to import newsprint on behalf of small and medium newspapers as they do not have the necessary infrastructure and the bargaining power for such imports.
- The training requirements of the journalists is yet another aspect which needs immediate attention. The press over the years has to become increasingly professional in nature. With a view to ensure that the press as a whole is capable of reporting and explaining and interpreting in their proper perspective various

developments taking place, it is imperative that additional facilities are created to enable journalists to have a broad educational preparation and specific training in journalism.

- Indian news agencies have not been able to operate effectively in the sphere of dissemination of national news abroad, and the gathering of foreign news for dissemination within the country. Foreign news agencies still dominate international news sections in leading newspapers. It should be the endeavour of the government to permit and strengthen the news agencies to become self-sufficient in these spheres. In this connection, renewed efforts should be made in revitalising the efforts taken in the wake of the Non-Aligned Conference, 1976 which led to the establishment of the newspool for exchange of news among third world countries.
- To strengthen the Indian news agencies, the sub-committee recommends that corporatisation of these news agencies with adequate equity base, as was suggested by the First Press Commission, should be seriously considered.
- Freedom of the editors, and editorial contents, insulated from the business and other interests of the owners, should be ensured through a proper institutional mechanism or guidelines to be evolved by the press themselves or by the Press Council of India. The issue of diversion of funds from the newspaper industry to other industries may be examined.
- The sub-committee feels that towards professionalisation of the print media, adequate institutional finance should be made available to the journalists, etc. through co-operatives on easy terms.

THE PRESS COUNCIL OF INDIA'S NORMS OF JOURNALISTIC CONDUCT

Ignorance and an inborn antipathy to any external pressure on one's inclination to do, speak and write that which one pleases, are often responsible for a blind resistance to any law, custom, tradition or norms. It is forgotten that some discipline and standard are necessary for a healthy and decent life, and they promote rather than thwart, the creative urges of the individual.

A distinction has to be made between those restraints which inhibit wholesome potentialities and those which encourage them. Freedom and creativity gain their content only in a society. Unless, life in a society is conducive to the growth of the personality of the individual, the raison d'etre of an organised living will be defeated.

Human beings being what they are, liberty frequently degenerates into licence and creativity into perversity; and the society itself becomes a cesspool of corrupt practices and pursuits. Tempering checks and constructive directions are necessary to preserve and promote decent values, robust creativity and healthy growth.

All customs and traditions, norms, mores and laws are born precisely to achieve this object. To the extent they promote that objective, they fulfil the purpose. The greatest single factor responsible for the human progress so far, is word. The invention of the word and communication through it, though only orally first, paved the way for human advancement.

The invention of the script and then of print took the graph of human achievement to new heights in a geometrically ascending scale. Today mankind finds itself amidst information explosion too fast to keep pace with and too difficult to assimilate, thanks to the mind-boggling progress in science and technology.

But the unbounded progress in the material sphere and in particular in the means of communication, itself warns us, that unless proper precautions are taken to control the method and the manner of the use of the word-spoken or written, typed, printed or copied, human society will be swept of its feet.

More wide-ranging and penetrating the sweep of the word, more the need to regulate its use, in the interest, of the peace, unity, fraternity and co-operation among the members of the society. All countries have therefore, throughout the ages tried to regulate the expression of the word, whatever the nature of the political regime, dictatorial or democratic.

The degree and the extent of the regulation have varied with times, and political, social, religious cultural climes; but the need for restriction of some kind or the other has been felt by all, all the time. Our constitution gives to every citizen the fundamental right of the freedom of speech and expression under Article 19 (1) (a) and at the same time makes its use subject to the restrictions mentioned clause (2) thereof.

The guarantee of the fundamental right does prevent the state from making any law, in so far as such law imposes reasonable restrictions on the exercise of the right, in the interest of the sovereignty and integrity of the state, the security of the state, friendly relations with foreign states, public order, decency and morality and in relation to the contempt of court, defamation or incitement to an offence.

The Press Council of India has been established with the objects of preserving the freedom of the press and of maintaining and improving the standards of newspapers and news agencies in the country. It is to further these objects, that the council is required among other things, to help newspapers and news agencies to maintain independence; to build up a code of conduct for newspapers agencies and journalists in accordance with high professional standards to ensure on their part the maintenance of high standards of public taste and to foster a due sense of the rights and responsibilities of citizenship and to foster the growth of a sense of responsibility and public service among all those engaged in the profession of journalism.

To discharge these functions entrusted to it, the council has to frame a code of ethics for those engaged in journalism and to enforce it. The council over the years has built up a code of ethics covering aspects of journalism which came to the fore from time to time and which needed to be dealt with at its end, keeping in mind the objects with which it has been established and the role it is expected to perform.

Since its last publication, there have been some additions to the ethical code on important aspects such as financial journalism and pre-poll and exit poll surveys. The council decided to publish and update code and the result is the present publication. This publication has been designed to be a trim and at the same time a comprehensive treatment on the subject.

Besides the ethics, the publication also contains references to the provisions of the constitution and of the various statute laws which have a bearing on the print media. It is hoped that it will be found useful by all concerned. The council hopes to publish its translation in regional languages in due course, for the council is of the view that the education in the code of ethics of journalists connected particularly with the small and regional language newspapers is very necessary if the code is to be effective. We have no doubt that we will succeed in getting assistance in this task from public-spirited individuals and associations.

PRINCIPLES AND ETHICS

The fundamental objective of journalism is to serve the people with news, views, comments and information on matters of public interest in a fair, accurate, unbiased, sober and decent manner. Towards this end, the press is expected to conduct itself in keeping with certain norms of professionalism universally recognised. The norms enunciated below and other specific guidelines appended thereafter, when applied with due discernment and adaptation to the varying circumstance of each case, will help the journalist to self-regulate his or her conduct.

1. *Accuracy and Fairness:* The press shall eschew publication of inaccurate, baseless, graceless, misleading or distorted material. All sides of the core issue or subject should be reported. Unjustified rumours and surmises should not be set forth as facts.

2. *Pre-publication Verification:* On receipt of a report or article of public interest and benefit containing imputations or comments against a citizen, the editor should check with due care and attention its factual accuracy-apart from other authentic sources with the person or the organisation concerned to elicit his/her or its version, comments or reaction and publish the same with due amendments in the report where necessary. In the event of lack or absence of response, a footnote to that effect should be appended to the report.

3. *Caution against Defamatory Writings:* A newspaper should not publish anything which is manifestly

defamatory or libellous against any individual organisation unless after due care and checking, they have sufficient reason to believe that it is true and its publication will be for public good.

4. Truth is no defence for publishing derogatory, scurrilous and defamatory material against a private citizen where no public interest is involved.
5. No personal remarks which may be considered or construed to be derogatory in nature against a dead person should be published except in rare cases of public interest, as the dead person cannot possibly contradict or deny those remarks.
6. The press shall not rely on objectionable past behaviour of a citizen for basing the scathing comments with reference to fresh action of that person. If public good requires such reference, the press should make pre-publication inquiries from the authorities concerned about the follow-up action, if any, in regard to those adverse actions.
7. The press has a duty, discretion and right to serve the public interest by drawing reader's attention to citizens of doubtful antecedents and of questionable character but as responsible journalists they should observe due restraint and caution in hazarding their own opinion or conclusion in branding these persons as 'cheats' or 'killers' etc. The cardinal principle being that the guilt of a person should be established by proof of facts alleged and not by proof of the bad character of the accused. In the zest to expose, the press should not exceed the limits of ethical caution and fair comments.
8. Where the impugned publication are manifestly injurious to the reputation of the complainant, the onus shall be on the respondent to show that they were true or to establish that they constituted for comment made in good faith and for public good.
9. *Parameters of the Right of the Press to Comment on the Acts and Conduct of Public Officials:* So far as the government, local authority and other organs/

institutions exercising governmental power are concerned, they cannot maintain a suit for damages for acts and conduct relevant to the discharge of their official duties unless the official establishes that the publication was made with reckless disregard for the truth. However, the judiciary which is protected by the power to punish for contempt of court and the parliament and legislatures, protected as their privileges are by Articles 105 and 194 respectively, of the constitution of India, represent exception to this rule.

10. Publication of news or comments/information on public officials conducting investigations should have a tendency to help the commission of offences or to impede the prevention or detection of offences or prosecution of the guilty. The investigative agency is also under a corresponding obligation not to leak out or disclose such information or indulge in disinformation.

11. The Official Secrets Act, 1923 or any other similar enactment or provision having the force of law equally bind the press or media though there is no law empowering the state or its officials to prohibit, or to impose a prior restraint upon the press/media.

12. Cartoons and caricatures in depicting good humour are to be placed in a special category of news that enjoy more liberal attitude.

13. *Right to Privacy:* The press shall not intrude or invade the privacy of an individual unless outweighed by genuine overriding public interest, not being a prurient or morbid curiosity. So, however, that once a matter becomes a matter of public record, the right to privacy no longer subsists and it becomes a legitimate subject for comment by press and media among others. Explanation: Things concerning a person's home, family, religion, health, sexuality, personal life and private affairs are covered by the concept of privacy excepting where any of these impinges upon the public or public interest.

14. *Caution against Identification:* While reporting crime involving rape, abduction or kidnap of women/females

or sexual assault on children, or raising doubts and questions touching the chastity, personal character and privacy of women, the names, photographs of the victims or other particulars leading to their identity shall not be published.

15. Minor children and infants who are the offspring of sexual abuse or 'forcible marriage' or illicit sexual union shall not be identified or photographed.
16. *Recording Interviews and Phone Conversation:* The press shall not tape-record anyone's conversation without that person's knowledge or consent, except where the recording is necessary to protect the journalist in a legal action, or for other compelling good reason.
17. The press shall, prior to publication, delete offensive epithets used by an interviewer in conversation with the press-person.
18. Intrusion through photography into moments of personal grief shall be avoided. However, photography of victims of accidents or natural calamity may be in larger public interest.
19. *Conjecture, Comment and Fact:* A newspaper should not pass on or elevate conjecture, speculation or comment as a statement of fact. All these categories should be distinctly stated.
20. *Newspapers to Eschew Suggestive Guilt:* Newspapers should eschew suggestive guilt by association. They should not name or identify the family or relatives or associates of a person convicted or accused of a crime, when they are totally innocent and a reference to them is not relevant to the matter reported.
21. It is contrary to the norms of journalism for a paper to identify itself with and project the case of any one party in the case of any controversy/dispute.
22. *Corrections:* When any factual error or mistake is detected or confirmed, the newspaper should publish the correction promptly with due prominence and with apology or expression of regrets in a case of serious lapse.

23. *Right of Reply:* The newspaper should promptly and with due prominence, publish either in full or with due editing, free of cost, at the instance of the person affected or feeling aggrieved/or concerned by the impugned publication, a contradiction/reply/clarification or rejoinder sent to the editor in the form of a letter or note. If the editor doubts the truth or factual accuracy of the contradiction/reply/clarification or rejoinder, he shall be at liberty to add separately at the end a brief editorial comment doubting its veracity, but only when this doubt is reasonably founded on unimpeachable documentary or other evidential material in his/her possession. This is a concession which has to be availed of sparingly with due discretion and caution in appropriate cases.

24. However, where the reply/contradiction or rejoinder is being published in compliance with the discretion of the Press Council, it is permissible to append a brief editorial note to that effect.

25. Right of rejoinder cannot be claimed through the medium of press conference, as publication of a news of a conference is within the discretionary powers of an editor.

26. Freedom of the press involves the readers' right to know all sides of an issue of public interest. An editor, therefore, shall not refuse to publish the reply or rejoinder merely on the ground that in his opinion the story published in the newspaper was true. That is an issue to be left to the judgement of the readers. It also does not behove an editor to show contempt towards a reader.

27. *Letters to Editor:* An editor who decides to open his columns for letters on a controversial subject, is not obliged to publish all the letters received in regard to that subject. He is entitled to select and publish only some of them either in entirety or the gist thereof. However, in exercising this discretion, he must make an honest endeavour to ensure that what is published is not one-sided but represents a fair balance between the views for and against with respect to the principal issue in controversy.

28. In the event of rejoinder upon rejoinder being sent by two parties on a controversial subject, the editor has the discretion to decide at which stage to close the continuing column.

29. *Obscenity and Vulgarity to be Eschewed:* Newspapers/journalists shall not publish anything which is obscene, vulgar or offensive to public good taste.

30. Newspapers shall not display advertisements which are vulgar or which, through depiction of a woman in nude or lewd posture, provoke lecherous attention of males as if she herself was a commercial commodity for sale.

31. Whether a picture is obscene or not, is to be judged in relation to three tests; namely

    (i) Is it vulgar and indecent?

    (ii) Is it a piece of mere pornography?

    (iii) Is its publication meant merely to make money by titillating the sex feelings of adolescents and among whom it is intended to circulate? In other words, does it constitute an unwholesome exploitation for commercial gain. Other relevant considerations are whether the picture is relevant to the subject matter of the magazine. That is to say, whether its publication serves any preponderating social or public purpose, in relation to art, painting, medicine, research or reform of sex.

32. *Violence not to be Glorified:* Newspapers/journalists shall avoid presenting acts of violence, armed robberies and terrorist activities in a manner that glorifies the perpetrators' acts, declarations or death in the eyes of the public.

33. Glorification/encouragement of social evils to be eschewed Newspapers shall not allow their columns to be misused for writings which have a tendency to encourage or glorify social evils like sati pratha or ostentatious celebrations.

34. *Covering Communal Disputes/clashes:* News, views or comments relating to communal or religious disputes/

clashes shall be published after proper verification of facts and presented with due caution and restraint in a manner which is conducive to the creation of an atmosphere congenial to communal harmony, amity and peace. Sensational, provocative and alarming headlines are to be avoided. Acts of communal violence or vandalism shall be reported in a manner as may not undermine the people's confidence in the law and order machinery of the state. Giving community-wise figures of the victims of communal riot, or writing about the incident in a style which is likely to inflame passions, aggravate the tension, or accentuate the strained relations between the communities/religious groups concerned, or which has a potential to exacerbate the trouble, shall be avoided.

35. Headings not to be sensational/provocative and must justify the matter printed under them. In general and particularly in the context of communal disputes or clashes-a. Provocative and sensational headlines are to be avoided; b. Headings must reflect and justify the matter printed under them; c. Headings containing allegations made in statements should either identify the body or the source making it or at least carry quotation marks.

36. *Caste, Religion or Community References:* In general, the caste identification of a person or a particular class should be avoided, particularly when in the context it conveys a sense or attributes a conduct or practice derogatory to that caste.

37. Newspapers are advised against the use of word 'scheduled caste' or 'harijan' which has been objected to by some persons.

38. An accused or a victim shall not be described by his caste or community when the same does not have anything to do with the offence or the crime and plays no part either in the identification of any accused or proceeding, if there be any.

39. Newspapers should not publish any fictional literature distorting and portraying religious characters in an

adverse light, transgressing the norms of literary taste and offending the religious susceptibilities of large sections of society who hold those characters in high esteem, invested with attributes of the virtuous and lofty.

40. Commercial exploitation of the name of prophets, seers or deities is repugnant to journalistic ethics and good taste.

41. *Reporting on Natural Calamities:* Facts and data relating to spread of epidemics or natural calamities shall be checked up thoroughly from authentic sources and then published with due restraint in a manner bereft of sensationalism, exaggeration, surmises or unverified facts.

42. *Paramount National Interest:* Newspapers shall, as a matter of self-regulation, exercise due restraint and caution in presenting any news, comment or information which is likely to jeopardise, endanger or harm the paramount interests of the state and society, or the rights of individuals with respect to which reasonable restrictions may be imposed by law on the right to freedom of speech and expression under clause (2) of Article 19 of the constitution of India.

43. Publication of wrong/incorrect map is a very serious offence, whatever the reason, as it adversely affects the territorial integrity of the country and warrants prompt and prominent retraction with regrets.

44. *Newspapers may Expose Misuse of Diplomatic Immunity:* The media shall make every possible effort to build bridges of co-operation, friendly relations and better understanding between India and foreign states. At the same time, it is the duty of a newspaper to expose any misuse or undue advantage of the diplomatic immunities.

45. *Investigative Journalism, its Norms and Parameters:* Investigative reporting has three basic elements. (a) It has to be the work of the reporter, not of others he is reporting; (b) The subject should be of public importance for the reader to know; (c) An attempt is being made to hide the truth from the people.

(i) The first norm follows as a necessary corollary from (a) that the investigative reporter should, as a rule, base his story on facts investigated, detected and verified by himself and not on hearsay or on derivative evidence collected by a third party, not checked up from direct, authentic sources by the reporter himself.

(ii) There being a conflict between the factors which require openness and those which necessitate secrecy, the investigative journalist should strike and maintain in his report a proper balance between openness on the one hand and secrecy on the other, placing the public good above everything.

(iii) The investigative journalist should resist the temptation of quickies or quick gains conjured up from half-baked incomplete, doubtful facts, not fully checked up and verified from authentic sources by the reporter himself.

(iv) Imaginary facts, or ferreting out or conjecturing the non-existent should be scrupulously avoided. Facts, facts and yet more facts are vital and they should be checked and cross-checked whenever possible until the moment the paper goes to press.

(v) The newspaper must adopt strict standards of fairness and accuracy of facts. Findings should be presented in an objective manner, without exaggerating or distorting, that would stand up in a court of law, if necessary.

(vi) The reporter must not approach the matter or the issue under investigation, in a manner as though he were the prosecutor or counsel for the prosecution. The reporter's approach should be fair, accurate and balanced. All facts properly checked up, both for and against the core issues, should be distinctly and separately stated, free from any one-sided inferences or unfair comments. The tone and tenor of the report and its language should be sober, decent and dignified, and not needlessly offensive, barbed, derisive or castigatory, particularly while commenting on the version of the person whose alleged activity or misconduct is being investigated. Nor should the investigative reporter conduct the proceedings and pronounce his verdict of guilt or innocence against the person whose alleged criminal acts and conduct were investigated, in a manner as if he were a court trying the accused.

(vii) In all proceedings including the investigation, presentation and publication of the report, the investigative journalist's newspaper should be guided by the paramount principle of criminal jurisprudence, that a person is innocent unless the offence alleged against him is proved beyond doubt by independent, reliable evidence.

(viii) The private life, even of a public figure, is his own. Exposition or invasion of his personal privacy or private life is not permissible unless there is clear evidence that the wrong-doings in question have a reasonable nexus with the misuse of his public position or power and has an adverse impact on public interest.

(ix) Though the legal provisions of criminal procedure do not in terms, apply to investigating proceedings by a journalist, the fundamental principles underlying them can be adopted as a guide on grounds of equity, ethics and good conscience.

46. *Confidence to be Respected:* If information is received from a confidential source, the confidence should be respected. The journalist cannot be compelled by the Press Council to disclose such source; but it shall not be regarded as a breach of journalistic ethics if the source is voluntarily disclosed in proceedings before the council by the journalist who considers it necessary to repel effectively a charge against him/her. This rule requiring a newspaper not to publish matters disclosed to it in confidence, is not applicable where:

(a) consent of the source is subsequently obtained; or

(b) the editor clarified by way of an appropriate footnote that since the publication of certain matters were in the public interest, the information in question was being published although it had been made 'off the record'.

47. *Caution in Criticising Judicial Acts:* Excepting where the court sits 'in-camera' or directs otherwise, it is open to a newspaper to report pending judicial proceedings, in a fair, accurate and reasonable manner. But it shall not publish anything—which, in its direct and immediate effect, creates a substantial risk of obstructing, impeding or prejudicing seriously the due administration of justice; or—is in the nature of a running commentary or debate, or records the paper's own findings, conjectures, reflection or comments on issues, sub judice and which may amount to arrogation to the newspaper the functions of the court; or—regarding the personal character of the accused standing trial on a charge of committing a crime. The newspaper shall not as a matter of caution, publish or comment on evidence collected as a result of investigative journalism, when, after the accused is arrested and charged, the court becomes seized of the case. Nor should they reveal, comment upon or evaluate a confession allegedly made by the accused.

48. While newspapers may, in the public interest, make reasonable criticism of a judicial act or the judgement of a court for public good; they shall not cast scurrilous aspersions on, or impute improper motives, or personal bias to the judge. Nor shall they scandalise the court or the judiciary as a whole, or make personal allegations of lack of ability or integrity against a judge.

49. The newspaper shall, as a matter of caution, avoid unfair and unwarranted criticism which, by innuendo, attributes to a judge extraneous consideration for performing an act in due course of his/her judicial functions, even if such criticism does not strictly amount to criminal contempt of court.

50. *Newspapers to Avoid Crass Commercialism:* While newspapers are entitled to ensure, improve or strengthen their financial viability by all legitimate means, the

press shall not engage in crass commercialism or unseemly cut-throat commercial competition with their rivals in a manner repugnant to high professional standards and good taste.

51. Predatory price wars/trade competition among newspapers, laced with tones disparaging the products of each other, initiated and carried on in print, assume the colour of unfair 'trade' practice, repugnant to journalistic ethics. The question as when it assumes such an unethical character, is one of the fact depending on the circumstances of each case.

52. *Plagiarism:* Using or passing off the writings or ideas of another as one's own, without crediting the source, is an offence against the ethics of journalism.

53. *Unauthorised Lifting of News:* The practice of lifting news from other newspapers publishing them subsequently as their own, ill-comports the high standards of journalism. To remove its unethicality, the 'lifting' newspaper must duly acknowledge the source of the report. The position of features articles is different from 'news'. Feature articles shall not be lifted without permission and proper acknowledgment.

54. The press shall not reproduce in any form offending portions or excerpts from a proscribed book.

55. *Non-return of Unsolicited Material:* A paper is not bound to return unsolicited material sent for consideration of publication. However, when the same is accompanied by a stamped envelope, the paper should make all efforts to return it.

56. *Advertisements:* Commercial advertisements are information as much as social, economic or political information. What is more, advertisements shape attitude and ways of life at least as much as other kinds of information and comment. Journalistic propriety demands that advertisements must be clearly distinguishable from editorial matters carried in the newspaper.

57. A newspaper shall not publish anything which has a tendency to malign wholesale or hurt the religious sentiments of any community or section of society.

58. Advertisements which offend the provisions of the Drugs and Magical Remedies (Objectionable Advertisement) Act, 1954, should be rejected.

59. Newspapers should not publish an advertisement containing anything which is unlawful or illegal, or is contrary to good taste or to journalistic ethics or proprieties.

60. Newspapers while publishing advertisements, shall specify the amount received by them. The rationale behind this is that advertisements should be charged at rates usually chargeable by a newspaper since payment of more than the normal rates would amount to a subsidy to the paper.

61. Publication of dummy advertisements that have neither been paid for, nor authorised by the advertisers, constitute breach of journalistic ethics.

62. Deliberate failure to publish an advertisement in all the copies of a newspaper offends against the standards of journalistic ethics and constitutes gross professional misconduct.

63. There should be no lack of vigilance or a communication gap between the advertisement department and the editorial department of a newspaper in the matter of considering the propriety or otherwise of an advertisement received for publication.

64. The editors should insist on their right to have the final say in the acceptance or rejection of advertisements, specially those which border on or cross the line between decency and obscenity.

65. An editor shall be responsible for all matters, including advertisements published in the newspaper. If responsibility is disclaimed, this shall be explicitly stated beforehand.

Guidelines on Specific Issues

(A) Guidelines for Observance by the Press in the Wake of Communal Disturbances 1969

Recognising that the press which enjoys the utmost freedom of expression has a great and vital role to play in educating and moulding public opinion on correct lines in regard to the need for friendly and harmonious relations between the various communities and religious groups forming the fabric of Indian political life and in mirroring the conscience of the best minds of the country to achieve national solidarity, the Press Council of India considers that this object would be defeated, communal peace and harmony disturbed and national unity disrupted if the press does not strictly adhere to proper norms and standards in reporting on or commenting on matters which bear on communal relations.

Without attempting to be exhaustive, the council considers the following as offending against journalistic proprieties and ethics:

1. Distortion or exaggeration of facts or incidents in relation to communal matters or giving currency to unverified rumours, suspicions or inferences as if they were facts and base their comments on them.
2. Employment of intemperate or unrestrained language in the presentation of news or views, even as a piece of literary flourish or for the purpose of rhetoric or emphasis.
3. Encouraging or condoning violence even in the face of provocation as a means of obtaining redress of grievances whether the same be genuine or not.
4. While it is the legitimate function of the press to draw attention to the genuine and legitimate grievances of any community with a view to having the same redressed by all peaceful, legal and legitimate means, it is improper and a breach of journalistic ethics to invent grievances, or to exaggerate real grievances, as these tend to promote communal ill-feeling and accentuate discord.

5. Scurrilous and untrue attacks on communities, or individuals, particularly when this is accompanied by charges attributing misconduct to them as due to their being members of a particular community or caste.
6. Falsely giving a communal colour to incidents which might occur in which members of different communities happen to be involved.
7. Emphasising matters that are not to produce communal hatred or ill-will, or fostering feelings of distrust between communities.
8. Publishing alarming news which are in substance untrue or make provocative comments on such news or even otherwise calculated to embitter relations between different communities or regional or linguistic groups.
9. Exaggerating actual happenings to achieve sensationalism and publication of news which adversely affect communal harmony with banner headlines or in distinctive types.
10. Making disrespectful, derogatory or insulting remarks on or reference to the different religions or faiths or their founders.

Guidelines issued by the Press Council for observance by the state governments and the media in relation to communal disturbances 1991

i. The state government should take upon themselves the responsibility of keeping a close watch on the communal writings that might spark off tension, destruction and death, and bring them to the notice of the council;
ii. The government may have occasion to take action against erring papers or editors. But it must do so within the bounds of law. If newsmen are arrested, or search-and-seizure operations become necessary, it would be healthy convention if such developments could be reported to the Press Council within 24 to 48 hours followed by a detailed note within a week;
iii. Under no circumstances must the authorities resort to vindictive measures like cut in advertisements,

cancellation of accreditation, cut in newsprint quota and other facilities;

iv. Provocative and sensational headlines should be avoided by the press;

v. Headings must reflect and justify the master primed under them;

vi. Figures of casualties given in headlines should preferably be on the lower side in case or doubt about their exactness and where the numbers reported by various sources differ widely;

vii. Headings containing allegations made in statements should either identify the person/body making the allegation or, at least, should carry quotation marks;

viii. News reports should be devoid of comments and value judgement;

ix. Presentation of news should not be motivated or guided by partisan feelings, nor should it appear to be so;

x. Language employed in writing the news should be temperate and such as may foster feelings or amity among communities and groups;

xi. Corrections should be promptly published with due prominence and regrets expressed in serious cases; and

xii. It will help a great deal if in-service training is given to journalists for inculcation of all these principles.

Guidelines issued by the Press Council on January 21-22, 1993 in the wake of the Ram Janambhoomi-Babri Masjid dispute. Guidelines for guarding against the commission of the following journalistic improprieties and unethicalities

1. Distortion or exaggeration of facts or incidents in relation to communal matters or giving currency to unverified rumours, suspicions or inferences as if they were facts and base their comment on them.

2. Employment of intemperate or unrestrained language in the presentation of news or views, even as a piece of literary flourish or for the purpose of rhetoric or emphasis.

3. Encouraging or condoning violence even in the face of provocation as a means of obtaining redress of grievance whether the same be genuine or not.
4. While it is the legitimate function of the press to draw attention to the genuine and legitimate grievances of any community with a view to having the same redressed by all peaceful legal and legitimate means, it is improper and a breach of journalistic ethics to invent grievances, or to exaggerate real grievances, as these tend to promote communal ill-feeling and accentuate discord.
5. Scurrilous and untrue attacks on communities, or individuals, particularly when this is accompanied by charges attributing misconduct to them as due to their being members of a particular community or caste.
6. Falsely giving a communal colour to incidents which might occur in which members of different communities happen to be involved.
7. Emphasising matters that are apt to produce communal hatred or ill-will, or fostering feelings of distrust between communities.
8. Publishing alarming news which are in substance untrue or make provocative comments on such news or even otherwise calculated to embitter relations between different communities or regional or linguistic groups.
9. Exaggerating actual happenings to achieve sensationalism and publication of news which adversely affect communal harmony with banner headlines or distinctive types.
10. Making disrespectful, derogatory or insulting remarks on or reference to the different religions or faiths or their founders.

(B) Coverage of Handouts of Militants/terrorists

Guiding principles arising out of a complaint against the publication of some ULFA handouts/threat notes by a newspaper of Assam. The Press Council has enunciated some general principles for the guidance of the press. These are in tune with the recommendations of the Press Council of India Report on

Punjab and Jammu and Kashmir, adopted by the Press Council in January, 1991. These guiding principles considered by the council in September 1992, are as follows:

Dictates or 'press notes' commanding newspapers to publish them, under duress or threats of dire consequence, emanating from elements wedded to violence, constitute "the gravest assault on the freedom of the press which is one of the surest guarantors of a democratic and plural society". Generally, such dictates or notes are not newsworthy per se. Their publication tends to demoralise the public and to affect adversely public, police and security. The publication not only compromises the freedom and independence of the newspaper concerned, but also constitutes an offence against the standards of journalistic ethics and professional responsibility.

This is not to say that if there is anything newsworthy in a 'press note' emanating from any source, it should be blacked-out altogether, because 'self-censorship' may be "no less dangerous for being insidious". The essential point is that editors must exercise due caution and circumspection in considering the dissemination of such press notes.

If the whole of the note is not pernicious, then it may be edited, its objectionable portions removed and language toned down so that whatever is truly newsworthy gets disseminated in a balanced manner. However, where the 'news' and the objectionable portions are inextricably mixed up, violating the entire warp and woof of the 'press note', it will be prudent to withhold its publication altogether.

This is not an easy way out, as the media's experience of militancy in Punjab has amply demonstrated. More than 50 media personnel have lost their lives in terrorist attacks and ignoring a militant press note can lead and has often led, to death of innocent and defenseless media persons.

Any show of editorial defence and courage is likely to be seen by defenseless employees of newspapers as exposing them to avoidable dangers. Editors and proprietors under these circumstances have little room for manoeuvres. A workable expedient that proved useful in Punjab, is for the government to be in close touch with newspapers so that objectionable and anti-national press notes from groups swearing by violence could be removed from newspapers before publication.

Even though this may be seen as a form of pre-censorship, this arrangement saved lives and spared newspapers from difficult and delicate choices. There is however a danger of a wilful administration using this process to muzzle the press and misuse its authority under the law to define 'objectionable material' on its own terms.

Strict procedures must therefore be laid down. Orders passed under any legislation in this regard from time to time in relation to publication of allegedly 'objectionable matter' should be subjected to some kind of appellate review so as to curb any propensity to arbitrary action. The principal legislation and rules made thereunder should also be periodically reviewed in the light of changing circumstances. These safeguards should be built into all such press legislation.

(C) Aids and the Media

The mass media should help set an agenda for the country to fight the Aids pandemic in co-ordination with the government, the medical profession and the voluntary agencies. So far, the media in India have treated Aids more as news than as a growing menace and scourge threatening both human lives and dignity.

An exploratory content-analysis study conducted by the Operations Research Group during 1989-90 revealed the inadequacy of print media coverage on Aids in India. The coverage of prominent urban dailies focussed more on clinical diagnostic research on Aids in western countries, and little on the Aids problem in India and its social implications.

There were very few independent reports on Aids and the sources of most stories were international agencies. Further, most stories were located in inside pages or in supplements, and, content-wise were superficial in nature. Since the disclosures of the survey, until 1992, the quality and quantity of newspaper coverage on Aids in India has not changed much while the relative quantity of Aids coverage is on the rise, and while a greater recognition exists on the part of the print media about the problem of Aids in India, newspapers are to quote experts, still 'reactive' rather than 'proactive'.

Do's and Don'ts

From sporadic news, Aids must become a campaign target for our mass media with the following components of dos and don'ts:

- The media must inform and educate the people, not alarm or scare them. The emphasis must be on the fact that HIV (Human immunodeficiency virus) can be prevented from going into unaffected humans. Aids takes around 10 years to develop and HIV is a virus which does not survive for long outside a body. Thus, it is not spread by casual contact, hugging or kissing or through food or water or through insects.
- The media must hammer home the point that Aids, through sexual transmission or blood infection, can be prevented. Minimum precaution of the use of condoms in sex, and sterilisation of skin-piercing instruments and their prompt disposal after use.
- The media must report every case pertaining to Aids, be it positive or negative. There must be a constant liaison between the media and the medical profession to report on latest developments and research findings.
- The media must highlight and crusade against such practice as quarantine, isolation and ostracism of Aids patients. Besides being an affront to human dignity, those practices will not help minimise Aids infection, and are injurious to public health as 'they give a false sense of security to people outside the stigmatised group that the threat of infection has been removed and the need for precaution minimised.' Also, such practices will drive the Aids problem underground and make the campaign against the scourge more difficult. Community education, using all the latest expertise of mass education and behavioural scientists and media experts, has to play a crucial role in spreading the message about preventing this dreaded infection. Option builders of

the society (political and religious leaders, movie and sports personalities, other famous persons) must take the leadership in educating the public about Aids and how to avoid contracting this infection. The innovative use of media and a positive reporting attitude of the media will go a long way in making the Aids awareness campaign a success.

- The media must force the authorities to impose rigorous blood-testing norms on prostitutes and professional women and issue periodical warnings to the public about areas where the incidence of Aids has high probability.
- The media must help the authorities in eliminating commercial blood collection and pre-testing of all blood donors for HIV and other diseases.
- The media must as a role respect the right to privacy of Aids patients and must not subject them to needless exposure and social stigma.
- Every mass medium must observe the terms of the final document of the international consultation of Aids and human rights, and promptly report the violation of such rights protecting the basic human rights to life and liberty, privacy and freedom of movement.

(D) Guidelines for Financial Journalists

1. The Press Council of India has counselled reporters/financial journalists/newspaper establishments to refrain from receiving any gifts/grants/concessions/facilities, etc., either in cash or kind which are likely to compromise free and unbiased reporting on financial matters.
2. The council in its report has observed that financial journalists today enjoy considerable influence over readers' minds and, therefore, they owe it to them to present a balanced and objective view of the financial dealings, status and prospects of a company. It observed that some companies are given excessive news coverage in the newspapers/magazines because they have issued advertisements to that print media. Sometimes, adverse reports are published of those companies which do not

give advertisements to the newspapers or magazines. Again, when a media is not happy with any company/ management for whatever reason, the negative aspects of the company are highlighted, while in the reverse situation, no negative aspects are brought to light. Some companies are also known to give gifts, loans, discounts, preferential shares, etc., to certain financial journalists to receive favourable and positive reports of the companies. At the same time, there is no mechanism for investors' education or for raising public opinion against such unhealthy practices.

3. The council feeling concerned over the malpractice in the corporate sector and after holding detailed deliberations and discussions with the representatives of financial institutions and journalists, has recommended the guidelines enumerated below for observance by the financial journalists:

   - The financial journalists should not accept gifts, loans, trips, discounts, preferential shares or other considerations which compromise or are likely to compromise his position.
   - It should be mentioned prominently in the report about any company that the report is based on information given by the company or the financial sponsors of the company.
   - When the trips are sponsored for visiting establishments of a company, the author of the report who has availed of the trip must state invariably that the visit was sponsored by the company concerned and that it had also extended the hospitality as the case may be.
   - No matter related to the company should be published without verifying the facts from the company and the source of such report should also be disclosed.
   - A reporter who exposes a scam or brings out a report for promotion of a good project, should be encouraged and awarded.

- A journalist who has financial interests such as share holdings, stock holdings, etc., in a company, should not report on that company.
- The journalist should not use for his own benefit or for the benefit of his relations and friends, information received by him in advance for publication.
- No newspaper owner, editor or anybody connected with a newspaper should use his relations with the newspaper to promote his other business interests.
- Whenever there is an indictment of a particular advertising agency or advertiser by the Advertising Council of India, the newspaper in which the advertisement was published must publish the news of indictment prominently.

(E) Guidelines Expected to be Observed by the Newspapers, Journalists, etc., while Publishing Reports on Elections

General elections are a very important feature of our democracy and it is imperative that the media transmits to the electorate fair and objective reports of the election campaign by the contesting parties. Freedom of the press depends to a large measure on the press itself behaving with a sense of responsibility.

It is, therefore, necessary to ensure that the media adheres to this principle of fair and objective reporting of the election campaign. The Press Council has, therefore, formulated the following guidelines to the media for observance during elections:

- It will be the duty of the press to give objective reports about elections and candidates. The newspapers are not expected to indulge in unhealthy election campaigns, exaggerated reports about any candidate/party or incident during the elections. In practice, two or three closely contesting candidates attract all the media attention. While reporting on the actual campaign, a newspaper may not leave out any important point raised by a candidate and make an attack on his or her opponent.

- Election campaign along communal or caste lines is banned under the election rules. Hence, the press should eschew reports which tend to promote feelings of enmity or hatred between people on the ground of religion, race, caste, community or language.
- The press should refrain from publishing false or critical statements in regard to the personal character and conduct of any candidate or in relation to the candidature or withdrawal of any candidate or his candidature, to prejudice the prospects of that candidate in the elections. The press shall not publish unverified allegations against any candidate/party.
- The press shall not accept any kind of inducement, financial or otherwise, to project a candidate/party. It shall not accept hospitality or other facilities offered to them by or on behalf of any candidate/party.
- The press is not expected to indulge in canvassing of a particular candidate/party. If it does, it shall allow the right of reply to the other candidate/party.
- The press shall not accept/publish any advertisement at the cost of public exchequer regarding achievements of a party/government in power.
- The press shall observe all the directions/orders/ instructions of the election commission/returning officers or chief electoral officer issued from time to time.

Guidelines for Pre-poll/Exit-poll Survey

The Press Council of India having considered the question of desirability or otherwise of publication of findings of pre-poll surveys and the purpose served by them, is of the view that the newspapers should not allow their forum to be used for distortions and manipulations of the elections and should not allow themselves to be exploited by interested parties.

- The Press Council, therefore, advises that in view of the crucial position occupied by the electoral process in a representative democracy like ours, the newspapers should be on guard against their precious forum being used for distortions and manipulations of the elections.

This has become necessary to emphasise today since the print media is sought to be increasingly exploited by the interested individuals and groups to misguide and mislead unwary voters by subtle and not-so-subtle propaganda on casteist, religious and ethnic basis as well as by the use of sophisticated means like the alleged pre-poll surveys. While the communal and seditious propaganda is not difficult to detect in many cases, the interested use of the pre-poll survey, sometimes deliberately planted, is not so easy to uncover. The Press Council, therefore, suggests that whenever the newspapers publish pre-poll surveys, they should take care to preface them conspicuously by indicating the institutions which have carried such surveys, the individuals and organisations which have commissioned the surveys, the size and nature of the sample selected, the method of selection of the sample for the findings and the possible margin of error in the findings.

- Further in the event of staggered poll dates, the media is seen to carry exit-poll surveys of the polls already held. This is likely to influence the voters where the polling is yet to commence. With a view to ensure that the electoral process is kept pure and the voters' minds are not influenced by any external factors, it is necessary that the media does not publish the exit-poll surveys till the last poll is held.
- The Press Council, therefore, requests the press to abide by the following guideline in respect of the exit-polls.

The Press Council Act, 1978

This act establishes a press council for the purpose of preserving the freedom of the press and of maintaining the standards of newspapers and news agencies in India. Be it enacted by parliament in the 29th year of the Republic of India as follows.

Chapter I Preliminary

1. Short title and extent-

    (1) This act may be called the Press Council Act, 1978.

    (2) It extends to the whole of India.

2. Definitions-In this act, unless the context otherwise requires,-

   (a) 'Chairman' means the chairman of the council;

   (b) 'Council' means the Press Council of India established under section 4; (c) 'Member' means a member of the council and includes its chairman;

   (d) 'Prescribed' means prescribed by rules made under this act;

   (e) The expressions 'editor' and 'newspaper' have the meaning respectively assigned to them in the Press and Registration of Books Act, 1867 (25 of 1867) and the expression 'working journalist' has the meaning assigned to it in the working Journalists and other Newspaper Employees (Conditions of Service) and Miscellaneous Provision Act, 1955 (45 of 1955).

3. Rule of construction respecting enactments not extending to the state of Jammu and Kashmir or Sikkim-Any reference in this act to a law which is not in force in the state of Jammu and Kashmir or Sikkim shall, in relation to that state, be constructed as a reference to the corresponding law, if any inverse in that state.

Chapter II Establishment of the Press Council

4. Incorporation of the council-

   (1) with effect from such date as the central government may, by notification in the official gazette, appoint, there shall be established a council by the name of the press council of India.

   (2) the said council shall be a body corporate having perceptual succession and a common seal and shall by the said name sue and bemused.

5. Composition of the council-

   (1) The council shall consist of a chairman and 28 other members.

   (2) The chairman shall be a person nominated by a committee consisting of the chairman of the council

of states (Rajya Sabha), the speaker of the house of the people (Lok Sabha) and a person elected by the members of the council under sub-section (6) and the nomination so made shall take effect from the date on which it is notified by the central government in the official gazette.

(3) Of the other members-

(a) Thirteen shall be nominated in accordance with such procedure as may be prescribed from among the working journalists, of whom six shall be editors of newspapers and the remaining seven shall be working journalists other than editors; so, however that the number of such editors and working journalists other than editors in relation newspapers published in Indian languages shall be not less than three and four respectively;

(b) Six shall be nominated in accordance with such procedure as may be prescribed from among persons who own or carry on the business of management of newspapers, so, newspapers, so, however, that there shall be two representatives from each of the categories of big newspapers, medium newspapers and small newspapers;

(c) One shall nominated in accordance with such procedure as may be prescribed from among persons who manage news agencies;

(d) Three shall be persons having special knowledge or practical experience in respect of education and science, law and literature and culture of whom respectively one shall be nominated by the University Grants Commission one by the Bar Council of India and one by the Sahitya Academy;

(e) Five shall be members of Parliament of whom three shall be nominated by the speaker from among the members of the House of the People

(Lok Sabha) and two shall be nominated by the chairman of the council of States (Rajya Sabha) from among its members: Provided that no working journalist who owns, or carries on the business of management of any newspaper shall eligible for nomination under clause (a): Provided further that the nominations under clause (a) and clause (b) shall be so made that among the persons nominated there is not more than one person interested in any newspaper or group of newspaper under the same control or management.

Explanation-for the purposes of clause (b), a 'newspaper' shall be deemed to be-

(i) 'Big newspaper' if the total circulation of all its editions exceeds 50,000 copies for each issue;

(ii) 'Medium newspaper' of the total circulation of all its editions exceeds 15,000 copies but does not exceed 50,000 copies for each issue;

(iii) 'Small newspaper' of the total circulation of all its editions does not exceed 15,000 copies for each issue.

(4) Before making any nomination under clause (a) clause (b) or clause (c) sub-section (3) the central government in the case of the first council and the retiring chairman of the previous council in the case of any subsequent council shall, in the prescribed manner, invite panels of names comprising twice the number to be nominated from such associations of persons of the categories referred to in the said clause (a) clause (b) or clause (c) as may be notified in this behalf by the central government in the case of the first council and by the council itself in the case of subsequent councils: Provided that where there is no association of persons of the category referred to in the said clause (c) the panels of names shall be invited from such news agencies as may be notified as aforesaid.

(5) The central government shall notify the names of persons nominated as members under sub-section (3) in the official gazette and every such nomination shall take effect from the date on which it is notify.

(6) The members of the council notified under sub-section (5) shall elect from among themselves in accordance with such procedure as may be prescribed, a person to be a member of the committee referred to in sub-section (2) and a meeting of the members of the council for the purpose of such election shall be prescribed over by a person chosen from among themselves.

6. Term of office and retirement of members-

(1) Save as otherwise provided in this section, the chairman and other members shall hold office for a period of three years: Provided that the chairman shall continue to hold such office until the council is reconstituted in accordance with the provisions of section five for a period of six months whichever is earlier.

(2) Where a person nominated as a member under clause (a) cláuse (b) or clause (c) of sub-section (3) of section 5 if censured under the provisions of sub-section (1) of section 14, he shall cease to be a member of the council.

(3) The term of office of a member nominated under clause (e) of sub-section (3) of section 5 shall come to an end as soon as he ceases to be a member of the House from which he was nominated.

(4) A member shall be deemed to have vacated his seat if he is absent without excuse, sufficient in the opinion of the council, from three consecutive meetings of the council.

(5) The chairman may resign his office by giving notice in writing to the central government and any other member may resign his office by giving notice in writing to the chairman and upon such resignation being accepted by the central government, or as the

case may be, the chairman, the chairman or the member shall be deemed to have vacated his office.

(6) Any vacancy arising under sub-section (2) sub-section (3) sub-section (4) or sub-section (5) or otherwise shall be filled, as soon as may be, nomination in the same manner in which the member vacating office was nominated and the member no nominated so nominated shall hold office for the remaining period in which the member in whose place he is nominated would have held office.

(7) A retiring member shall be eligible for re-nomination for not more than one term.

7. Conditions of service of members-

(1) The chairman shall be a whole-time officer and shall be paid such salary as the central government may think fit, and the other members shall receive such allowances of fees for attending the meetings of the council as may be prescribed.

(2) Subject to the provisions of sub-section (1) the condition of service of members shall be such as may prescribed.

(3) It is hereby declared that the office of a member of the council shall not disqualify its holder for being chooses, as or for being a member of either House of Parliament.

8. Committees of the council-

(1) For the purpose of performing its function under this act, the council may constitute from among its members such committees for general or special purposes as it may deem necessary and every committee so constituted shall perform such functions as are assigned to it by the council.

(2) The council shall have the power to co-opt as members of any committee constitute under sub-section (1) such other number of persons, not being members of the council, as it thinks fit.

(3) Any such member shall have the right to attend any meeting of the committee on which he is so co-opted and to take part in the discussions thereat, but shall not have the right to vote and shall not be a member for any other purpose.

9. Meetings of the council and committees-The council or any committee thereof shall meet at such times and places and shall observe such trolls of procedure in regard to the transaction of business at its meetings as may be provided by regulations made under this act.

10. Vacancies among members or defect in the constitution not to invalidate acts and proceedings of the council-No act or proceeding of the council shall be deemed to be invalid by reason merely of the existence of any vacancy in, or any defect in the constitution of, the council.

11. Staff of the council-

(1) subject to such rules as may be made by the central government in this behalf, the council may appoint a secretary and such other employees as it may think necessary for the efficient performance of its function under this act.

(2) the terms and conditions of service of the employees shall be such as may be determined by regulations.

12. Authentication of orders and other instruments of the council-All orders and decisions of the council shall be authenticated by the signature of the chairman or any other member authorised by the council in this behalf and other instruments issued by the council shall be authenticated by the signature of the secretary or any other officer of the council authorised in manner in this behalf.

Chapter III Powers and functions of the council

13. Objects and functions of the council-

(1) the objects of the Cancun shall be to preserve the freedom of the press and to maintain and improve the standards of newspapers and news agencies in India.

(2) The council may, in furtherance of its objects, perform the following functions, namely-

(a) to help newspapers and news agencies to maintain their independence;

(b) to build up a code of conduct for newspapers news agencies and journalists in accordance with high professional standards;

(c) to ensure on the part of newspapers news agencies and journalists, the maintenance of high standards of public taste and foster a due sense of both the rights and responsibilities of citizenship;

(d) to encourage the growth of a sense of responsibility and public service aiming all those engaged in the profession of journalism;

(e) to keep under review any development likely to restrict the supply and dissemination of news of public interest and importance;

(f) to keep under review cases of assistance received by any newspaper or news agency in India from any foreign source including such cases as are referred to it by the central government or are brought to its notice by any individual, association of persons or any other organisation: Provided that nothing in this clause shall preclude the central government from dealing with any case of assistance received by a newspaper or news agency in India from any foreign source in any other manner it thinks fit;

(g) to undertake studies of foreign newspapers, including those brought out by any embassy or other representatives in India of a foreign state, their circulation and impact.

Explanation-For the purpose of this clause, the expression 'foreign state' has the meaning assigned to it in section 87A of the code of civil procedure, 1908 (5 of 1908);

(h) to promote a proper functional relationship among sell classes of persons engaged in the production or publication of newspapers or in news agencies: Provided that nothing in this Calais shall be deemed to confer on the council any functions in regard to disputes to which the Industrial Disputes Act, 1947 (14 of 1947) applies;

(i) to concern itself developments such as concentration of or other aspects of ownership of newspapers and news agencies which may affect the independence of the press;

(j) to indurate such studies as may be entrusted to the council and to espousers its opinion in regard to any matter referred to it by the central government;

(k) to do such other acts as may be incidental or conductive to the discharge of the above functions.

14. Power to censure-

(1) where on receipt of a complaint made to it or otherwise, the council has reason believe that a newspaper or news agency has offended against the standards or journalist ethics or public taste or that an editor or a working journalist has committed any professional; misconduct, the council may, after giving the newspaper, or news agency, the editor or journalist concerned an opportunity of being heard, hold an inquiry in such annett as may be provided by regulations made under this act and, if it is satisfied that it is necessary so to do, it may, for reasons to be recorded in writing, warn, admonish or censure the newspaper, the news agency, the editor or the journalist or disapprove the conduct of the editor or the journalist, as the case may be: Provided that the council may not take cognisance of a complaint if in the opinion of the chairman there is no sufficient ground for holding an inquiry.

(2) If the council is of the opinion that it is necessary or expedient in the public interest so to do, it may require any newspapers to publish therein in such manner as the council thinks, fir any particulars relating to any inquiry under this section against a newspaper or news agency, an editor or a journalist working therein, including the name of such newspaper, news agency, editor or journalist.

(3) Nothing in sub-section (1) shall be deemed to empower the council to hold an inquiry into any matter in respect of which any proceeding is pending in a court of law.

(4) The decision of the council under sub-section (1) or sub-section (2) as the case may be shall be final and shall not be questioned in any court of law.

15. General powers of the council-

(1) For the purpose of performing its functions or holding any inquiry under this act, the council shall have the same powers throughout Indies are vested in a civil court while trying a suit under the code of civil procedure 1908 (5 of 1908) in respect of the following matters, namely:

(a) summoning and enforcing the attendance of persons and examining them on oath;

(b) requiring the discovery and inspection of documents;

(c) receiving evidence on affidavits;

(d) requisitioning any public record or copies thereof from any court or office;

(e) issuing commissions for the examination of witness or documents; and (f) any other matter which may be prescribed.

(2) Nothing in sub-section (1) shall be deemed to compel any newspaper news agency editor or journalist to disclose the source of any news ore information published by that newspaper or received or reported be that news agency editor or journalist.

(3) Every inquiry held by the council shall be deemed to be a judicial proceeding within the meaning of sections 193 and 228 of the Indian Penal Code (45 of 1860).

(4) The council may, it if considers it necessary for the purpose of carrying out its objects or for the performance of any of its function under this act, make such observation as it may think, fir, in any of its decisions or reports, respecting the conduct of any authority, including government.

16. Levy of fees-

(1) The council may, for the purpose performing its functions under this act, levy such fees, at such rates and in such manner as my be prescribed from registered newspapers and news agencies and different rates may be prescribed for different newspapers banging regard to their circulation and other matters.

(2) Any fees payable to the council under sub-section (21) may be recovered as an areas of land revenue.

17. Payments to the council-The central government may after due appropriation made by Parliament by law in this behalf, pay to the council by way of grants such sums of money as the central government may consider necessary for the performance of the functions of the council under this act.

18. Fund of the council-

(1) The council shall have its own fund; and the fees collected by it all such sums as may from time to time be paid to it by the central government and all grants and advances made to it by any other authority or person shall be credited to the fund and all payments by the council shall be made therefrom.

(2) All moneys belonging to the fund shall be deposited in such banks or invested in such manner as may subject to the approval of the central government, be decided by the council.

(3) The council may spend such sums as it thinks fit or for performing its functions under this act, and such sums shall be treated as expenditure payable out of the fund of the council.

19. Budget-The council shall prepare, in such form and at such time each year as may be prescribed a budget in respect of the financial year next ensuing showing the stimulated receipts and expenditure and copies thereof shall be forwarded to the central government.

20. Annual report-The council shall prepare once every year, in such form and at such time as may be prescribed an annual report giving summary of its activities during the previous year, and giving an account of the standards of newspapers and news agencies and factors affecting them, and copies thereof, together with the statement of accountants audited in the manner prescribed under section 22 shall be forwarded to the central government and the government shall cause the same to be laid before both houses of Parliament.

21. Interim reports-Without prejudice to the provisions of Section 20, of the council may prepare at any time during the course or a year a report giving a summary of such of its activities during the year as it considers to be of public importance and copies thereof shall be forwarded to the central government and the government shall cause to be laid before both Houses of Parliament.

22. Accounts and audit-The accounts of the council shall be maintained and audited in such as may in consultation with the comptroller and auditor of India be prescribed.

Chapter IV Miscellaneous

23. Protection of action taken in good faith-

(1) No suit or other legal proceeding shall lie against the council or any member thereof or any person acting under the direction of the council in respect of anything which is in good faith done intended to be done under this act.

(2) No suit or other legal proceeding shall lie against any newspaper in respect of the publication of any matter therein under the authority of the council.

24. Members, etc., to be public servants-Every member of the council and every officer or other employee appointed by the council shall be deemed to be a public servant within the meaning of section 21 of the Indian Penal code (45 of 1860).

25. Power to make rules-

(1) The central government may, be notification in the official gazette, make rules to carry out the purposes of this ct. Provided that when the council has been established no such rules shall be made without consulting the council.

(2) In particular and without prejudice to the generality of the foregoing power such rules may provide for all or any of the following matters, namely:

(a) the procedure for nomination of members of the council under clauses (a) (b) and (c) of sub-section 5;

(b) the manner in which panels of names may be invited under sub-section (4) of section 5;

(c) the procedure for election of a number of the committee referred to in sub-section (2) of section 5 under sub-section (6) of that section;

(d) the allowances of fees to be paid to the members of the council for attending the meetings of the council, and other conditions of service of such members under sub-section 91) and (2) of section 7;

(e) the appointment of the secretary and other employees of the council under section ·I1;

(f) the matters referred to in clause (f) of sub-section (1) of section 15;

(g) the rates at which fees may be levied by the council under section 16 and the manner in which such fees any be levied;

(h) the form in which and the time within which the budget and annual report are to be prepared by the council under section 19 and 20 respectively;

(i) the manner in which the accounts of the council are to be maintained and audited under sections (3) every rule made under this section shall be laid as soon as may be after it is made, before each house of parliament while it is in session for a total period of 30 days which may be comprised in one session or into or more successive sessions, and if before the expiry of the session immediately following the session or the successive sessions aforesaid, both houses agree in making any modification in the rule or both houses agree that the rule should not be made the rule shall thereafter have effect only in such modified form or be of no effect, as the case may be; so however that any such modification or annulment shall be without prejudice to the validity of anything done under that rule.

26. Power to make regulations-The council may make regulations not inconsistent with this act and the rules made thereunder for-

(a) regulating the meeting of the council or any committee thereof and the procedure for conducting the business thereat under section 9;

(b) specifying the terms and conditions of service of the employees, appointed by the council under sub-section (2) of section 11;

(c) regulating the manner of holding any inquiry under this act;

(d) delegating to the chairman or the secretary of the council, subject to such conditions as it may think fit to impose, any of its powers under sub-section (3) of section 18;

(e) any other matter for which provision any be made by regulations under this act; Provided that the regulations made under clause (b) shall be made only with the price approval of the central government.

27. Amendment of Act 25 of 1867-In sub-section (1) of section 8C of the Press and Registration of Books Act, 1867, for the words 'consisting of a chairman and another member to be appointed by the central government', the words and figures 'consisting of a chairman and another member to be nominated by the Press Council of India, established under section 4 of the Press Council Act 1978, from among its members' shall be substituted.

*(Section 27 of the Press Council Act, 1978 repealed vide the Repealing and Amending Act, 1988, Section 2, Sch.I: upon amendment of Sec. 8 (c) of Press and Registration Act, 1867 to incorporate the above mentioned words and figures).

Published in the Gazette of India
Part III Section 4
Gazette Extraordinary Press Council of India
Notification
New Delhi dated November 14, 1979

In exercise of powers conferred by clause (c) of section 26 of the Press Council Act, 1978 (37 of 1978), and all other powers 'hereunto enabling, the Press Council of India hereby makes the following regulations, namely:

1. Short title and commencement:

   (1) These regulations, may be called the Press Council (Procedure for Inquiry) Regulations, 1979

   (2) They shall come into force on the date of their publication in the official gazette.

2. Definitions:

   (a) 'Act' means the Press Council Act, 1978 (37 of 1978).

   (b) 'Committee' means the inquiry committee constituted by the council under Section 8 (1) of the act for the purpose of inquiry into complaints under Sections 13 (2) and 14 (1) of the act

(c) 'Council' means the Press Council of India constituted under the act;

(d) 'Complainant' means a person or authority making a complaint to the council regarding a newspaper, news agency, editor or other working journalist, in the case of complaints under section 14 (1) of the act, and with regard to complaints relating to other matters, means a person making a complaint to the council in respect of any matter which the council has jurisdiction to entertain, examine and pronounce its views upon, and

(e) 'Matter' means an article, news-item, news-report, or any other matter 'which is published by a newspaper or transmitted by a news agency by any means whatsoever and includes a cartoon, picture, photograph strip or advertisement which is published in a newspaper:

3. Contents of complaint in respect of a newspaper, news agency, editor or other working journalist under section 14 (1) of the act:

(1) where a person makes a complaint to the council in respect of the publication or non-publication of any matter in any newspaper or news agency, under section 14 (1) of the act he shall

(a) furnish the name and address of the newspaper, news agency, editor or other working journalist against which or whom the complaint is preferred and in cases where the complaint relates to the publication of matter in a newspaper or to the transmission by a news agency, forward along with the complaint a cutting of the matter complained of in original and such other particulars as are relevant to the subject-matter of the complaint; and where the complaint is in respect of non-publication of matter, the original or a copy of the matter, non-publication of which is complained of;

(b) state in what manner the publication or non-publication of the matter complained of is objectionable within the meaning of section 14 (1) of the act;

(c) before filing the complaint before the council, draw the attention of the newspaper, news agency, editor or other working journalist concerned, to the matter appearing in the newspaper etc. or to the non-publication there of which, in the opinion of the complainant, is objectionable and he shall also furnish to the newspaper, news agency, editor or the working journalist, as the case may be, the grounds for holding such opinion. The complainant shall, along with the complaint, enclose a copy of the letter written by him to the newspaper, news agency, editor or other working journalist together with a copy of the reply, if any received by him, provided that the chairman may in his discretion waive this condition;

(d) in case where the complaint is that an editor or a working journalist has committed any professional misconduct, other than the way of the publication or non-publication of any matter in a newspaper, the complainant shall set out clearly in detail the facts which according to him justify the complaint and the provisions of clause (c) above shall also apply to such complaints.

(e) In every case place all other relevant facts before the council; and

(f) (i) In the case of a complaint relating to the publication or non-publication of any matter in respect of newspaper or news agency the same shall be lodged with the council within the following periods of its publication or non-publication: A. Dailies, news agencies and weeklies... within two months B. In all other cases... within four months Provided that a relevant publication of an earlier date may be referred to in the complaint.

(ii) In the case of a complaint against an editor or working journalist under clause (d) above the same shall be lodged within four months of the misconduct complained of:

Provided that the council may, if satisfied that the complainant has acted promptly, but that the delay in filing the complaint within the period prescribed under subclause (i) or sub-clause (ii) of regulation (3)1(f) has been caused by reason of the time taken to comply with the condition laid down in sub clause (c) supra or on account of other sufficient cause condone the delay and entertain the complaint. The power of condonation shall be exercised by the chairman, subject to the approval of the council.

(2) The complainant while presenting the complaint shall at the foot thereof make and subscribe to a declaration to the effect:

(i) that to the best of his knowledge and belief he has placed all the relevant facts before the council and that no proceedings are pending in any court of law in respect of any matter alleged in the complaint.

(ii) that he shall inform the council forthwith if during the pendency of the inquiry before the council any matter alleged in the complaint becomes the subject-matter of any proceeding in a court of law.

4. Return of complaint:

(1) Where a complainant does not comply with the requirements of regulation 3, the chairman may return the complaint asking the complainant to bring it in conformity with such requirements and represent it within such time as he may fit in that behalf.

(2) The complainant shall be informed of the reasons for the return of the complaint.

5. Issue of notice:

   (1) As soon as possible, and in any case not later than 15 days from the date of receipt of a complaint, under the direction of the chairman, a copy thereof shall be sent to the newspaper, news agency, editor or other working journalist against which or whom the complaint has been made, under regulation three along with a notice requiring the newspaper, news agency, editor or other working journalist, as the case may be, to show cause why action should not be taken under section 14 of the act.

   Provided that in appropriate cases the chairman shall have the discretion to extend time for the issuance of the notice.

   Provided further that the chairman may decide not to issue a notice to show cause to the newspaper, news agency, editor or working journalist where, in his opinion, there is no sufficient ground for holding an inquiry. The council at its next meeting shall be apprised by the chairman of the reasons for his decision not to issue a 'showcause' notice and it may pass such orders as it deems fit.

   (2) The notice issued under sub-regulation (I) above shall be sent to the newspaper, news agency, editor or other working journalist concerned by registered post, acknowledgment due, at the address furnished in the complaint.

6. Filing of written statement:

   (1) The newspaper, news agency, editor or other working journalist against which or whom the complaint is made may, within 14 days from the date of service of the copy of the complaint and notice under regulation 5 or within such further time as may be granted by the chairman in this behalf, submit a written statement in reply to the complaint.

   (2) A copy of the written statement when received shall be forwarded to the complainant for his information.

(3) After receipt of the complaint or written statement, the chairman may, if he considers necessary, call for any further information either from the complainant or the respondent newspaper, news agency, editor or working journalist, as the case may be, in order to clarify matters appearing in the complaint or written statement and in doing so, may call for such documents or further statements as he might consider necessary. All the document and statements called for by him shall form part of the record and shall be placed before the committee at the time of the inquiry.

7. Power to call for additional particulars etc: The committee may after considering the complaint and the written statement, call for such additional particulars or documents or relevant to the subject-matter of the case as it may consider necessary from both the parties or either of them.

8. Rejection of complaint of the same nature previously inquired into:

(1) Where at any time in the course of the inquiry into the complaint it appears to the committee that the subject-matter of the complaint is substantially the same as, or has been covered by any former complaint dealt with by the council under these regulations, the committee shall hear the complainant, if he desires to be heard and also if the committee considers it necessary, the newspaper, news agency, editor or other working journalist, as the case may be, and make its recommendation to the council which may pass such order as may be considered necessary and the same shall be duly communicated to the parties.

9. Inquiry by the committee: Notice of the time, date and place of hearing shall be served on the complainant as well as on the newspaper, news agency, editor and working journalist, as the case may be, and shall be sent by registered post, acknowledgment due. In the inquiry

before the committee, the parties shall be entitled to adduce relevant evidence, oral or documentary, and make submissions in support of their contentions.

(2) At the close of the inquiry, the committee shall make a report of its findings on the allegations contained in the complaint together with its reasons and submit the record of the case to the council.

10. Decision by the council:

(1) The council shall after perusing the record of the case, pass orders giving its decision or it may remit the case to the committee for such further inquiry as the council may deem necessary and after receipt of its report dispose of the case.

(2) Every case shall be determined by a majority of votes of the members of the council present and voting, and in the event of the votes being equal, the chairman shall have a casting vote and shall exercise the same.

(3) The order of the council shall be communicated in writing to the parties to the case.

11. Appearance of parties etc: In any inquiry under these regulations, the editor, news agency or other working journalist, or any authority including government, or the newspaper through its editor, against which or whom a complaint has been made may appear in person, or with the permission of the committee or council as the case may be, by a counsellor or a duly authorised representative.

12. Restrictions on power of members to discuss and vote in certain cases: No members of the committee shall vote or take part in the discussion of, and no member of the council shall vote or take part in the discussion of any complaint coming up for consideration at a meeting of the committee or the council if the case is one in which he is personally involved or has any direct or indirect interest by himself or his partner, or in which he is interested professionally on behalf of a client or as an agent or representative for any newspaper, news

agency, editor or other working journalist as the case may be.

13. Power to take suo motu action: The chairman may suo motu issue notice or, as the case may be, take action in respect of any matter which falls within the mischief of section 14 (1) of the act or in respect of or relating to any matter falling under section 13 (2) thereof and thereupon the procedure prescribed by these regulations from regulation five onwards shall be followed as if it were a complaint under regulation three.

14. Procedure in respect of complaints etc. under section 13: The procedure prescribed by these regulations in respect of complaints under section 14 (1) of the act shall apply, as far as may be, to complaints or representations received by the council with regard to any subject falling within the provisions of section 13.

15. Procedure in matters not provided for in these regulations:

The council as also the committee shall have the power to regulate their own procedure in respect of any matter for which no provision or inadequate provision is made in these regulations and shall also have the power in appropriate cases to hold inquiries in camera.

The Working Journalists and Other Newspaper Employees (Conditions of Service) and Miscellaneous Provisions Act, 1955

The Working Journalists and other Newspaper Employees (Conditions of Service) and Miscellaneous Provisions Act, 1955, together with the Working Journalists (Conditions of Service) and Miscellaneous Provisions Rules 1975, covers rights of journalists like leave (including maternity) and holidays, payment of gratuity, retrenchment, hours of work, compensation for overtime and the setting-up of a wage board.

Chapter 1 (Preliminary)

(1) (a) Short title and commencement:

This act may be called Working Journalists and other Newspaper Employees (Conditions of service) and Miscellaneous Provisions Act, 1955.

(b) It extends to the whole of India, except the state of Jammu and Kashmir.

(2) (a) Definitions:

(b) 'Newspaper' means any printed periodical work containing public news or comments on public news and includes such other class of printed periodical work as many, from time to time, be notified in this behalf by the central government in the official gazette.

(c) 'Newspaper employees' means any working journalists and includes any other person employed to do any work in or in relation to any newspaper establishment.

(d) 'Newspaper establishment' means an establishment under the control of any person or body of persons, whether incorporated or not for any production or publication of one or more newspaper or for conducting any news agency or syndicate.

(f) 'Working journalists' means a person whose principal avocation is that of a journalist and (who is employed as such, either whole-time or part-time in, or in relation to, one or more newspaper establishment), and includes an editor, a leader writer, news-editor, sub-editor, feature-writer, copy-tester, reporter, correspondent, cartoonist, news-photographer and proof-reader, but does not include any such person who-(a) is employed mainly in a managerial or administrative capacity or (b) being employed in a supervisory capacity, performs, either by the nature of duties attached to his office of by reasons of the power vested in him, and function mainly of a managerial nature.

Chapter 2 Working journalist

(3) Sec 25-f of the aforesaid act, in its application to working journalist, shall be construed as in Cl.

(a) thereof, for the period of notice referred to therein in relation to the retrenchmcnt of a workman, the following periods in relation to the retrenchment of a working journalist has been substituted, namely- (a) six months, in case of an editor, (b) three months, in case of any other working journalists.

Termination of service without notice-effect thereof- where a journalist was permitted to continue into employment even after he has attained the age of superannuation, but later on his service were terminated without giving him notice or retrenchment compensation, it was held by the court that the action of the management of the company in terminating the services was illegal and improper.

(4) Special provisions in respect of certain cases of retrenchment:

Where at any time between July 14, 1954 and March 12, 1955, any working journalist had been retrenched, he shall be entitled to receive from employer-

(a) Wages for one month at the rate to which he was entitled immediately before his retrenchment, unless he has been given one month notice in writing before such retrenchment; and

(b) Compensation which shall be equivalent to 15 days average pay for every completed years of service under that employer or any part thereof in excess of six months.

(5) Payment of gratuity: Where

(a) any working journalist has been in continuous service, whether before or after the commencement of this act for not less than three years in any newspaper establishment and

(i) his services are terminated by the employer in relation to that newspaper establishment for any reason whatsoever, otherwise than a punishment inflicted by way of disciplinary action or

(ii) he retires from services on reaching the age of superannuation or

(b) any working journalist has been in continuous service whether before or after the commencement of this act for not less than 10 years in any newspaper establishment and he voluntarily resigns on or after July 1, 1961 from services in that newspaper establishment on any ground what so ever other than on the ground of conscience or,

(c) any working journalist has been in continuous service whether before or after the commencement of this act for not less than three years in any newspaper establishment and he voluntarily resigned on or after July 1, 1961, from services in that newspaper establishment on any ground whatsoever other than on the ground of conscience or

(d) any working journalist dies while he is in service in any newspaper establishment

(6) Hours of work

(1) Subject to any rules that may be made under this act, no working journalist shall be required or allowed to work in any newspaper establishment for more than 144 hours during any periods of four consecutive weeks, exclusive of time for meals.

(2) Every working journalist shall be allowed during any period of seven consecutive days rest for a period of not less than 24 consecutive hours, the period between 10 pm and 6 pm being included therein (Explanation-for the purpose of this section, 'week' means a period of seven days beginning at midnight on Saturday.)

The maximum hour of work for any period of consecutive weeks is 144 hours.

Working Journalists (Conditions of Service) and Miscellaneous Provisions Rules, 1975

Chapter 3 Hours of work

(1) Special provisions regarding editor, etc (hours of work)-The provision of this chapter shall not apply

to editor, or to correspondents, reporters or news photographers

(2) Not withstanding any thing contained in sub rule (1) the following provision shall apply to every correspondent, reporter, news photographer stationed at the place at which the newspaper (in relation to person is employed) namely

(a) Subject to such agreement as may be arrived at either collectively or individually between the parties concerned, every correspondent, reporter or news photographer shall, once he enters upon duty on any day, be deemed to be on duty throughout that day till he finishes all the work assigned to him during the day:

Provided that if such correspondent, reporter or news photographer has had at his disposal for rest any interval or intervals for a total period of two hours or less between any two or more assignments of work, he shall not be on duty during such period. Provided further that where the total period of such interval or intervals exceeds two hours, he shall be deemed to be on duty during the period which is in excess of the said period of two hours.

(b) Any period of work in excess of 36 hours during any week (which shall be considered as a unit of work for the purpose of this subrule) shall be compensated by rest during the succeeding week and shall be given in one or more spells of not more than three hours each.

Provided that where the aggregate of the excess hours worked falls short of three hours, the duration of rest shall be limited only to such excess.

(8) Normal working days. The number of hours which shall constitute a normal working day for working journalists exclusive of time for meals shall exceed six hours per day in case of a day shift and five and half hours per

day in case of night shift and no working journalist shall ordinarily be required or allowed to work for longer than the number of hours constituting a normal working day.

(10) Compensation for overtime work. When a working journalist works for more than six hours on any day in the case of day shift, and more than five and half hours in case of night shift, he shall in respect of that overtime work, be compensated in the form of hours of rest equal in number to the hours for which he has worked overtime.

Chapter 4 Holidays

(13) The number of holidays in a year

A working journalist shall be entitled to 10 holidays in a calendar year and

(15) Shall be entitled to wages on all holidays if he was on duty.

(16) A working journalist shall be entitled to wages for weekly day of rest if he was on duty.

Chapter 5 Leave

Without prejudice to such holidays, casual leave or other kind of leave as may be prescribed, every working journalist shall be entitled to-

(25) (a) Earned leave on full wages for not less than one-eleventh of the period spent on duty, provided that he shall cease to earn such leave when the earned leave due amounts to 90 days.

(28) Leave on medical certificate: 1) A working journalist shall be entitled to leave on medical certificate on one-half of wages for not less than one-eighteenth of the period of service.

(29) Maternity leave-

(1) A female working journalist who has put in not less than one year's service in the newspaper establishment in which she is for the time being employed shall be granted maternity leave on full

wages on production of a medical certificate from an authorised medical practitioner for a period which may extend for three months from the date of its commencement or six weeks from the confinement whichever is earlier.

(2) Leave of any other may be granted in continuation of maternity leave.

(3) Maternity leave shall also be granted in case of miscarriage, including abortion, subject to the condition that the leave does not exceeds six weeks.

(30) Quarantine leave-Quarantine leave on full wage shall be granted by newspaper establishment on the certificate of authorised medical practitioner for a period not exceeding 21 days or in exceptional circumstances, 30 days.

(31) Extraordinary leave-A working journalist who has no leave to his credit may be granted, at the discretion of newspaper establishment in which such working journalist is employed leave not due.

(33) Study leave may be granted in same pattern.

(34) Casual leave-(1) A working journalist shall be eligible for casual leave at the discretion of newspaper establishment for 15 days in a calendar year.

Setting of the Wage Board

For the purpose of fixing or revising rates of wages in respect of working journalists, the central government shall as and when necessary constitute a wage board which shall consist of-

(a) Three persons representing employers in relation to newspaper establishments

(b) Three persons representing working journalists

(c) Four independent persons, one of whom shall be a person who is or has been a judge of high court or supreme court and who shall be appointed by the government as the chairman.

The Working Journalists and other Newspaper Employees (Conditions of Service) and Miscellaneous Provisions Rules, 1957.

In exercise of the powers conferred by section 29 of the Working Journalists (Conditions of Service) and Miscellaneous Provisions Act, 1955 (45 of 1955), the Central Government hereby makes the following Rules, namely-1. Vide S.R.O. 1737, dated 23rd May, 1957.

Chapter I: Preliminary

1. Short title-These rules may be called the Working Journalists (Conditions of Service) and Miscellaneous Provisions Rules, 1957.
2. Definitions-In these rules, unless the context otherwise requires,-
   (a) 'Act' means the Working Journalists (Conditions of Service) and Miscellaneous Provisions Act, 1955 (45 of 1955);

   (b) 'Authorised medical practitioner' means a registered medical practitioner designated as such under rule 24 and where no such practitioner has been designated, any registered medical practitioner;

   (c) 'Average pay' shall have the meaning assigned to it in the Industrial Disputes Act, 1947 (14 of 1947);

   (d) 'Competent officer' means an office designated as such under rule 17;

   (f) 'Form' means a form appended to these rules;

   (g) 'Leave' means earned leave, leave on medical certificate, maternity leave, extraordinary leave, leave not due, casual leave, study leave or quarantine leave;

   (h) 'Earned leave', means leave admissible under clause (a) of section 7 of the act;

   (i) 'Leave on medical certificate' means leave admissible under clause (b) of section 7 of the act;

(j) 'Leave not due' means leave which is not due to a working journalist but which may be granted to him in anticipation of its being earned subsequently;

(k) 'Quarantine leave' means leave of absence from duty by reason of the presence of an infectious disease in the family or household of a working journalist;

(l) 'Study leave' means leave granted to a working journalist to enable him to undergo any special course of training which may be of use to him in his journalistic career; and

(m) Shifts': 'day shift' means a shift when any hours of work of the shift do not fall between the hours of 11 pm and 5 am; 'night shift' means a shift when any hours of work fall between the hours of 11 pm and 5 am.

Chapter II: Gratuity

3. Payment of gratuity-Gratuity shall be paid to a working journalist or, in the case of his death, his nominee or nominees or, if there is no nomination in force at the time of the death of the working journalist, his family, as soon as possible after it becomes due and in any case not later than three months.

4. Gratuity due to a deceased working journalist to whom payable-On death of a working journalist-

   (a) If a nomination made by him in accordance with Rule 5 subsists, the gratuity shall be paid to his nominee or nominees in accordance with such nomination; and

   (b) If no nomination subsists or if that nomination relates only to a part of the gratuity, the amount of the gratuity or the part thereof to which the nomination does not relate, as the case may be, shall be paid to his family.

5. Nominations-

   (1) A working journalist shall, as soon as he completes three years of continuous service, or in the case of

those who have completed three years of continuous service at the commencement of the act, as soon as may be after these rules come into force, make a nomination in form A conferring the right to receive any gratuity payable under the act, in the event of this death before the amount has become payable of, where the amount has become payable, before the payment has been made.

[Where the nominee is a minor, a working journalist shall appoint any person in Form AA to receive the gratuity in the event of working journalist's death during the minority of the nominee.]

(2) A working journalist may, in his nomination distribute the amount that may be come due to him amongst his nominees at his own discretion.

(3) A nomination made under sub-rule (1) 4 may at any time be modified by the working journalist after giving a written notice of his intention to do so in Form B. If the nominee predeceases the working journalist, the interest of the nominee shall revert to the working journalist, who may make a fresh nomination in accordance with these rules.

(4) A nomination or its modification shall take effect, to the extent it is valid on the date on which it is received by the newspaper establishment.

6. Deductions from gratuity-The gratuity will be subject to deductions on account of overpayments made to a working journalist by the newspaper establishment liable to pay such gratuity and monies borrowed by the working journalist from such newspaper establishment.

Chapter III: Hours of work

7. Special provisions regarding editor's etc.-

(1) The provision of this chapter shall not apply to editors, or to correspondents, reporters or news-photographers.

(2) Notwithstanding anything contained in sub-rule (1), the following provisions shall apply to every correspondent, reporter or news-photographer stationed at the place at which the newspaper (in relation to which any such person is employed) is published, namely:

(a) Subject to such agreement as may be arrived at either collectively or individually between the parties concerned, every such correspondent, reporter or news photographer shall, once he enters upon duty on any day, be deemed to be on duty throughout that day in he finishes all the work assigned to him during that day: provided that if such correspondent, reporter or news-photographer has had at his disposal for rest any interval or intervals for a total period of two hours or less between any two or more assignments of work, he shall not be deemed to be on duty during Such period; provided further that where the total period of such interval or intervals exceeds two hours, he shall be deemed to be on duty during the period, which is in excess of the said period of two hours;

(b) Any period of work in excess of 36 hours during any week (which shall be considered as a unit of work for the purposes of this sub-rule) shall be compensated by rest during the succeeding week and shall be given in one or more spells of not less than three hours each; provided that where the aggregate of the excess hours worked falls short of three hours, the duration of rest shall be limited only to such excess.

8. Normal working day-The number of hours which shall constitute a normal working day for a working journalist exclusive of the time for meals shall not exceed six hours per day in the case of a day shift and five and half hours per day in the case of a night shift and no

working journalist shall ordinarily be required or allowed to work for longer than the number of hours constituting a normal working day.

9. Interval for rest-Subject to such agreement as may be arrived at between a newspaper establishment and working journalists employed in that establishment, the periods of work for working journalists shall be so fixed that no working journalist shall work for more than four hours in the case of day shift and three hours in the case of night shift before lie had had an interval of rest, in the case of day shift for one hour, and in the case of nigh shift for half an hour.
10. Compensation for overtime work-When a working journalist works for more than six hours on any day in the case of a day shift and more than five-and-a-half hours in the case of a night shift lie shall, in respect of that overtime work, be compensated in the form of hours of rest equal in number to the hours for which he has worked overtime.
11. Conditions governing night shifts-No working journalist shall be employed on a night shift continuously for more than one week at a time or for more than one week in any period of 14 days: provided that, subject to the previous approval of the state labour commissioner or any authority appointed by the state government in this behalf, the limit prescribed in this rule may be exceeded where special circumstances so require.
12. Interval preceding change of shift-In the case of change of shift from night shift to day shift or vice versa, there shall be an interval of not less than 24 consecutive hours between the two shifts and in the case of a change from one day shift to another day shift or from one night shift to another night shift there shall be interval of not less than 12 consecutive hours. Provided that no such interval may be allowed if such interval either coincides with, or falls within, the interval enjoyed by a working journalist under sub-section (2) of section 6 of the act.

Chapter IV: Holidays

13. Number of holidays in a year-A working journalist shall be entitled to 10 holidays in a calendar year.
14. Compensatory holidays-If a working journalist is required to attend on a holiday, a compensatory holiday shall be given to him, within 30 days immediately following the holiday, on a day mutually agreed upon by him and his employer.
15. Wages for holidays-A working journalist shall be entitled to wages on all holidays as if he was on duty.
16. Wages for weekly day of rest-A working journalist shall be entitled to wages for the weekly day of rest as if he was on duty.

Chapter V: Leave

17. Competent officers-Every newspaper establishment may designate one or more officers in that establishment as competent officers for the purposes of this chapter.
18. Application for leave-
    (1) A working journalist who desires to obtain leave of absence shall apply in writing to the competent officer.
    (2) Application for leave, other than casual leave, leave on medical certificate and quarantine leave, shall be made not less than one month before the date of commencement of leave, except in urgent or unforeseen circumstances.
19. Recording of reason for refusal or postponement of leave-If leave is refused or postponed, the competent officer shall record the reasons for such refusal or postponement, as the case may be, and send a copy of the order to the working journalist.
20. Affixing of holidays to leave-Holidays, other than weekly days of rest, shall not be prefixed or suffixed to any leave without the prior sanction of the competent officer.
21. Holidays intervening, during period of leave-A holiday, including a weekly rest day, intervening during any

leave granted under these rules shall form part of the period of leave.

22. Recall before expiry of leave-

    (1) A newspaper establishment may recall a working journalist on leave if that establishment considers it necessary to do so. In the event of such recall such working journalist shall be entitled to travelling allowance if at the time of recall he is spending his leave at a place other than his headquarters.

    (2) The traveling allowance, which shall be paid to a working journalist under sub-rule (1), shall be determined in accordance with the rules of the newspaper establishment governing traveling allowance for journeys undertaken by working journalists in the course of their duties.

23. Production of medical certificate of fitness before resumption of duty-A working journalist who has availed himself of leave for reasons of health may, before he resumes duty, be required by his employer to produce a medical certificate of fitness from an authorised medical practitioner, any registered medical practitioner or the medical officer who issued the medical certificate under sub-rule (2) of rules 28.

24. Designation of authorised medical practitioner-Every newspaper establishment may designate one or more registered medical practitioner as authorised medical practitioners for the purposes of these rules.

25. Earned leave-

    (1) A working journalist shall be entitled to earned leave on full wages for a period not less than one month for every 11 months spent on duty: Provided that he shall cease to earn such leave when the earned leave due amounts to ninety days.

    (2) The period spent on duty shall include the weekly days of rest, holidays, casual leave and quarantine leave.

26. Wages during earned leave-A working journalist on earned leave shall draw in wages equal to his average monthly wages earned during the period of 12 complete months spent on duty, or if the period is less than 12 complete months, during the entire such period, immediately preceding the month in which the leave commences.

27. Cash compensation for earned leave not availed of-

(1) When a working journalist voluntarily relinquishes his post or retires from service on reaching the age of superannuation, he shall be entitled to cash compensation for earned leave not availed of unto a maximum of 30 days: Provided that a working journalist who has been refused earned leave due to him shall be entitled to get cash compensation for the earned leave so refused: Provided further that in the case of a working journalist who the while in service and who has not availed himself of the earned leave due to him immediately preceding the date of his death, his heirs shall be entitled to cash compensation for the leave not so availed of.

(2) When a working journalist's services are terminated for any reason, whatsoever, other than as punishment inflicted by way of disciplinary action, he shall be entitled to cash compensation for earned leave not availed of unto a maximum of 90 days.

(3) The cash compensation shall not be less than the amount of wages due to a working journalist for the period of leave not availed of, the relevant wage being that which would have been payable to him had he actually proceeded on leave on the day immediately preceding the occurrence of any of the events specified in sub-rules (1) or (2), as the case may be.

28. Leave on medical certificate-

(1) A working journalist shall be entitled to leave on medical certificate on one-half of the wages at the rate of not less than one month for every 18 months

of service: Provided that he shall cease to earn such leave when the leave on medical certificate amounts to 90 days.

(2) The medical certificate shall be from an authorised medical practitioner: Provided that when a working journalist has proceeded to a place other than his headquarters with the permission of his employer and falls in, he may produce a medical certificate from any registered medical practitioner: Provided further that the employer may, when the registered medical practitioner is not in the service of the government, arrange at his own expense, the medical examination of the working journalist concerned, by any government medical officer not below the rank of a civil assistant surgeon or any other medical officer in charge of a hospital run by a local authority or a public organisation at that place like the Kasturba Gandhi Trust, Kamladevi Nehru Trust or Tata Memorial Trust.

(3) Leave on medical certificate may be taken in continuation with earned leave provided that the total duration of earned leave and leave on medical certificate taken together shall not exceed 120 days at any one time.

(4) A working journalist shall be entitled at his option to convert leave on medical certificate on one-half of the wages to half the amount of leave on full wages.

(5) The ceiling laid down in the provisos to sub-rule (1) and sub-rule (3) on the accumulation and total duration of leave may be relaxed by the competent officer in the cases of working journalists suffering from lingering illness such as tuberculosis.

(6) Leave on medical certificate or converted leave on medical certificate referred to in sub-rules (1) and (4) may be granted to a working journalist at his request not withstanding that earned leave is due to him.

29. Maternity leave-

(1) A female working journalist who has put in not less than one year's service in the news paper establishment in which she for the time being employed shall be granted maternity leave on full wages for a period which he may extend unto three months from the date of its commencement or six weeks from the date of confinement whichever be earlier.

(2) Leave of any other kind may also be granted in continuation of maternity leave.

(3) Maternity leave shall also be granted in cases of miscarriage, including abortion, subject to the condition that the leave does not exceed six weeks.

30. Quarantine leave-Quarantine leave on full wages shall be granted by the newspaper establishment on the certificate of the authorised medical practitioner designated as such under rule 24 or where, there is no such authorised medical practitioner by a district public health officer or other municipal health officer of similar status, for a period not exceeding 21 days, or, in exceptional circumstances, 30 days. Any leave necessary for quarantine purposes in excess of that period shall be adjusted against any other leave that may be due to the working journalist.

31. Extraordinary leave-A working journalist who has no leave to his credit may be granted extraordinary leave without wages at the discretion of the newspaper establishment in which such working journalist is employed.

32. Leave not due-A working journalist who has no leave to his credit may be granted at the discretion of the newspaper establishment in which such working journalist is employed leave not due.

33. Study leave-A working journalist may be granted study leave with or without wages at the discretion of the newspaper establishment in which such working journalist is employed.

34. Casual leave-

(1) A working journalist shall be eligible for casual leave at the discretion of the newspaper establishment for 15 days in a calendar year: Provided that not more than five days' casual leave shall be taken at any one time and such leave shall not be combined with any other leave.

(2) Casual leave not availed of during a calendar year will not be carried forward to the following year.

35. Wages during casual leave-A working journalist on casual leave shall be entitled to wages as if he was on duty.

Chapter VI: Miscellaneous

35A. Manner of giving notice under section 12 of the act-Notice required to be given under proviso to clause (a) of sub-section (2) of section 12 of the act shall in Form H and shall be published in the Official Gazette and in leading newspapers.

36. Application under section 17 of the act-An application under section 17 of the act shall be made in Form C to the government of the state, where the central office or the branch office of the newspaper establishment in which the newspaper employee is employed, is situated.

37. Maintenance of registers, records and muster rolls-Every newspaper establishment shall prepare and maintain the following registers, records and muster-rolls:

(i) A register of employees in Form D.

(ii) Service registers in respect of all working journalists in Form E.

(iii) Leave registers in respect of all working journalists in Form F.

(iv) A muster roll in Form G: Provided that the leave register in Form F and the muster-roll in Form G may not be maintained by the newspaper establishments to which the Minimum Wages Act, 1948 and/or the Shops and Commercial

Establishments Act of the state concerned apply and which are required under those acts of the rules made thereunder to maintain such or similar forms.

38. Effect of rules and agreements inconsistent with these rules-The provisions of these rules shall have effect notwithstanding anything inconsistent therewith contained in any other rule or agreement or contract of service applicable to a working journalist: Provided that where under any schedule, agreement or contract of service or otherwise, a working journalist is entitled to benefits in respect of any matter which are more favourable to him than those to which he would be entitled under these rules, the working journalist shall continue to be entitled to the more favourable benefits in respect of that matter, notwithstanding that he receives benefit in respect of other matters under these rules.

5

Freedom of Press Worldwide

AN OVERVIEW

Every year, the Reporters Without Borders organization establishes a ranking of countries in terms of their freedom of the press. The list is based on responses to surveys sent to journalists that are members of partner organisations of the RWB, as well as related specialists such as researchers, jurists and human rights activists. The survey asks questions about direct attacks on journalists and the media as well as other indirect sources of pressure against the free press, such as pressure on journalists by non-governmental groups. RWB is careful to note that the index only deals with press freedom, and does not measure the quality of journalism.

In 2003, the countries where press was the most free were Finland, Iceland, the Netherlands and Norway.

In 2004, apart from the above countries, Denmark, Ireland, Slovakia, and Switzerland were tied at the top of the list, followed by New Zealand and Latvia. The countries with the least degree of press freedom were ranked with North Korea having the worst, followed by Burma, Turkmenistan, Eritrea, China (mainland only), Vietnam, Nepal, Saudi Arabia, and Iran.

Non-democratic States

According to Reporters Without Borders, more than a third of the world's people live in countries where there is no press freedom. Overwhelmingly, these people live in countries where there is no system of democracy or where there are serious deficiencies in the democratic process. Freedom of the press is an extremely problematic concept for most non-democratic systems of government since, in the modern age, strict control of access to information is critical to the existence of most non-democratic governments and their associated control systems and security apparatus. To this end, most non-democratic societies employ state-run news organisations to promote the propaganda critical to maintaining an existing political power base and suppress (often very brutally, through the use of police, military, or intelligence agencies) any significant attempts by the media or individual journalists to challenge the approved "government line" on contentious issues. In such countries, journalists operating on the fringes of what is deemed to be acceptable will very often find themselves the subject of considerable intimidation by agents of the state. This can range from simple threats to their professional careers (firing, professional blacklisting) to death threats, kidnapping, torture, and assassination.

Reporters Without Borders reports that, in 2003, 42 journalists lost their lives pursuing their profession and that, in the same year, at least 130 journalists were in prison as a result of their occupational activities.

In 2005, 63 journalists and 5 media assistants were killed worldwide.

- The Lira Baysetova case in Kazakhstan.
- In Nepal, Eritrea and China (mainland only), journalists may spend years in jail simply for using the "wrong" word or photo.
- The George R. Gongadze case in Ukraine.

HISTORY

England

The English revolution of 1688 resulted in the supremacy of Parliament over the Crown and, above all, the right of revolution. The main theoretical inspirator of Western liberalism was John Locke. Having decided to grant some of his basic freedoms in the state of nature (natural rights) to the common good, the individual placed some of his rights in trusteeship with the government. A social contract was entered into by the people, and the Sovereign (*i.e.* government) was instructed to protect these individual rights on behalf of the people, argues John Locke in his book Two Treatises of Government.

Until 1694, England had an elaborate system of licensing. No publication was allowed without the accompaniment of a government-granted license. Fifty years earlier, at a time of civil war, John Milton wrote his pamphlet Areopagitica. In this work Milton argued forcefully against this form of government censorship and parodied the idea, writing "when as debtors and delinquents may walk abroad without a keeper, but unoffensive books must not stir forth without a visible jailer in their title." Although at the time it did little to halt the practice of licensing it would be viewed later a significant milestone in press freedom.

Milton's central argument was that the individual is capable of using reason and distinguishing right from wrong, good from bad. In order to be able to exercise this ration right, the individual must have unlimited access to the ideas of his fellow men in "a free and open encounter". From Milton's writings developed the concept of "the open market place of ideas": When people argue against each other, the good arguments will prevail. One form of speech that was widely restricted in England was the law of seditious libel that made criticizing of the government a crime. The King was above public criticism and that statements critical of the government were forbidden, according to the English Court of the Star Chamber. Truth was not a defense to seditious libel because the goal was to prevent and punish all condemnation of the government.

John Stuart Mill approached the problem of authority versus liberty from the viewpoint of a 19th century utilitarian: The individual has the right of expressing himself so long as he does not harm other individuals. The good society is one in which the greatest number of persons enjoy the greatest possible amount of happiness. Applying these general principles of liberty to freedom of expression, Mill states that if we silence an opinion, we may silence the truth. The individual freedom of expression is therefore essential to the well-being of society.

Mill's application of the general principles of liberty is expressed in his book On Liberty: "If all mankind minus one, were of one opinion, and one, and only one person were of the contrary opinion, mankind would be no more justified in silencing that one person, than he, if he had the power, would be justified in silencing mankind".

Germany

The dictatorship of Adolf Hitler largely suppressed freedom of the press through Joseph Goebbels' Propaganda Ministry. As the Ministry's name implies, propaganda did not carry the negative connotations that it does today (or did in the Allied countries); how-to manuals were openly distributed by that same ministry explaining the craft of effective propaganda. The Ministry also acted as a central control-point for all media, issuing orders as to what stories could be run and what stories would be suppressed. Anyone involved in the film industry—from directors to the lowliest assistant—had to sign an oath of loyalty to the Nazi Party, due to opinion-changing power Goebbels perceived movies to have. (Goebbels himself maintained some personal control over every single film made in Nazi Europe.) Journalists who crossed the Propaganda Ministry were routinely imprisoned or shot as traitors.

India

The Indian Constitution, while not mentioning the word "press", provides for "the right to freedom of speech and expression" (Article 19(1)a). However this right is subject to restrictions under subclause (2), whereby this freedom can be restricted for reasons of "sovereignty and integrity of India, the security of the State, friendly relations with foreign States, public order, preserving decency, preserving morality, in relation to contempt of court, defamation, or incitement to an offence". Laws such as the Official Secrets Act and Prevention of Terrorism Act (PoTA) have been used to limit press freedom. Under PoTA, person could be detained for upto six months for being in contact with a terrorist or terrorist group. PoTA was repealed in 2006, but the Official Secrets Act 1923 continues.

For the first half-century of independence, media control by the state was the major constraint on press freedom. Indira Gandhi famously stated in 1975 that All India Radio is "a

Government organ, it is going to remain a Government organ..." With the liberalization starting in the 1990s, private control of media has burgeoned, leading to increasing independence and greater scrutiny of government. Organizations like Tehelka and NDTV have been particularly influential, e.g. in bringing about the resignation of powerful Haryana minister Vinod Sharma.

United States

John Hancock was the first person to write newspapers in the British colonies in North America were published "by authority," that is, under license from and as the mouthpiece of the colonial governors. The first regularly published newspaper was the Boston News-Letter of John Campbell, published weekly beginning in 1704. The early colonial publishers were either postmasters or government printers, and therefore unlikely to challenge government policies.

The first independent newspaper in the colonies was the New-England Courant, published in Boston by James Franklin beginning in 1721. A few years later, Franklin's younger brother, Benjamin, purchased the Pennsylvania Gazette of Philadelphia, which became the leading newspaper of the colonial era.

During this period, newspapers were unlicensed, and able freely to publish dissenting views, but were subject to prosecution for libel or even sedition if their opinions threatened the government. The notion of "freedom of the press" that later was enshrined in the United States Constitution is generally traced to the seditious libel prosecution of John Peter Zenger by the colonial governor of New York in 1735. In this instance of jury nullification, Zenger was acquitted after his lawyer, Andrew Hamilton, argued to the jury (contrary to established English law) that there was no libel in publishing the truth. Yet even after this celebrated case, colonial governors and assemblies asserted the power to prosecute and even imprison printers for publishing unapproved views.

During the American Revolution, a free press was identified by Revolutionary leaders as one of the elements of liberty that they sought to preserve. The Virginia Declaration of Rights (1776) proclaimed that "the freedom of the press is one of the greatest bulwarks of liberty and can never be restrained but by despotic governments." Similarly, the Constitution of Massachusetts (1780) declared, "The liberty of the press is essential to the security of freedom in a state: it ought not, therefore, to be restrained in this commonwealth." Following these examples, the First Amendment to the United States Constitution restricted Congress from abridging the freedom of the press and the closely associated freedom of speech.

John Locke's ideas had inspired both the French and American revolutions. Thomas Jefferson wanted to unite the two streams of liberalism, the English and the French schools of thought. His goal was to create a government that would provide both security and opportunity for the individual. An active press was essential as a way of educating the population. In order to be able to work freely, the press must be free from control by the state. Jefferson was a person who himself suffered great calumnies of the press. Despite this, in his second inaugural address, he proclaimed that a government that could not stand up under criticism deserved to fall.

Jefferson said: "No experiment can be more interesting than that we are now trying, and which we trust will end in establishing the fact, that man may be governed by reason and truth. Our first object should therefore be, to leave open to him all avenues of the truth".

In 1931, the U.S. Supreme Court decision in Near v. Minnesota used the 14th Amendment to apply the freedom of the press to the States. Other notable cases regarding free press are:

- New York Times Co. v. United States: The Supreme Court upheld the publication of the Pentagon Papers.
- New York Times Co. v. Sullivan: The Court decided that in order for written words to be libel, it must be, first of all, false. It must also be published with the deliberate intent to ruin someone's reputation.

In Branzburg v. Hayes (1972), the Court placed limits on the ability of the Press to refuse a subpoena from a Grand Jury by claiming Freedom of the Press. The issue decided in the case was whether a reporter could refuse to "appear and testify before state and Federal grand juries" by claiming such appearance and testimony "abridges the freedom of speech and press guaranteed by the First Amendment." The 5-4 decision was that such a protection was not provided by the First Amendment.

Notable Exceptions

In 1798, not long after the adoption of the Constitution, the governing Federalist Party attempted to stifle criticism by means of the Alien and Sedition Acts. (It was notable that the Sedition Act made criticism of Congress, and of the President, a crime, but not criticism of the Vice-President. Jefferson, a non-Federalist, was Vice-President at the time the Act was passed.) These restrictions on freedom of the press proved very unpopular and worked against the Federalists. Thomas Jefferson was among those who opposed the Acts, and he was elected President in the election of 1800. Jefferson then pardoned all those convicted under the Acts. He made it a principle not to ask what they had done, but only whether they had been charged under the Acts.

In his first Inaugural Address in 1801 he reiterated his longstanding commitment to freedom of speech and of the press: "If there be any among us who would wish to dissolve this Union or to change its republican form, let them stand undisturbed as monuments of the safety with which error of opinion may be tolerated where reason is left free to combat it."

The Espionage Act of 1917 and the Sedition Act of 1918, which amended it, imposed restrictions on the free press during wartime. It carried fines of $10,000 and up to 20 years imprisonment for people publishing "... disloyal, profane, scurrilous, or abusive language about the form of government of the United States or the Constitution of the United States, or the military or naval forces of the United States..." In Schenck v. United States (1919), the Supreme Court upheld the laws, setting the "Clear and present danger" standard. Congress repealed both laws in 1921, and Brandenburg v. Ohio (1969) revised the "Clear and present danger" test to the "Imminent lawless action" test, which is less restrictive.

1988: Hazelwood School District vs. Kuhlmeier: The Supreme Court upheld that the principal of a school has the right to review and block controversial articles of a school paper funded by the school and published in the school's name.

In the United States in 2005, interpretation of the Bipartisan Campaign Reform Act may consider political statements as being the equivalent of campaign donations. Because access to Internet statements are weakly controlled, the campaign value of statements is not known in advance and a high ultimate value may trigger large fines for violations. This particularly threatens Internet statements by individuals, and ambiguous definitions of membership in the press make the possible effects ambiguous.

IMPLICATIONS OF NEW TECHNOLOGIES

Many of the traditional means of delivering information are being slowly superseded by the increasing pace of modern technological advance. Almost every conventional mode of media and information dissemination has a modern counterpart that offers significant potential advantages to journalists seeking to maintain and enhance their 'freedom of speech'. A few simple examples of such phenomena include:

Terrestrial Television versus Satellite Television: Whilst terrestrial television is relatively easy to manage and manipulate, satellite television is much more difficult to control as journalistic content can easily be broadcast from other jurisdictions beyond the control of individual governments. An example of this in the Middle East is the satellite broadcaster Al Jazeera. This Arabic language media channel operates out of the 'relatively liberal' state of Qatar, and often presents views and content that are problematic to a number of governments in the region and beyond. However, because of the increased affordability and miniaturisation of satellite technology (e.g. dishes and receivers) it is simply not practicable for most states to control popular access to the channel.

Web-based Publishing (e.g., blogging) vs. Traditional Publishing: Traditional magazines and newspapers rely on physical resources (e.g. offices, printing presses) that can easily be targeted and forced to close down. Web-based publishing systems can be run using ubiquitous and inexpensive equipment and can operate from any global jurisdiction, to get control over web publications, nations and organisations, are using Geolocation and Geolocation software.

Voice Over Internet Protocol (VOIP) vs. Conventional Telephony: Although conventional telephony systems are easily tapped and recorded, modern VOIP technology can employ sophisticated encryption systems to evade central monitoring systems. As VOIP and similar technologies become more widespread they are likely to make the effective monitoring of journalists (and their contacts and activities) a very difficult task for governments.

Naturally, governments are responding to the challenges posed by new media technologies by deploying increasingly sophisticated technology of their own (a notable example being China's attempts to impose control of through a state run internet service provider that controls access to the Internet) but it seems that this will becomes an ever increasingly difficult task as nimble, highly motivated journalists continue to find ingenious novel ways to exploit technology and stay one step ahead of the generally slower moving government institutions that they necessarily do battle with.

Journalism ethics and standards include principles of ethics and of good practice to address the specific challenges faced by professional journalists. Historically and currently these principles are most widely known to journalists as their professional "code of ethics" or the "canons of journalism." The basic codes and canons commonly appear in statements drafted by both professional journalism associations and individual print, broadcast, and online news organizations.

While various existing codes have some differences, most share common elements including the principles of-truthfulness, accuracy, objectivity, impartiality, fairness and public accountability-as these apply to the acquisition of newsworthy information and its subsequent reportage to the public.

Like many broader ethical systems, journalism ethics include the principle of "limitation of harm." This often involves the withholding of certain details from reports such as the names of minor children, crime victims' names or information not materially related to particular news reports release of which might, for example, harm someone's reputation.

EVOLUTION AND PURPOSE OF CODES OF JOURNALISM

The principles of good journalism are directed toward bringing the highest quality of news reporting to the public, thus fulfilling the mission of timely distribution of information in service of the public interest. To a large degree, the codes and canons evolved via observation of and response to past ethical lapses by journalists and publishers.

Today, it is common for terms of employment to mandate adherence to such codes equally applicable to both staff and free-lance journalists; journalists may face dismissal for ethical failures. Upholding professional standards also enhances the reputation of and trust in a news organization, which boosts the size of the audience it serves.

Journalistic codes of ethics are designed as guides through numerous difficulties, such as conflicts of interest, to assist journalists in dealing with ethical dilemmas. The codes and canons provide journalists a framework for self-monitoring and self-correction as they pursue professional assignments.

Codes of Practice

While journalists in the United States and European countries have led in formulation and adoption of these standards, such codes can be found in news reporting organizations in most countries with freedom of the press. The written codes and practical standards vary somewhat from country to country and organization to organization, but there is a substantial overlap among mainstream publications and societies.

One of the leading voices in the U.S. on the subject of Journalistic Standards and Ethics is the Society of Professional Journalists. The Preamble to its Code of Ethics states:

Public enlightenment is the forerunner of justice and the foundation of democracy. The duty of the journalist is to further those ends by seeking truth and providing a fair and comprehensive account of events and issues. Conscientious journalists from all media and specialties strive to serve the public with thoroughness and honesty. Professional integrity is the cornerstone of a journalist's credibility. The Radio-Television News Directors Association, an organization exclusively centered on electronic journalism, maintains a code of ethics centering on—public trust, truthfulness, fairness, integrity, independence and accountability.

Examples of journalistic codes of ethics held by international news gathering organizations may be found as follows:

- *British Broadcasting Corporation:* Editorial Guidelines.
- *Canadian Broadcasting Corporation:* Journalistic Standards and Practices
- *Al Jazeera:* Code of Ethics.
- Code of Journalists of the Republic of Slovenia

Common Elements

The primary themes common to most codes of journalistic standards and ethics are the following.

Objectivity

- Unequivocal separation between news and opinion. In-house editorials and opinion (Op-Ed) pieces are clearly separated from news pieces. News reporters and editorial staff are distinct.
- Unequivocal separation between advertisements and news. All advertisements must be clearly identifiable as such.
- Reporter must avoid conflicts of interest-incentives to report a story with a given slant. This includes not taking bribes and not reporting on stories that affect the reporter's personal, economic or political interests.
- Competing points of view are balanced and fairly characterized.
- Persons who are the subject of adverse news stories are allowed a reasonable opportunity to respond to the

adverse information before the story is published or broadcast.

- Interference with reporting by any entity, including censorship, must be disclosed.

Sources

- Confidentiality of anonymous sources.
- Avoidance of anonymous sources when possible.
- Accurate attribution of statements made by individuals or other news media.
- Pictures, sound, and quotations must not be presented in a misleading context (or lack thereof). Simulations, reenactments, alterations, and artistic imaginings must be clearly labelled as such, if not avoided entirely.
- Plagiarism is strongly stigmatized and in many cases illegal.

Accuracy and Standards for Factual Reporting

- Reporters are expected to be as accurate as possible given the time allotted to story preparation and the space available, and to seek reliable sources.
- Events with a single eyewitness are reported with attribution. Events with two or more independent eyewitnesses may be reported as fact. Controversial facts are reported with attribution.
- Independent fact-checking by another employee of the publisher is desirable
- Corrections are published when errors are discovered
- Defendants at trial are treated only as having "allegedly" committed crimes, until conviction, when their crimes are generally reported as fact (unless, that is, there is serious controversy about wrongful conviction).
- Opinion surveys and statistical information deserve special treatment to communicate in precise terms any conclusions, to contextualize the results, and to specify accuracy, including estimated error and methodological criticism or flaws.

Slander and Libel Considerations

- Reporting the truth is never libel, which makes accuracy and attribution very important.
- Private persons have privacy rights that must be balanced against the public interest in reporting information about them. Public figures have fewer privacy rights.
- Publishers vigorously defend libel lawsuits filed against their reporters

HARM LIMITATION PRINCIPLE

During the normal course of an assignment a reporter might go about-gathering facts and details, conducting interviews, doing research, background checks, taking photos, video taping, recording sound—should he or she report everything learned? If so, how should this be done? The principle of limitation of harm means that some weight needs to be given to the negative consequences of full disclosure, creating a practical and ethical dilemma. The Society of Professional Journalists' code of ethics offers the following advice, which is representative of the practical ideals of most professional journalists. Quoting directly:

- Show compassion for those who may be affected adversely by news coverage. Use special sensitivity when dealing with children and inexperienced sources or subjects.
- Be sensitive when seeking or using interviews or photographs of those affected by tragedy or grief.
- Recognize that gathering and reporting information may cause harm or discomfort. Pursuit of the news is not a license for arrogance.
- Recognize that private people have a greater right to control information about themselves than do public officials and others who seek power, influence or attention. Only an overriding public need can justify intrusion into anyone's privacy.
- Show good taste. Avoid pandering to lurid curiosity.

- Be cautious about identifying juvenile suspects or victims of sex crimes.
- Be judicious about naming criminal suspects before the formal filing of charges.
- Balance a criminal suspect's fair trial rights with the public's right to be informed.

Presentation

Ethical standards should not be confused with common standards of quality of presentation, including:

- Correctly spoken or written language (often in a widely spoken and formal dialect, such as Standard English)
- Clarity
- Brevity (or depth, depending on the niche of the publisher)

SELF-REGULATION

In addition to codes of ethics, many news organizations maintain an in-house Ombudsman whose role is, in part, to keep news organizations honest and accountable to the public. The ombudsman is intended to mediate in conflicts stemming from internal and or external pressures, and to maintain accountability to the public for news reported. Also, to foster self-criticism and to encourage adherence to both codified and uncodified ethics and standards.

An alternative is a news council, an industry-wide self-regulation body, such as the Press Complaints Commission, set up by UK newspapers and magazines. Such a body is capable perhaps of applying fairly consistent standards, and of dealing with a higher volume of complaints, but may not escape criticisms of being toothless.

ETHICS AND STANDARDS IN PRACTICE

As with other ethical codes, there is perennial concern that the standards of journalism are being ignored. One of the most controversial issues in modern reporting is media bias, especially on political issues, but also with regard to cultural and other issues. Sensationalism is also a common complaint. Minor factual errors are also extremely common, as almost anyone who is familiar with the subject of a particular report will quickly realize.

There are also some wider concerns, as the media continue to change, for example that the brevity of news reports and use of sound-bites has reduced fidelity to the truth, and may contribute to a lack of needed context for public understanding. From outside the profession, the rise of news management contributes to the real possibility that news media may be deliberately manipulated. Selective reporting (spiking, double standards) are very commonly alleged against newspapers, and by their nature are forms of bias not easy to establish, or guard against.

This section does not address specifics of such matters, but issues of practical compliance, as well as differences between professional journalists on principles.

STANDARDS AND REPUTATION

Among the leading news organizations that voluntarily adopt and attempt to uphold the common standards of journalism ethics described herein, adherence and general quality varies considerably. The professionalism, reliability and public accountability of a news organization are three of its most valuable assets. An organization earns and maintains a strong reputation, in part, through a consistent implementation of ethical standards, which influence its position with the public and within the industry.

Among the most respected western English-language publications, programs and broadcast networks are:

- Washington Post
- New York Times
- Wall Street Journal
- The Christian Science Monitor
- British Broadcasting Corporation (BBC)
- Canadian Broadcasting Corporation (CBC)

- The Globe and Mail, Canada
- The Cable News Network (CNN)
- Corporation for Public Broadcasting, which supports two news platforms:
  - o National Public Radio (NPR)
  - o Public Broadcasting Service (PBS), known in particular for The NewsHour with Jim Lehrer and Frontline

GENRES AND ETHICS

Advocacy journalists-a term of some debate even within the field of journalism-by definition tend to reject "objectivity", while at the same time maintaining many other common standards and ethics.

Creative nonfiction and Literary journalism use the power of language and literary devices more akin to fiction to bring insight and depth into often book-length treatment of the subjects about which they write. Such devices as dialogue, metaphor, digression and other such techniques offer the reader insights not usually found in standard news reportage. However, authors in this branch of journalism still maintain ethical criteria such as factual and historical accuracy as found in standard news reporting. Yet, with brilliant prose, they venture outside the boundaries of standard news reporting in offering richly detailed accounts. One widely regarded author in the genre is Joyce Carol Oates, as with her book on boxer Mike Tyson.

New Journalism and Gonzo journalism also reject some of the fundamental ethical traditions and will set aside the technical standards of journalistic prose in order to express themselves and reach a particular audience or market segment.

Tabloid journalists are often accused of sacrificing accuracy and the personal privacy of their subjects in order to boost sales. Supermarket tabloids are often focused on entertainment rather than news. A few have "news" stories that are so outrageous that they are widely read for entertainment purposes, not for information. Some tabloids do purport to maintain common journalistic standards, but may fall far short in practice. Others make no such claims.

Some publications deliberately engage in satire, but give the publication the design elements of a newspaper, for example, The Onion, and it is not unheard of for other publications to offer the occasional, humorous articles appearing on April Fool's Day.

RELATIONSHIP WITH FREEDOM OF THE PRESS

In countries without freedom of the press, the majority of people who report the news may not follow the above-described standards of journalism. Very often non-free media are prohibited from criticizing the national government, and in many cases are required to distribute propaganda as if it were news. Various other forms of censorship may restrict reporting on issues the government deems sensitive.

VARIATIONS, VIOLATIONS AND CONTROVERSIES

There are a number of finer points of journalistic procedure that foster disagreements in principle and variation in practice among "mainstream" journalists in the free press. Laws concerning libel and slander vary from country to country, and local journalistic standards may be tailored to fit. For example, the United Kingdom has a broader definition of libel than does the United States.

Accuracy is important as a core value and to maintain credibility, but especially in broadcast media, audience share often gravitates toward outlets that are reporting new information first. Different organizations may balance speed and accuracy in different ways. The New York Times, for instance, tends to print longer, more detailed, less speculative, and more thoroughly verified pieces a day or two later than many other newspapers. 24-hour television news networks tend to place much more emphasis on getting the "scoop." Here, viewers may switch channels at a moment's notice; with fierce competition for ratings and a large amount of airtime to fill, fresh material is very valuable. Because of the fast turn-around, reporters for these networks may be under considerable time pressure, which reduces their ability to verify information.

Laws with regard to personal privacy, official secrets, and media disclosure of names and facts from criminal cases and civil lawsuits differ widely, and journalistic standards may vary accordingly. Different organizations may have different answers to questions about when it is journalistically acceptable to skirt, circumvent, or even break these regulations. Another example of differences surrounding harm reduction is the reporting of preliminary election results. In the United States, some news organizations feel that it is harmful to the democratic process to report exit poll results or preliminary returns while voting is still open. Such reports may influence people who vote later in the day, or who are in western time zones, in their decisions about how and whether or not to vote. There is also some concern that such preliminary results are often inaccurate and may be misleading to the public. Other outlets feel that this information is a vital part of the transparency of the election process, and see no harm (if not considerable benefit) in reporting it.

TASTE, DECENCY AND ACCEPTABILITY

Audiences have different reactions to depictions of violence, nudity, coarse language, or to people in any other situation that is unacceptable to or stigmatized by the local culture or laws (such as the consumption of alcohol, homosexuality, illegal drug use, scatological images, etc.). Even with similar audiences, different organizations and even individual reporters have different standards and practices. These decisions often revolve around what facts are necessary for the audience to know.

When certain distasteful or shocking material is considered important to the story, there are a variety of common methods for mitigating negative audience reaction. Advance warning of explicit or disturbing material may allow listeners or readers to avoid content they would rather not be exposed to. Offensive words may be partially obscured or bleeped. Potentially offensive images may be blurred or narrowly cropped. Descriptions may be substituted for pictures; graphic detail might be omitted. Disturbing content might be moved from a cover to an inside page, or from daytime to late evening, when children are less likely to be watching.

There is often considerable controversy over these techniques, especially concern that obscuring or not reporting certain facts or details is self-censorship that compromises objectivity and fidelity to the truth, and which does not serve the public interest. For example, images and graphic descriptions of war are often violent, bloody, shocking and profoundly tragic. This makes certain content disturbing to some audience members, but it is precisely these aspects of war that some consider to be the most important to convey. Some argue that "sanitizing" the depiction of war influences public opinion about the merits of continuing to fight, and about the policies or circumstances that precipitated the conflict. The amount of explicit violence and mutilation depicted in war coverage varies considerable from time to time, from organization to organization, and from country to country.

CAMPAIGNING IN THE MEDIA

Many print publications take advantage of their wide readership and print persuasive pieces in the form of unsigned editorials that represent the official position of the organization. Despite the ostensible separation between editorial writing and news gathering, this practice may cause some people to doubt the political objectivity of the publication's news reporting. (Though usually unsigned editorials are accompanied by a diversity of signed opinions from other perspectives.)

Other publications and many broadcast media only publish opinion pieces that are attributed to a particular individual (who may be an in-house analyst) or to an outside entity. One particularly controversial question is whether media organizations should endorse political candidates for office. Political endorsements create more opportunities to construe favoritism in reporting, and can create a perceived conflict of interest.

Investigative Methods

Investigative journalism is largely an information-gathering exercise, looking for facts that are not easy to obtain by simple requests and searches, or are actively being concealed, suppressed or distorted. Where investigative work involves undercover journalism or use of whistle-blowers, and even more if it resorts to covert methods more typical of private detectives or even spying, it brings a large extra burden on ethical standards.

Anonymous sources are double-edged-they often provide especially newsworthy information, such as classified or confidential information about current events, information about a previously unreported scandal, or the perspective of a particular group that may fear retribution for expressing certain opinions in the press. The downside is that the condition of anonymity may make it difficult or impossible for the reporter to verify the source's statements. Sometimes sources hide their identities from the public because their statements would otherwise quickly be discredited. Thus, statements attributed to anonymous sources may carry more weight with the public than they might if they were attributed. The Washington press has been criticized in recent years for excessive use of anonymous sources, in particular to report information that is later revealed to be unreliable. The use of anonymous sources increased markedly in the period before the 2003 invasion of Iraq.

Science Issues

The mainstream press is often criticized for poor accuracy in reporting science news. Many reporters are not scientists, and are thus not familiar with the material they are summarizing. Technical information is also difficult to contextualize for lay audiences, and short-form reporting makes providing background, context, and clarification even harder. Food scares are an example of the need for responsible science journalism, as are stories connected with the safety of medical procedures.

Examples of Ethical Dilemmas

One of the primary functions of journalism ethics is to aid journalists in dealing with many ethical dilemmas they may encounter. From highly sensitive issues of national security to everyday questions such as accepting a dinner from a source, putting a bumper sticker on one's car, publishing a personal opinion blog, a journalist must make decisions taking into account things such as the public's right to know, potential threats, reprisals and intimidations of all kinds, personal integrity, conflicts between editors, reporters and publishers or management, and many other such conundrums. The following are illustrations of some of those.

- The Pentagon Papers dealt with extremely difficult ethical dilemmas faced by journalists. Despite government intervention, The Washington Post, joined by The New York Times, felt the public interest was more compelling and both published reports. (The cases went to the Supreme Court where they were merged and are known as New York Times Co. v. United States, 403 U.S. 713
- The Washington Post also once published a story about a listening device that the United States had installed over an undersea Soviet cable during the height of the cold war. The device allowed the United States to learn where Soviet submarines were positioned. In that case, Post Executive Editor Ben Bradlee chose not to run the story on national security grounds. However, the Soviets subsequently discovered the device and, according to Bradlee, "It was no longer a matter of national security. It was a matter of national embarrassment." However, the U.S. government still wanted The Washington Post not to run the story on the basis of national security, yet, according to Bradlee, "We ran the story. And you know what, the sun rose the next day."
- The Ethics Advice Line, a joint venture, public service project of Chicago Headline Club Chapter of the Society of Professional Journalists and Loyola University Chicago Center for Ethics and Social Justice, provides some examples of typical ethical dilemmas reported to their ethical dilemma hot-line and are typical of the kinds of questions faced by many professional journalists.

A partial listing of questions received by The Ethics Advice Line:

- Is it ethical to make an appointment to interview an arsonist sought by police, without informing police in advance of the interview?

- Is lack of proper attribution plagiarism?
- Should a reporter write a story about a local priest who confessed to a sex crime if it will cost the newspaper readers and advertisers who are sympathetic to the priest?
- Is it ethical for a reporter to write a news piece on the same topic on which he or she has written an opinion piece in the same paper?
- Under what circumstances do you identify a person who was arrested as a relative of a public figure, such as a local sports star?
- Free-lance journalists and photographers accept cash to write about, or take photos of, events with the promise of attempting to get their work on the AP or other news outlets, from which they also will be paid. Is that ethical?
- Can a journalist reveal a source of information after guaranteeing confidentiality if the source proves to be unreliable?

ONLINE NEWSPAPER

Modern printed newspapers all over the world are developing and running web newspapers. Going online created more opportunities for newspapers for instance, it allows newspapers to effectively compete with broadcast journalism in presenting breaking news online in a more timely manner than printing allows. The credibility and strong brand recognition of well-established newspapers, and the close relationships they have with advertisers (particularly in the case of local newspapers), are also seen by many in the newspaper industry as strengthening their chances of survival. The movement away from the printing process can also help decrease costs.

Not only do they allow for instant updating of news stories in text but allowing equal opportunities for access for disabled groups as well as adding more interesting features for the viewers to use leading to more interest and more advert opportunities. As distinctions between modes of communication become blurred, and as mass communication transforms itself every day with innovation; anyone who has a cell phone on a hike in the woods may now be in instant contact with news and events worldwide.

Web/online newspapers are not precisely like blogs or forum sites; however, it is not unusual for newspaper reporters and editors to maintain blogs, or for newspapers to add forums to their websites, for easy response from readers. Online newspapers must abide by the same legalities as do their sister publications. Professional journalists have some advantages, as editors are normally aware of the potential for legal problems. The big difference over blog and forum sites as to online newspaper and news sites is that blog and forum sites are not media based websites. As bloggers and independent citizen-journalists become more prevalent on the web, the potential for an explosion in lawsuits looms as they are not regulated in the same way as it is down to the public and not professional reporters to post stories in most cases. Blog sites can contain misleading information that could be seen as libel, questions regarding negligence or actual malice, or suits regarding invasion of privacy torts (such as appropriation, intrusion, private facts and false light). This problem was brought up in November 2006 the issue about blog sites and newspaper sites when it hit national headlines in the UK.

The Press Complaints Commission director Tim Toulmin told a London conference on race at the end off 2006:-"We're not in favour of regulating the internet. You can't regulate it. But unless there is a voluntary code there are no forms of redress. The flow of information should not be regulated by the government." In fact the PCC did cover online newspapers, but not blog and forum news sites. Soft-copy newspapers are much like hard-copy newspapers and have the same legal boundaries, such as laws regarding libel, privacy and copyright, also apply to online publications in most countries, like in the UK. Also in the UK the data protection act also applies to online newspapers and news pages. As well as the PCC rules in the UK. But the distinction was not very clear to the public in the UK as to what was a blog or forum site and what was an online newspapers. In 2007 a ruling was passed in 2007 to formally regulate UK based online newspapers, news audio and news video websites covering the responsibilities expected of them and to clear up who is and who are not online publications in the UK.

News reporters in progressive newsrooms throughout the country are being taught to shoot video and to write in the succinct manner necessary for the Internet news pages. Many are learning how to implement blogs and the ruling by the UK's PCC should help this development of the internet. Journalism students in schools around the world are being taught about the "convergence" of all media and the need to have knowledge and skills involving print, broadcast and web.

Responses to this sea-change in the competitive environment have varied. Some newspapers have attempted to integrate the internet into every aspect of their operations, for example with reporters writing stories for both print and online, and classified advertisements appearing in both media; others operate websites that are more distinct from the printed newspaper. Many in both camps believe that newspapers will increasingly leave breaking news to online and broadcast media, with print publications focused on comment and analysis.

The moderator of television's longest-running program began his career in news delivering armfuls of newspapers in Buffalo, N.Y. Decades have passed, but Tim Russert of NBC's Meet the Press said during a press conference at Mount Union College that he can't imagine doing his job without print news. "I am very reliant on newspapers. I read them all, six or seven a day," said the former paperboy. Although he could scour the internet for news, Russert said, "I still like to hold a newspaper; it's part of my upbringing." Russert, 55, who is also a political analyst for NBC Nightly News and The Today Show, said this in response to Akron Beacon Journal reporter Sandra M. Klepach's questions while delivering Tuesday's Schooler Lecture at Mount Union College's Timken Building.

Examples of Hard Copies Online

It would be difficult to find a daily newspaper in the UK or United States, in fact in the world, in the 21st Century, that does not have or share a website. Most student newspapers even have websites. At the same time, broadcast media have established websites in similar fashion. Media transitions in the beginning of the century have blurred the boundaries between print, broadcast and the internet. Websites are available now even on cellphones, and broadcasts on cellphones and all kinds of computers.

In the United States, from Hawaii to Maine, newspaper websites in particular have come online, and over the years have undergone transitions in design and content. Newspapers, wary of the Internet and desiring to compete, began in the mid 1990s with strong investment in local staffing for web newspapers. Over the decade, most have reduced their web staffing and automated many features, including placement of news and advertising. Consolidation and cost-cutting measures have come at the behest of corporate or chain headquarters, and components of web design and implementation have, in many respects, become centralized. At first, newspapers attempted to individualize their offerings with unique and sometimes gaudy web pages, but soon found a need to simplify for the reader with smaller headlines and briefer stories on their fronts. Now, however, with the need for revenue beckoning, splashy animated ads and unlimited gimmickry, advertising videos and come-ons interfere with access to newspaper pages online. While most newspapers now have film clips online, these are studded with advertisements. Newspapers find themselves in hot competition for local classified ads with such services as Craigslist, and have lost much ground to mammoth web advertising from Google. Google and Yahoo in 2006 went on record saying that they wanted to have media partnerships to increase their profits on both sides because the search engine can attract traffic and sell ads using the publication's brand name while mutually drawing visitors back to the magazine's home page.

Very few newspapers in the year 2006 will claim to have made money from their websites, which are most free to all viewers. Declining profit margins and declining circulation in daily newspapers have forced executives to contemplate new methods of obtaining revenue from websites, without charging for subscription. This has been difficult. Newspapers with specialized audiences such as The Wall Street Journal or the

Chronicle of Higher Education, successfully charge subscription fees. Many of the web papers have simplified their URLs so that, for instance, miami.com will take you to The Miami Herald whose website first appeared in the mid-1990s. The Los Angeles Times features a web site, as do all of the large dailies in California. As with most newspapers, the website can also be reached by the name of the paper, as in latimes.com. The Washington Post, USA Today, The New York Times, and all major newspapers in the United States are reached easily.

Examples of Soft Copy Newspapers

Many small newspapers supplement or compete with the larger newspapers in their cities through websites and in other electronic formats as well as having hard copy newspapers.

Online-only Newspapers

With the introduction of the internet, web based newspapers have also started to be produced as online only publications. To be a Web-Only newspaper they must be web published only and must not be part of or have any connection to hard copy formats. To be classed as a Online Only Newspaper the paper must also be regularly updated at a regular time and keep to a fixed news format, like a hardcopy newspaper. They must also be only published by professional media companies, be regarded under the national and international press rules and regulations and have 80% or above news content. For example, in 2000 an independent web only newspaper was introduced in the UK called Southport Reporter. It is a weekly regional newspaper that is not produced or run in any format other than soft-copy on the internet by its publishers PCBT Photography. Unlike blog sites and other news websites it is run as a newspaper and is recognized by media groups in the UK, like the NUJ and/or the IFJ. Also they fall under the UK's PCC rules.

Soft-copy News Sheets

A news sheet is a paper that is on one or two pages only. Soft-copy sheets are like online newspapers, in that the have to be predominately news, not advert or gossip based. These sheets can be updated periodically or regularly, unlike a newspaper. They must also like a newspaper be regarded as a news outlet by media groups and governments like newspapers. An online edition updated when appropriate, as in the small webpaper in Tallahassee, Florida, can bee seen by looking at THE TALLAHASSEE NEWS.

Future

The development of electronic newspapers, will very soon be replacing hard-copy printed papers via electronic paper. In February 2006, the Flemish daily De Tijd of Antwerp announced plans to distribute an electronic-ink version of the paper to selected subscribers. This will be the first such application of electronic ink to newspaper publishing. Also the future of newspapers see newspapers section.

NEWS STYLE

News style or news writing is the particular prose style used for news reporting (*i.e.*. in newspapers) as well as in news items that air on radio and television. News style encompasses not only vocabulary and sentence structure, but also the way in which stories present the information in terms of relative importance, tone, and intended audience.

News writing attempts to answer all the basic questions about any particular event in the first two or three paragraphs: Who? What? When? Where? and Why? and occasionally How? (*i.e.* "5 W's"). This form of structure is sometimes called the "inverted pyramid," to refer to decreased importance of information as it progresses.

Overview

While newspapers, like encyclopedias, generally adhere to an expository writing mode and style, this has changed over time as journalism ethics and standards have (debatably) increased to become more objective and less sensationalistic. There are debated degrees of professionalism among particular news agencies, and their reputability or public value, according to professional standards of idealism and depending on what the reader wants from a news story, may be tied to their ability to be objective. In its most ideal form, news writing strives to be intelligible to the vast majority of potential readers, as well as to be engaging and succinct. Within the limits created by these goals, news stories also aim for a kind of comprehensiveness. However other factors are involved, some of which are practical and derived from the media form, and others stylistic.

Among the larger and more respected newspapers, fairness and balance is a major factor for the presentation of information. Commentary is usually confined to a separate section, though each paper may have a different overall slant. Editorial policy dictates the use of adjectives, euphemisms, and idioms. Papers with an international audience for example, usually use a more formal style of writing.

The specific choices made by a news outlet's editor or editorial board are often collected in a style guide or stylebook; common commercial stylebooks are the "AP Style Manual" and the "US News Style Book". The main goals of news writing can be summarized by the ABCs of journalism: accuracy, brevity, and clarity..

Terms and Structure

Journalistic prose is explicit and precise, and tries not to rely on jargon. As a rule, journalists will not use a long word when a short one will do. They use subject-verb-object construction and vivid, active prose. They offer anecdotes, examples and metaphors, and they rarely depend on colorless generalizations or abstract ideas. News writers try to avoid using the same word more than once in a paragraph (sometimes called an "echo" or "word mirror").

The most important structural element of a story is the lede-namely contained in the story's first sentence. Lede (pronounced/lid/) is a traditional spelling, from the archaic English, used to avoid confusion with the printing press type formerly made from lead, or the typographical term "leading". The lede is usually the first sentence, or in some cases the first two sentences, and is ideally 20-25 words in length. The top-loading principle applies especially to ledes, but the unreadability of long sentences constrains its size. This makes writing a lede an optimization problem, in which the goal is to articulate the most encompassing and interesting statement that a writer can make in one sentence, given the material with which he or she has to work. While a rule of thumb says the lede should answer most or all of the 5 Ws, few ledes can fit all of these.

Inverted Pyramid

Journalism instructors usually describe the organization or structure of a news story as an inverted pyramid. The journalist top-loads the essential and most interesting elements of his or her story, with supporting information following in order of diminishing importance.

This structure enables readers to quit reading at any point and still come away with the essence of a story. It allows people to enter a topic to the depth that their curiosity takes them, and without the imposition of details or nuances that they would consider irrelevant.

Newsroom practicalities represent another rationale. The inverted pyramid structure enables sub-editors and other news staff to quickly create space for ads and late-breaking news simply by cutting paragraphs from the bottom ("cutting", literally, at the papers that still use traditional paste up techniques). The structure frees sub-editors to truncate stories at almost any length that suits their needs for space.

Poor structure typically begins with a faulty lede. Steeped in the raw material of their interviews and research, apprentice news writers often fail to anticipate what readers will find most interesting or to sum up the information quickly. These elements of their story they present only after their lede and in an article's later paragraphs. This is the reason for the popular newsroom admonition: "Don't bury the lede!"

Some writers start their stories with the "1-2-3 lede". This format invariably starts with a 5W opening paragraph, followed by an indirect quote that serves to support a major element of the first paragraph, and then a direct quote to support the indirect quote.

Feature Style

News stories aren't the only type of material that appear in newspapers and magazines. Longer articles, such as magazine cover articles and the pieces that lead the inside sections of a newspaper, are known as features. Feature stories differ from straight news in several ways. Foremost is the absence of a straight-news lede, most of the time. Instead of offering the essence of a story up front, feature writers may attempt to lure readers in.

A feature's first paragraphs often relate an intriguing moment or event, as in an "anecdotal lede". From the particulars of a person or episode, its view quickly broadens to generalities about the story's subject.

The section that signals what a feature is about is called the nut graf or billboard. Billboards appear as the third or fourth paragraph from the top, and may be up to two paragraphs long. Unlike a lede, a billboard rarely gives everything away. This reflects the fact that feature writers aim to hold their readers' attention to the end, which requires engendering curiosity and offering a "payoff." Feature paragraphs tend to be longer than those of news stories, with smoother transitions between them. Feature writers use the active-verb construction and concrete explanations of straight news, but often put more personality in their prose.

NEWS BROADCASTING

Television news refers to the practice of disseminating current events via the medium of television. News Bulletins are programmes lasting from seconds to hours that provide updates on world, national, regional or local news events. Television channels may provide news bulletins as part of a regular program that is aired daily or more often at standard times. Less often, television shows may be interrupted or replaced by "news flashes" to provide news updates on current events of great importance or sudden events of great importance.

A newscast typically consists of the coverage of various news events and other information, either produced locally by a radio or television station newsroom, or by a broadcast network. It may also include such additional material as sports coverage, weather forecasts, traffic reports, commentary and other material that the broadcaster feels is relevant to their audience.

In some parts of the world there are 'rolling news' TV channels that broadcast news 24 hours a day.

Television news consists of several different elements, introduced by a news presenter or presenters. The presenters read 'links' and do interviews.

Most news stories come in the form of short 'packages'. These are pre-recorded reports usually lasting from one to five minutes. News reporters gather and edit together interview clips, pictures and their own 'pieces to camera' to tell a story. They script and record a 'voice-over' to explain the pictures and link the elements together.

Some stories are done as live reports. This can be a reporter on the scene of a story either being interviewed by a studio presenter (sometimes known as a 'two-way'), a reporter interviewing one or more other people, or simply live pictures and sound of an event.

The sound and pictures are sent back to the TV station via fixed cable links, bounced off a satellite from a vehicle carrying a satellite dish (a 'sat truck'), or sent through microwave radio transmissions from a vehicle carrying a microwave transmitter. With the growth of "rolling news" channels the use of live material has increased enormously and TV reporters are now often judged as much on their ability to perform live in front of a camera as on their package-making or writing skills.

TV news programs are put together by producers, who decide what goes in and what gets left out, and how long and in what form each story is presented. They put together 'running orders'-a list of the stories in what they decide is the right order.

INVESTIGATIVE JOURNALISM

Investigative journalism is a kind of journalism in which reporters deeply investigate a topic of interest, often involving crime, political corruption, or some other scandal. De Burgh (2000) states that: "An investigative journalist is a man or woman whose profession it is to discover the truth and to identify lapses from it in whatever media may be available. The act of doing this generally is called investigative journalism and is distinct from apparently similar work done by police, lawyers, auditors and regulatory bodies in that it is not limited as to target, not legally founded and closely connected to publicity".

An investigative journalist may spend a considerable period researching and preparing a report, sometimes months or years, whereas a typical daily or weekly news reporter writes items concerning immediately available news. Most investigative journalism is done by newspapers, wire services and free-lance journalists. An investigative journalist's final report may take the form of an expose.

There is no more important contribution that we can make to society than strong, publicly-spirited investigative journalism.
—Tony Burman, editor-in-chief of CBC News

The Investigation: The investigation will often require an extensive number of interviews and travel; other instances might call for the reporter to make use of activities such as surveillance techniques, analysis of documents, investigations of the performance of any kind of equipment involved in an accident, patent medicine, scientific analysis, social and legal issues, and the like. Investigative journalism requires the scrutiny of details, fact-finding, and physical effort. An investigative journalist must have an analytical and incisive mind with strong self-motivation to carry on when all doors are closed, when facts are being covered up or falsified and so on.

Some of the means reporters can use for their fact-finding:

- studying neglected sources, such as archives, phone records, address books, tax records and license records
- anonymous sources (for example whistle-blowers)
- going undercover

Investigative journalism can be contrasted with analytical reporting. According to De Burgh (2000) analytical journalism takes the data available and reconfigures it, helping us to ask questions about the situation or statement or see it in a different way, whereas investigative journalists go further and also want to know whether the situation presented to us is the reality.

Professional References

In The Reporter's Handbook: An Investigator's Guide to Documents and Techniques, Steve Weinberg defined investigative journalism as:

Reporting, through one's own initiative and work product, matters of importance to readers, viewers or listeners. In many cases, the subjects of the reporting wish the matters under scrutiny to remain undisclosed. There are currently university departments for teaching investigative journalism. Conferences are conducted presenting peer reviewed research into investigative journalism.

ASSIGNMENT EDITOR

In journalism, an assignment editor is an editor-either at a newspaper, or radio or television station-who selects, develops and plans reporting assignments, either news events or feature stories, to be covered by reporters.

An assignment editor often fields calls from the public, who give news tips, or information about a possible story or event to be covered. Sometimes, these calls may:

- Alert editors about a disaster-perhaps something as minor as a car accident or as major as a large industrial fire with mass casualties.
- Be someone wishing to make a complaint about corporate or governmental practices, or have information or an opinion about a major decision that a local or state government is making.
- Be something as minor as a child building the world's largest sand castle or a budding entrepreneur wanting to promote his/her product.

Other times, the news tip may come in the form of a news release, which may either promote an event, meeting, etc.; or alert editors and reporters about an upcoming news conference. Sometimes, assignment editors must sift through hundreds of news releases each day.

Whatever the case, it is the assignment editor's job to determine what news tips and news releases are the most newsworthy, and then decide which reporter to assign a story to. Those assignments are often determined based on the reporter's experience, skills and his/her beat (e.g., police, courts, schools, city hall, county, etc.).

If a major story develops-such as a disaster or economic development-an assignment editor may enlist several reporters (in addition to whomever usually covers that beat) to cover various angles of a story. For instance, if the story is about a plant closing, one reporter may be asked to do the main story about the closing, while other reporters may be asked to do stories on such things as employee reaction, reaction from business and community leaders, a history of the plant (and other plant closings, if appropriate), etc.

Required Background

An assignment editor often has at least one year of experience working for a particular news organization, and has good knowledge of the community in which he/she works and lives. Sometimes, it may be a journalist's first job as an editor, with other editorial sections-such as copy, section, managing and chief editors-higher in seniority.

At many smaller daily and weekly newspapers, the role of assignment editor is often combined with an editor's other duties (e.g., an assistant editor who also lays out the pages also may be asked to assign stories to reporters).

6

Mass Media Today

During the recent years mass media has invaded the life of a common man in a big way. Upto seventies, mass media mainly remained confined to cinema, newspaper and radio. It was in the early eighties that audio-visual electronic medium in the form of television invaded the Indian scenario in a big way. The Government created huge infrastructure for spread of television network in the country. During this decade itself, advent of computers and Video Cassette Recorders (VCR) also supplemented the audio-visual media, putting well established medium of cinema to shade. During the early nineties, satellite television revolutionised the audio-visual media by reaching most of the households in the urban areas. The latest invasion of audio-visual electronic media has suddenly increased the demand for professionals in journalism, technicians and other service individuals. These careers not only offer excellent opportunities, salaries, challenge and satisfaction of work, but also provide an opportunity for self-employment in various fields.

PRINT MEDIA

An old saying goes "pen is mightier than sword". The saying is not just a rhetoric. It reflects the power of print media. Being the most important media, print media pertains to broad activity of publication of newspapers, magazines and books and all persons connected with this activity have their contribution in successful running of this medium. While writing of books and contributing to magazines is largely a self-employment occupation, publication of newspapers and magazines involves a huge work force such as editors, technicians, printing technicians, composers, etc. In all these jobs the options of either working on desk or working in the field are available to the candidates. Reporters and correspondents generally operate in the field and submit their reports or stories on local, national or international issues pertaining to politics, trade, commerce, defence, sports, etc. One special category of reporters and correspondents operates in the field of investigative journalism.

This category of reporting pertains to investigation on the issues of public importance. This type of journalism and reporting attracts public attention instantaneously. Special attention in such reporting is required in the authenticity of information, selection of issues of public interest and succinct reporting in interesting and convincing language. In case of magazine reporting, many a times the reports, stories and features are contributed by free-lance reporters and part-time amateur writers. To pursue the career as a reporter one may attain bachelor's degree or post-graduate diploma in journalism. Some of the universities offer post graduate diplomas of 9-month duration while others offer post-graduate one-year diploma in Public Relations or post graduate degree in mass-communication.

Latest trend in this regard is that big groups of newspapers advertise the posts of trainees in any of the above categories for which all graduates are eligible. After conducting the entrance examination, suitable graduate trainees, with flair for writing are selected and employed. In other words, now the formal academic qualification for being a reporter, copy writer or correspondent is not an essential qualification. Similarly, for writing features or analytical articles in magazines, one need not have any formal and professional academic qualification.

What is required is in-depth knowledge, command over the language concerned and outstanding analytical capability. Broadly speaking, anyone keen to pursue this career in any capacity must have outstanding general awareness, good perception, an eye for details and very keen observation. In turn, the career offers challenge, immense job satisfaction and fairly good compensation. For acquiring general awareness regular reading of newspapers, magazines and books on variety of topics is a must. Discussions on current topics also go a long way in widening the horizons of knowledge. For the beginners, it is better to consult a good book on the background to current affairs so that further knowledge is strengthened after acquiring fundamental knowledge. Latest edition of "Current Affairs and Backgrounders" published by M/s Khanna Brothers (Publishers) Pvt Ltd is an ideal book for this purpose. Command over the concerned language is not a capability which can be acquired overnight. Regular and intensive reading as well as regular writing practice not only improves the command over the language, but also improves the flair for writing.

Candidates seriously pursuing this career should also go in for academic degree/diploma in Journalism/Public Relations/ Mass Communication from a good university or institute to have an edge over others.

AUDIO-VISUAL MEDIA

The requirement of personnel for the audio and audio-visual media is a little different than that for the print media. Traditionally, Radio has been the audio media having farthest reach. It was only with effect from the early eighties that Radio started getting replaced by Television. In most of the cases TV just supplemented the Radio. Despite the recent invasion by Doordarshan channels and Satellite and Cable TV, importance of Radio has not been undermined. The percentage of population covered by Radio is much more than the TV, mainly due to better technical infrastructure, longer range of short wave radio and cheaper cost and running cost of radio and transistors. Hence, Radio still remains very important medium.

Radio needs various types of personnel which includes announcers, news-readers, news-composers, writers, producers, commentators, and various categories of radio artists like singers, musicians, drama artists, narrators, etc. There is also a growing demand for good programmes and producers of such programmes. Audio-visual media is the strongest form of medium, but has limited reach. The earliest form of audio-visual medium was cinema which had very limited reach and people had to spend some money to have an access to it. Cinema, however, still enjoys the most glamorous place in the entire media. In this feature, Cinema as career in audio-visual media has been left out and will be covered later in a separate feature on careers.

Television, satellite and cable TV offer varied opportunities for career seekers. This medium offers excellent opportunities for newsreaders, composers, announcers, technicians, commentators, producers, models, actors, cameramen, script writers, etc. In addition to the Government-run Doordarshan, all other companies in the field of television, be it in production, direction, acting, cable operation and satellite TV operation, are handled by the individuals or private companies.

The choice of career is available in a variety of fields, not only with Doordarshan but with commercially-run media companies also. Candidates seeking any type of career in audio-visual electronic media must have characteristics like artistic inclination, expertise in own field of activity, pleasing personality, adaptability, general awareness, quick reflexes, flexibility and imagination. All these qualities must be coupled with the required technical and academic qualifications and professional competence. In case of announcers and newsreaders the qualities of good voice and presentable and photogenic face are additional requirements.

Good flow of spoken language and command over the language concerned are also pre-requisites in these cases. Capabilities to compare and compose become added qualifications. In addition to programmes and news, three other aspects of advertisement, engineering and management are also of paramount importance in TV and other electronic media. Technical and professional staff provide engineering services and act from behind the screen. These personnel are responsible for providing support services so essential for good quality of transmission, colour combinations, creation of support infrastructure for transmission, day-to-day management of video recording, time-management and other related aspects.

How to Join

Career in News-reading and announcing does not require any professional or technical qualifications. Any simple graduate with good command over the language, with pleasing face and personality, accurate pronunciation and a good voice can hope to enter this career. Experience of stage and theatre also helps a candidate. Most important of all these qualities is the aptitude for a particular job and keen interest in it. To provide technical support service, trainee Transmission Executives are recruited. The recruitment for trainee Transmission Executives is made by the Staff Selection Commission (SSC).

SSC holds a selection test and all candidates who are between 18 to 25 years of age and have diploma from National School of Drama (NSD) and Film and Television Institute of India (FTII), Pune are eligible to take test. After selection, trainee Transmission Executives are made responsible for making timely transmission of scheduled programmes. They are also expected to ensure proper quality of transmission. This is achieved by properly conceptualising the programme, their timings and ensuring technical precision. Transmission Executives may rise to the levels of Programme Executive, Assistant Station Director or even Station Directors.

The higher level managerial posts are held by the officers of Central Information Service (Group-A). Recruitment to this service is made by the combined Civil Services Examination which is held by the Union Public Service Commission every year. It is one of the allied services in this examination and recruitment for this service takes place every year. Officers from this service also hold senior level posts in All India Radio and in the Department of Information and Broadcasting. In addition, technical positions like cameramen, make-up-men, video technicians, editors, etc need specific technical qualifications and specific experience in the related fields.

JOURNALISM

Journalism fascinates many young people who have a keen desire of seeing their name in print. Anyone who has written something for the college paper believes a career in journalism can be pursued. This feature points out that a career in journalism means more than merely writing well. As we receive a number of queries from our readers who want to become famous journalists and editors, we decided to describe in detail the requirements of newspapers and television channels today. This feature describes the skills required, as also the upside and the downside of the field. It also gives information about how one can become a journalist, the qualities that are required to be a successful one and addresses of some of the well known institutes. To an outsider, journalism is an exciting field in which fame and fortune can be achieved if one is able to write well. The names of some famous journalists come easily to mind. Khushwant Singh, who writes columns in several newspapers; M.J. Akbar, the editor of The Asian Age; and Shobha De, former editor of Stardust and now a celebrated writer. Opportunities in the field have also multiplied with the boom in magazines and television channels.

Each of these requires people who can report and interpret events in a coherent and interesting manner. To assess whether you can be a famous journalist, you have to first know the skills that are required. The first is a good command over language. You must be able to express yourself well. A course in journalism will help sharpen these skills.

But this is not all. What is required is the ability to collect information and report events quickly. If you are in a television channel, it may mean going on camera as the event is happening, often a difficult task. In newspapers one has to write out the story before the deadline and it must contain all the correct information and the drama. Even a small error can destroy the credibility of the journalist. So journalism is just not about being able to write well alone.

The nature of a journalist's job is also changing. With news becoming competitive and personality-oriented, the job of a TV journalist often means waiting outside the offices or homes of politicians for hours and trying to catch a "sound byte" as the leader comes out.

The pursuit of truth does not extend beyond getting a small segment in the news programme. In this race, there is no room for being creative or following stories that one may like to. Threats of law-suits have made news channels and newspapers increasingly wary about publishing scoops and many of the investigative stories are just killed. There is little room for creativity in today's news organisations.

Increasing Scope

Once you accept these limitations, a career in journalism may be a good option. Some years back there was a boom in television channels which led to an increase in opportunities for aspiring journalists. Many print journalists shifted to television. Salaries had jumped. Today, there is a shakeout among the channels, which has led to the opportunities being reduced drastically. Newspapers and magazines continue to employ journalists, but with circulations and profitability under stress, three has been a decrease in opportunities somewhat. However, this situation may be linked to the economic slowdown and things may become better once the economy picks up. It may be mentioned that there are over 4,000 newspapers in 100 languages registered in India and the scope for employment will always exist, despite difficulties.

Avenues in journalism have multiplied because of unexpected growth in two new areas: (a) Niche publications; and (b) Web editing. We explain these below: Niche Publications: This means special purpose publications catering to particular industries, for example, travel and tourism, hotels, textiles or computers. Many such publications have been started in the past few years. These "niche" publications may not have the mass circulations of newspapers but are highly profitable. However, to work in them one needs to have journalistic skills as well as industry knowledge. Hence, MBAs are employed in business publications while computer experts find jobs in information technology magazines. The idea is to develop a specialisation and build on it. In the future, journalists with specialised skills in an industry may be more in demand than those with mere writing skills.

WEB EDITING

Another avenue has opened up in recent times and that is because of the Internet. Many newspapers and magazines have web editions and require skilled people to maintain their sites. Web newspapers have also started, which do not have print editions. This has opened up a great opportunity but here those journalists would be required who have knowledge of websites and how to make them attractive. The work involves content creation, layout, graphics and text on the Web newspage. The scope of journalists is, therefore, increasing by the day, though the role has changed a great deal. Earlier, journalists collected their daily quota of news at the Press Club and this was rehashed for publication the next day. Today, however, a journalist must be a professional like any other and must have technical skills as well.

Develop the Necessary Skills

One major shortcoming of the Indian press has been its failure to follow up stories. Scandals are reported but soon forgotten because the press finds something else to report. This has led to the unfortunate situation where newspapers are not taken seriously any more. If this continues, the privileges enjoyed by journalists may well become a thing of the past. The day of famous editors is also over.

Today, different editors are employed for different sections and there is no one person who is all powerful in a newspaper organisation, except perhaps the owner. Do not thus think of a career in journalism because of privileges that you might get. Instead, get a specialisation and try to make a name in your chosen field. The modern journalist should have skills of expression as well as technical skills. Even if you are a reporter, you will have to type in your stories on a page-making and publishing software. Nor is it necessary to have a journalism degree. One can belong to any discipline and hope to join journalism if one has demonstrated qualities of writing and reporting. Niche magazines, in any case, want specialists and not mere journalists. On the other hand, a journalism degree will help you acquire skills and also enable you an entry into a newspaper or television organisation. The ideal thing might be to zero-in on your area of specialisation, acquire a degree, and then do journalism.

This may be a better career option than doing just a journalism course. To acquire fame, of course, one has to be a good journalist. Merely getting a journalism degree does not make you good at your job. First, one must have the capability of getting information. This means that you must have a "head for the news". Then, you must have the perseverance and grit to obtain the information, considering the fact that most people do not like to part with information. Finally, you must have the ability to transform the information into an interesting story.

Future Prospects

After your basic training, you are ready to enter the world of journalism. Whether you wish to join TV journalism or a newspaper, you can expect to be a reporter at a starting salary of Rs 5,000 per month. Growth is fast, especially if you show an aptitude for the job. After a few years you can expect to be a senior reporter and move in the salary of around Rs 10,000 and thereafter it all depends on how famous and good you become. A sub-editor's job consists of editing what others have written and prepare the pages that will be printed.

The schedule is usually unearthly, with shifts ending at 2 or 3 am, which means that social life has to be discarded. Once you get used to it, however, it becomes enjoyable. In TV journalism one can start as a reporter or do some research work and later become a correspondent and anchor. There are thousands of people who want to become newsreaders and anchors but they lack training. There are few institutes available which can train you to become a newsreader. Even if you have training, it is a tough field, since newsreaders are employed on contract.

Presenters are given the boot for minor mistakes. In Doordarshan the situation is worse and requires political patronage. Think of this option only as part-time work or look for employment in organisations like NDTV or Sun TV. Another option could be to start out on your own and become a private producer. If you have an idea about a programme that can click, approach a company which supplies programmes to channels.

BRIDGING ACADEMIA AND JOURNALISM

For much of the last century, journalism has been a major influence on the way we perceive the world. Whether we live in a democratic society with a central tenet of press freedom, in an environment where state-controlled media direct our thinking, or somewhere between the two, the information we gather through newsprint, television and radio broadcasting is enormously influential. Political life today is conducted largely through the media, which increasingly sets the agenda and judges success and failure, truth and lies, within some framework of undeclared criteria. Recent years have seen the growth of global media corporations and, in counterpoint, the rise of the 'citizen reporter' publishing first-hand information on the Internet. Increasingly, as allegations of 'spin' abound, it can be hard to know which media sources to trust-and how far.

Closely scrutinising those with power and calling them to account is one of the core principles of journalism, yet journalism itself is not often on the receiving end of such inspection. Against this backdrop, in September 2006 Oxford launched the Reuters Institute for the Study of Journalism, based in the Department of Politics and International Relations. This ground-breaking research institute, which has been established with £1.75 million funding from the Reuters Foundation, will provide high-calibre analysis of the practice of journalism in all media forms, examining both its ethical framework and evolution and the realities of journalistic practice.

By bringing together academic rigour and the expertise of working journalists, the Reuters Institute will strive to further our understanding of journalism and the challenges it faces as the digital age dissolves our local and national boundaries.

The Director of the Institute is Dr Sarmila Bose, whose respected academic career at universities in the UK, USA and India has been complemented by her work as a broadcast and print journalist, particularly in the area of electoral politics and public policy issues for the Indian press.

The Director of Journalism is John Lloyd, contributing editor of the Financial Times. The Institute's Advisory Committee is chaired by the Chancellor, Lord Patten, and its Steering Committee by Tim Gardam, Principal of St Anne's College and former Director of Television at Channel 4. Other Steering Committee members include Geert Linnebank, Editor-in-Chief of Reuters, and Professor Timothy Garton Ash, a regular contributor to the Guardian and the New York Times.

The establishment of the Reuters Institute boosts a growing engagement on the part of the University with the media. For almost 25 years, Reuters Fellowships have allowed distinguished mid-career journalists from around the world to take time out from the daily tyranny of deadlines and spend study breaks of one to three terms using the University's facilities, whilst being welcomed as Visiting Scholars at Green College. Since 1996, the Centre for Socio-Legal Studies has been home to the Programme in Comparative Media Law and Policy, which examines issues such as media regulation and the legal and social implications of new media technologies.

The more recently established Oxford Internet Institute is examining the ways in which the Internet is pushing the borders of what we mean by journalism and how it should be controlled, and within the Saïd Business School, the study of media management and media strategy is creating real excitement. Through a combination of innovative research and seminars around the world with high-profile participants, the University is taking a genuinely international approach.

The Reuters Institute will reinforce this global perspective, whilst being firmly anchored within the University's academic programme. 'Our task will be to bring together scholars and practitioners from the world of journalism to study the content of news media and the issues it raises', says Dr Bose. 'We are an institute for the study of journalism, not a school of journalism, and that, together with our global outlook, probably makes us unique. We hope to draw in scholars from all parts of the University, including areas like medicine, science and philosophy, and we are also keen to extend the links we are already forging with a number of colleges and centres.'

'We have five core areas where we will initially focus our research', she adds.

'First, the challenge of freedom and responsibility in journalism. We want to look at established open societies, such as Western Europe, the USA and India, where freedom of the media is constitutionally guaranteed and is part of democratic society, but examine the ways in which, in practice, there may not be complete freedom.

Secondly, we want to compare the situation in emerging societies that were formerly closed, for example Russia.

Thirdly, we want to look at journalistic coverage of scientific and medical issues, building on work already ongoing at Green College; and fourthly, we want to study business and economics journalism, working with our legal and business school colleagues to create an international dimension. Finally, we will examine the representation of religion in media, starting with the representation of Islam.' A three-year research project that compares journalism across Europe has just begun, funded by the Swedish Ax:son Johnson Foundation.

As befits an organisation working on issues of relevance to the world of practice, the Reuters Institute is keen to ensure that its findings are aired and debated in the media-and fed back to its practitioners. As well as academic publications, books, seminars and articles, the Institute website will host a running commentary on the media itself and include space for blogging. 'We've had great interest from both academics and journalists who are keen to share their experiences and ideas', says Dr Bose. 'By creating a real partnership between these worlds, we intend to study the content of journalism in global comparison, combining the analytic rigour of Oxford and policy relevance to the world of practice.'

Bibliography

Baker, C. Edwin: *Advertising and a Democratic Press,* Princeton NJ: Princeton University Press, 1994.

Ball, Rick: *Meet the Press: Fifty Years of History in the Making,* New York, McGraw-Hill, 1998.

Bliss, Edward: *Now the News: The Story of Broadcast Journalism,* New York, Columbia University Press, 1991.

Bruce D. Itule: *Visual Editing: A Graphic Guide for Journalists,* Belmont, CA: Wadsworth, 1990.

Cannadine, David: *History and the Media*, New York, Palgrave Macmillian, 2004.

Clint C. Wilson.: *A History of the Black Press,* Washington, DC: Howard University Press, 1997.

Colin Sparks: *Communication and Citizenship: Journalism and the Public Sphere in the New Media Age,* New York: Routledge, 1991.

Craig, Richard: *Online Journalism: Reporting, Writing and Editing for New Media*, Belmont, CA: Thomson/Wadsworth, 2005.

Dardenne, Robert: *A Free and Responsible Student Press: An Ideal Vision of How Community and Communication Can Preserve Scholastic Journalism,* St.Petersburg, The Poynter Institute for Media Studies, 1996.

David, B.: *The Civil War and the Press,* New Brunswick, NJ: Transaction Publishers, 2000.

David, Paul: *Communities of Journalism: A History of American Newspapers and Their Readers,* Urbana, University of Illinois Press, 2001.

Dizard, Jr. Wilson: *Old Media/New Media: Mass Communication in the Information Age,* New York, Longman, 2000.

Donald, A.: *American Journalists,* Oxford, Oxford University Press, 1997.

Earl, R.: *Writing for Mass Communication,* White Plains, NY: Longman, 1996.

Ehrlich, Matthew C. *Journalism in the Movies.* Urbana: University of Illinois Press, 2004.

Farrar, Howard: *The Baltimore Afro-American, 1892-1950,* Westport CT, Greenword Press, 1998.

Fedler, Fred: *Lessons from the Past: Journalists' Lives and Work, 1850-1950,* Prospect Heights, Waveland Press, 2000.

George M. Killenberg: *The Conversation of Journalism: Communication, Community, and News,* Westport, CT: Praeger, 1994.

Ghiglione, Loren:*The American Journalist: Paradox of the Press,* Washington, Library of Congress, 1990.

Gillmor, Dan: *We the Media: Grassroots Journalism by the People, for the People,* Sebastopol, CA: O'Reilly Media, 2004.

Hanno, Hardt: *Picturing the Past: Media, History and Photography,* Champaign, IL: University of Illinois Press, 1999.

Harrison, S.L.: *Cavalcade of Journalists 1900-2000,* Miami, Wolf Den Books, 2002.

Henry, Lewis: *The Black Press in the Middle West, 1865-1985,* Westport, CT: Greenwood Press, 1996.

Hudson, Frederick: *Journalism in the United States from 1690-1872,* New York, Routledge, 2000.

James, C.: *Online Journalism: Principles and Practices of News for the Web,* Scottsdale, AZ: Holcomb Hathaway, 2005.

Jerry, W.: *In the News: American Journalists View Their Craft,* Wilmington, Scholarly Resources, 2000.

John Nerone: *The Form of News: A History,* New York, Guilford Press, 2001.

Jon, E.: *The Mammoth Book of Journalism: An Anthology of the 100 Greatest Newspaper Articles,* New York, Carrol & Graf., 2003.

Kawamoto, Kevin: *Digital Journalism: Emerging Media and Changing Horizons of Journalism,* Lanham, MD: Rowman & Littlefield, 2003.

Kessler, Lauren: *The Dissident Press,* Newbury Park, CA: Sage, 1984.

Kitano, Harry: *The Ethnic Press in the United States,* Westport, CT: Greenwood Press, 1987.

Kolodzy, Janet: *Convergence Journalism: Writing and Reporting Across the News Media*, Llanham, MD: Rowman & Littlefield, 2006.

Langman, Larry: *The Media in the Movies,* Jefferson, NC: McFarland & Company, 1997.

Lynne Olson: *The Murrow Boys: Pioneers on the Front Lines of Broadcast Journalism,* Boston, Houghton Mifflin Company, 1996.

Margaret, A.: *History of the Mass Media in the United States, An Encyclopedia,* Chicago, Fitzroy Dearborn Publishers, 1998.

Martin, Paul E.: *Black Press, Britons and Immigrants: Alternative Press and Society*, Kingston, Jamaica: Vintage Communications, 1998.

Nancy L. Roberts: *The Press and America: An Interpretive History of the Mass Media*, Boston, Allyn and Bacon, 1999.

Newton, Eric: *Crusaders, Scoundrels, Journalists: The Newseum's Most Intriguing Newspeople*, New York, Times Books, 1999.

Peter Burke: *A Social History of the Media from Gutenberg to the Internet*, Malden, Blackwell, 2001.

Robert W. Snyder: *Defining Moments in Journalism*, New Brunswick, NJ: Transaction Publishers, 1998.

Robert, V.: *Mass Media,* New York, Garland Publishing, 1987.

Ross, Lillian: *Reporting Back: Notes on Journalism*, Washington, DC: Counterpoint, 2002.

Sims, Norman: *Literary Journalism in the Twentieth Century*, New York, Oxford University Press, 1990.

Stacks, John F.: *Scotty: James B. Reston and the Rise and Fall of American Journalism*, Boston, Little, Brown & Company, 2003.

Sterling, John Michael: *Stay Tuned: A History of American Broadcasting*, Mahwah, NJ: Lawrence Erlbaum Associates, 2002.

Streitmatter, Rodger: *Mightier Than the Sword: How the News Media Have Shaped American History*, Boulder, CO: Westview Press, 1997.

Stuart Adam: *Journalism: The Democratic Craft*, New York, Oxford, 2006

Thomas, Leonard: *The Power of the Press: The Birth of American Political Reporting*,New York, Oxford University Press, 1986.

Ward, Hiley H.: *Mainsteams of American Media History*, Needham Heights, MA: Allyn & Bacon, 1997.

Willard, G.: *Main Currents in the History of American Journalism*, New York: Houghton Mifflin, 1927.

William Serrin: *Muckraking: The Journalism that Changed America*, New York, New Press, 2002.

Wolk, Roland: *Introduction to Online Journalism*, Boston, Allyn & Bacon, 2001.

Wolseley, Ronald E.: *Black Achievers in American Journalism*, Nashville, James C. Winston Publishing, 1995.

Index

P

R

□□□